The Illustrated History of

Women's
Golf

The Illustrated History of

Women's Golf

by Rhonda Glenn

Foreword by Mickey Wright

Taylor Publishing Company
Dallas, Texas

For My Mother and Father

Frontispiece: Rosamond Vahey putting on the 18th green in a match with Virginia Van Wie in a U.S. Women's Amateur Championship of the thirties.

Published by Taylor Publishing Company
1550 West Mockingbird Lane
Dallas, Texas 75235

Photo credits follow index.

Designed by Smithermans

Library of Congress Cataloging in Publication Data

Glenn, Rhonda.
    The illustrated history of women's golf / Rhonda Glenn.
        p.   cm.
    Includes index.
    ISBN 0-87833-743-1 : $34.95
    1. Golf for women—History.   I. Title.
    GV966.G57   1991
    796.352'082—dc20   91-3900
                                                             CIP

Printed in the United States of America

10   9   8   7   6   5   4   3   2   1

Acknowledgments

This book was the idea of Janet Seagle, the very talented curator of the USGA Museum at Golf House. Frankly, I wouldn't have undertaken a project of this scope without her urging. In 1983 Miss Seagle said, "We need a book on the history of women's golf, and you should write it."

In the intervening years, I'd receive batches of ancient newspaper clippings and magazine articles from Miss Seagle—a sort of silent prod to keep going. She also set up invaluable interviews with Glenna Collett Vare, Maureen Garrett, and Enid Wilson, among others. I'm very pleased that she consented to be the book's art consultant, personally choosing more than one hundred of the photographs. Janet Seagle is one of golf's hidden assets, a fine player who has made many wonderful contributions to the game's literature. I very much appreciate her generosity and inspiration.

One of golf's subtle qualities is that it attracts good people; the phrase "for the good of the game" isn't a hollow one. A number of people who love golf contributed greatly to this book, and it wouldn't exist without the generosity of spirit of a few sterling golfers, primarily Mickey Wright, Kathy Whitworth, Judy Bell, Patty Berg, Maureen Garrett, and George Eberl.

Miss Wright encouraged the project by encouraging its writer. She spent long hours reminiscing and sharing previously untold experiences and, over a period of five years, gave me new insight into the golf swing. Additionally, she shared rare films of her magnificent golf swing and clippings about her life in the game. She remains an inspiration.

Miss Whitworth has believed in this book since the first word was written. Her keen insights about players of the last thirty-five years were crucial to its completion, and she contributed wonderful memories of the early years of American professional golf. She also opened doors, giving me access to players I may not otherwise have met, and has helped my understanding of golf as it is played at the highest level.

Miss Bell, one of golf's greatest volunteers, generously shared her knowledge and perspective. This was just one of many projects to which she devotes her incredible energy, yet she made many keen suggestions and was always ready with a word of encouragement.

The delightful Patty Berg was equally generous. Her stories about Babe Zaharias, the early LPGA Tour, and her own tremendous life were valuable as well as entertaining. Miss Berg is a national treasure, and her great spirit has inspired me for nearly thirty years.

Mrs. Garrett was a gracious hostess during my research in Britain, serving tea, gourmet meals, and wonderful anecdotes of British players. Her dedication to the game was a constant reminder that women's golf first began in the British Isles.

My friend George Eberl of *Golf Journal*, a superb writer, remains the best editor I know. His unflagging support and critiques were invaluable.

Friend and professional golfer Peggy Wilson gave heaps of encouragement and shared her vast collection of writings on the women's game. Polly Riley generously shared clippings that go back to the 1930s.

Fellow journalist Barbara Holsomback, with her great nuts-and-bolts knowledge of writing and editing, made this book better. Miss Holsomback helped organize the book and outline the chapters, and was a valuable critic.

Katherine Williams was a patient and helpful researcher who did excellent surveys on the early status of women. I'm fortunate to have a sister so willing to contribute to my projects, and I thank her for her great moral support as well as her solid research.

Sheila Luginbuel, a fine young golfer and budding journalist, interviewed Anne Sander and Edean Ihlanfeldt for the chapter on the golden years of amateur golf. Karen Bednarsky, who became curator of Golf House when Miss Seagle retired, and Andy Mutch were also generous and supportive in their extensive photo research. DeAnna Lunden was an excellent copy editor whose suggestions were always valuable.

Mary Kelly, of Taylor Publishing Company, helped guide the project to completion, and I'm very grateful for her enthusiasm and care.

I very much appreciate the work of Jim Donovan, the book's editor. Mr. Donovan is a sports buff as well as a fine craftsman, and his ideas and careful work improved this project tremendously. It is only because of the enthusiasm of Mrs. Kelly and Mr. Donovan that this book is in your hands today.

Molly Gourlay, Mervyn Barton, Marlene Stewart Streit, Bertha Bowen, and Ann Gregory contributed vital interviews. Richard S. Taylor, Robert Sommers, and Joan Flynn Dreyspool, three of the game's finest writers, are always an inspiration. Katherine Graham, Mary Capouch, and Kay Jackson, longtime members of the USGA Women's Committee, were most encouraging.

In an indirect way, this book couldn't have been written without the very positive influence of Henry Lindner, Barbara Romack, George McCampbell, Al Polagyi, and Wilfrid Reid. Many years ago they shared their knowledge with a young golfer, exemplifying the great generosity of spirit that keeps the game alive. My life is richer because I've been fortunate enough to have enjoyed such fine friends.

And, in the largest sense, I appreciate the unwavering encouragement of my father, Ranford E. Glenn, and my mother, Rhanolda Glenn. Their love of history, literature, and golf have been a lifelong inspiration. I'll always be grateful.

Alexa Stirling hits out of a bunker during the 1921 U.S. Women's Amateur finals.

Contents

	Foreword	xi
	Introduction	xiii
	Prologue	1
1	No Longer Content	5
2	The Suffragettes	21
3	The Curtis Cup Begins	41
4	Grace vs. Power	65
5	The British Rebel	85
6	Golf's Great Loss	105
7	The Freckled Fireplug	121
8	Barnstorming	149
9	Catherine the Great	177
10	Golf's Golden Girl	199
11	The Modern Monarch	249
12	The Lopez Phenomenon	279
	Appendix: *The Record Book of Women's Golf*	309
	References	333
	Index	335

By 1925, when this photo was taken of the first tee of the Old White Golf Course at the Greenbrier in West Virginia, women golfers were very much in fashion.

Foreword

Ifirst met Rhonda Glenn twenty-five years ago when we were paired together in the St. Petersburg Open. As we chatted on the first tee, I learned that she was majoring in journalism. Today she has become one of the few women to have combined her great love for competitive golf and writing into a career, one of the results of which is this history of women's golf.

Joyously, this is not just a dry chronology of golf events and participants. The author has brought to life for us the social atmosphere for women in the different periods, from the sixteenth century to the present.

Her tireless research for eight years has provided us with a flawless journalistic history, but more important, her sensitive creative abilities have given us an enjoyable and highly readable "up-close and personal" look at the women in the record books.

Within these pages you'll read of the early struggling years of our professional tour and of the glory years of women's amateur golf. Almost two hundred photographs provide a fine visual history, while the tournament results and records are the only such published collection.

My heroines and friends are accurately portrayed in this book. Perhaps you'll meet some new ones here for yourself.

Mickey Wright

Elizabeth Abbott attempts to hole a putt on the eighth green at Pebble Beach.

Introduction

Hope and Terror

It is another bitter Texas spring, and good golf weather is at least a month away, but tomorrow I will tee it up with Polly.

Last night a norther blew down. Rain pummeled the wood shingles until I feared for the roof, and the wind howled. The daffodils took some hard licks, and this morning they looked a little defeated. There's no greenness yet. Through my window I can see the 10th fairway of the old Creek course rolling off down the hill, still brown as straw.

Polly won't mind. At sixty-three she is enjoying golf now more than ever. After a fifteen-year hiatus she has rediscovered it, and she attacks the game with a frenzy, practicing and planning her tournaments. She has lost twenty pounds, and her eyes, behind her glasses, have a fine new light. Her swing is coming around. She stomps up to the tee, squints down the fairway, and her stocky body propels the tee shot to the preferred side in a good high draw.

Polly is Polly Riley. She was on six Curtis Cup teams and was captain in 1962. In the 1948 Women's Texas Open she beat Babe Zaharias, 10 and 9, in the 36-hole final. Most people don't know that. They also don't know that the feisty Miss Riley, a lifelong amateur, knocked the socks off the pros in 1950 when she won the very first LPGA tournament, the Tampa Open. Polly, Claire Doran, and Grace DeMoss scared the hell out of the pros that year.

She still has all the shots: that good draw, the spanking little 4-wood, and an 8-iron run-up shot that she nips up to the hole. She can still hit them all—she just can't hit them as often.

When we play, Polly bubbles. She chats away, a font of anecdotes about Glenna, Estelle, Aniela, and Babe. She says she's going to write a book. Some day. They all say that.

Until at least the mid-1930s, all women golfers were amateurs. There was great newspaper coverage, no television, and very few of the players wrote books. But it would be a shame if all of that effort, the self-discipline, the work and soul-searing doubt, the joy of the pursuit and the huge relief of victory, were lost.

Our earliest players were students. They researched swing theories and sought out instruction, each one grinding away in years of lonely solitude on far-flung practice tees. They even studied golf conduct: acceptance speeches, the deportment of stoicism for match play, and what the gracious youngster should say upon defeating a veteran ("I was awfully lucky").

Most players were at least borderline well-to-do, others married well, but a lot of them held a variety of jobs to finance their seemingly futile lifestyles: work hard to simply get to the tournament, play, perhaps win a cup, and return home to work again. Polly must have had about a hundred jobs. She even knit headcovers, on commission, while on the amateur circuit.

All that effort.

Women have been playing competitive golf for nearly one hundred years now. At times when I look out through the window of my study, my drifting mind sees them in a long parade, hundreds of them, women of the past who teed it up with the same degree of hope and terror. Alexa Stirling, Glenna Collett, Charlotte Cecilia Pitcairn Leitch, and the rest. . . . In my mind they stalk single file across the fairway below, beyond the big lake, and up over the bleak, leafless horizon in their bustles and straw hats and hobnail boots, their white duck skirts and flapper dresses and cloche hats, their cashmere sweaters and fine tweeds and wool berets.

What is important is not the victories. Many of them won tournaments, and a handful were great players. But there is glory here, and what matters is the effort.

When I think of all the players who made this trip before we did, sometimes I can even hear the bagpipes. Women's golf, *real* women's golf, the organization and competition end of it, got its start in the British Isles. . . .

Prologue

Golf's First Monarch: Mary, Queen of Scots

There was a moment, right at the beginning, when the game's most famous female player—a woman entangled in court intrigue and several overlapping love affairs—gave golf an awful reputation. Mary, Queen of Scots, began to officially rule her kingdom in 1559 and, in spite of the heavy burdens of the crown, court life took on a certain sizzle during her reign. In quick succession she married Francis, son of Henry II, King of France; Henry Stewart, Lord Darnley; and James, Earl of Bothwell, all the while entertaining a number of court "favorites."

Golf had been declared unlawful in Scotland three times, but under Mary's reign it experienced a sort of revival. The Scots didn't invent golf—it was probably first played by the Dutch—but the Scots clasped it to their bosom and can be credited with nurturing it and later spreading the word of golf throughout the world.

Mary was an avid player, having possibly picked up a form of the game in France. She took to the Scottish linksland with vigor, even making an appearance or two at St. Andrews. Her lasting contribution to the game is the origination of the word *caddie*, which came about when Mary brought a number of *cadets*, sons of French noblemen who

Mary, Queen of Scots. Testimony about her golf helped convict her of treason.

served as pages, back to Scotland after the death of her first husband. The Scots pronounced the French *cadet* as "caddie." Sporting a great pleated collar and heavy gowns of silk and rich velvet, Mary strolled with her *cadets* around Scotland's first golf links; so crude were the links that players agreed to a starting and ending point to determine the length of a round.

Mary apparently had interests other than golf. In 1565, after the death of her first husband, Francis, she married Lord Darnley. Darnley was a lusty fellow, a ladies' man who galloped around the country in hot pursuit of Scotland's fairest maids, a habit he neglected to drop after his marriage. Meanwhile, Mary commiserated with David Rizzio, her court favorite of the time. Darnley may have felt Mary's friendship with Rizzio went entirely too far, and Lord Darnley is widely credited with Rizzio's murder.

Darnley was having other problems, having contracted "an obnoxious disease, probably syphilis," and was recovering from the ailment when the house in which he was staying was blown up by a massive gunpowder explosion. Darnley was found in the garden, strangled. Many suspected that Mary was involved, and many more were sure that James, Earl of Bothwell, was involved. Here Mary made a fatal mistake, mourning poor Darnley's death with a few brisk rounds of golf on the playing fields around Seton. After a not-quite-decent interval of three months, she married the Earl of Bothwell. The people of Scotland were outraged.

The Presbyterians looked with disfavor on the whole bloody and lecherous gang. In 1567, after only eight eventful years on the throne, Mary's followers deserted her and she was forced to abdicate. In England the prudent Elizabeth I was on the throne, and Mary was brought to trial for what amounted to treason. Mary's rounds of golf after Darnley's death came back to haunt her and were recounted at her trial as evidence of her ruthless coldheartedness. She was charged with "compassing and imaging . . . matters tending to the death and destruction of the Queen of England."

In 1587 golf's first famous woman player was convicted and beheaded.

Women's golf went into something of a decline after that.

But the game bloomed, slumped, and bloomed again until, three hundred and some years later, the world's finest young women athletes were playing golf for trophies, honor, and the new riches of the professional tour.

1

No Longer Content

One bright day in June 1893, a small band of women trundled north on the road from London to a bumpy little course in Lancashire. The women tramped around the clubhouse yard in heavy, sensible shoes, their long skirts trailing in the dust. They wore stiff-collared white blouses with long leg-of-mutton sleeves. Flat straw hats held their hair in place. When someone suggested they assemble for a photograph, there was a momentary flutter of confusion, but finally they settled into their places, a few on chairs, others standing. Today, all that we have of the moment is a photograph of thirty-five very somber women who do not appear to be on the cutting edge of anything. Yet the faces in the old photograph have an air of resolute purpose, as if the women knew that they were about to be taken seriously.

They were "no longer content to be regarded as a purveyor of fun in mixed foursomes, or as a member of some race apart who should be confined to scratching in a nice little hen-run with dear little holes of 20 yards or so whilst the menfolk looked on in amused tolerance," wrote Eleanor Helme.

This was the first women's golf championship, organized by the

Ladies Golf Union in England, with a shove from the LGU's forceful secretary, Issette Pearson.

The championship was conceived under dire predictions of doom from some male golfers. While organizing the tournament, LGU officials asked a leading British golf official about their chances for success, and the man's written testimony leaves no doubt as to where he stood on the issue of distaff golf.

> 1. Women never have and never can unite to push any scheme to success. . . .
>
> 2. They will never go through *one* Ladies Championship with credit. Tears will bedew, if wigs do not bestrew, the green.
>
> 3. Constitutionally and physically women are unfitted for golf. They will never last through two rounds of a long course in a day. Nor can they ever hope to defy the wind and weather encountered on our best links even in spring and summer. Temperamentally the strain will be too great for them. *The first ladies' championship will be the last,* unless I and others are greatly mistaken. The L.G.U. seems scarcely worth while."

Women were willing to tolerate the amused laughter of men in order to play this new and fascinating game. "There were still glorious opportunities for the comic papers, had they realized it, in those clothes of ours," Helme wrote, "but nobody knew how funny they were and golf was certainly no laughing matter."

These women looked very nearly comedic swinging a club, bound up in their dark, heavy clothes and making timid little passes at the ball. Most women in their class had never been encouraged to try anything more physical than climbing into a carriage, and that with the aid of a gentleman's arm.

In fact, it was said of one well-known Victorian woman, Lady Ida Sitwell, that she not only did not know how to lace up her own shoes, she would have been humiliated by the knowledge.

In spite of their seeming helplessness, women had actually been hacking around the world's golf courses for well over three hundred years.

Catherine of Aragon, the first of Henry VIII's eight wives, followed the game devotedly in 1513, while Henry was off at war and ransacking the French town of Therouanne.

"I shall not so often hear from the King," Catherine wrote wistfully to a friend, ". . . I thank God to be busy with the Golfe."

In spite of her enthusiasm, there's no evidence that Catherine actually played the game, and it's more likely that she was a keen observer.

In 1567 Mary, Queen of Scots, got into her scrapes with the game and is the first known woman player.

In 1810 golf became decidedly more democratic when Scottish fishwives played on the links at Musselburgh in the first known women's tournament. They were no doubt tempted by the prizes—a new creel and skull, which was a fish basket balanced on the head, and two fine Barcelona handkerchiefs.

By the 1860s British women were establishing their own clubs. The St. Andrews Ladies' Golf Club formed in 1867, and by 1886 it had five hundred members. Another ladies' club formed at Westward Ho! in North Devon in 1868.

This was the tail end of the Victorian era's sober society, when life was lived within the strict confines of family, strong religious beliefs, and Victorian sensibility. Now golf gave women a sort of freedom. It was a game, but a complex one, and it offered a free-swinging grace, pastoral adventure, the beauty of the sun, and the wind blowing fresh across the moors.

Yet the profound question of whether women could play golf seriously, and play it well, would go unanswered until earnest players lined up for national competition. Women's golf would be no more clearly defined than the tedious monotony of croquet unless women would willingly put themselves on the line in something more than a friendly round. They needed to play for something more than Barcelona handkerchiefs; they needed a national championship.

The time seemed hardly ripe for such an innovative idea. Although Queen Victoria was in her fifty-sixth year on the throne and growing ever more feeble, she kept a solid grip on the empire's morality, and her attitudes were deeply ingrained in British society. Women had not been encouraged into any all-out physicality, although they were beginning to compete seriously in tennis, and there was even a national tennis championship.

The woman athlete faced several hazards; the first was her wardrobe—the dark, heavy clothing lined with endless buttons and punishing whalebone stays. Such costumes were *de rigueur*, even for sports. The sight of an ankle was a near-scandal, and in everyday conversation the human anatomy was denied completely. Legs were still called "limbs."

Women who played serious golf faced other obstacles. At most courses they were prohibited from entering the clubhouse, except on the day of the annual mixed-foursome, when they entered by the back door. For the remainder of the season they changed their shoes and stored their clubs in a single room of a small cottage or an improvised dressing room made of corrugated iron, perhaps eight feet square.

The Wimbledon ladies had a clubhouse of their own, one considered unusually posh for the times, where an attendant served tea or a simple lunch to the players in a small lounge and adjoining tea room. But Wimbledon was the most palatial of all British golf clubs. At most clubs women made do with humble rooms or buildings that

Issette Pearson, founder of England's Ladies Golf Union.

One of the difficulties faced by early women golfers was their confining wardrobe, such as long flowing skirts and whalebone stays.

were little more than shacks. Not that they had to recover from a great deal of strenuous effort on the course; they were usually restricted to playing a short nine-hole ladies' course or, worse, the club's putting course.

Clearly, if they were going to improve their own playing conditions, they would need to work at it. They needed an organization of some sort, preferably a national society that could sponsor a championship, and their leader should be someone who could safely maneuver their cause through the tricky maze of social prejudice and male resistance.

Issette Pearson was a woman for the times. She was a skilled player and a member of the Wimbledon Club and, although she became a controversial leader, in golf she found her life's work.

Women's golf has enjoyed an array of wildly diverse personalities—swashbucklers, socialites, great beauties, great clowns, tragic figures, and a monarch or two. In this vast group of individualists, Issette Pearson had a niche of her own.

A large, stately woman, she could be an intimidating foe. "Miss Pearson is as despotic as the Czar of Russia," wrote one journlist, after losing an argument to her. But she was also greatly loved by many. She offered support and advice to young players and a sympathetic ear to friends.

Miss Pearson dressed in a severe style, wearing only high-necked frocks, and her thick forbidding eyebrows slashed darkly across a stern forehead.

Her friend Mabel Stringer admitted that Issette was an autocrat, one who could not tolerate interference in any of her schemes, but if "it was proved feasible or wrong, then she was instantly ready to acknowledge herself at fault and abandon the project."

Miss Pearson had the added handicap of treading on new ground.

"As an organiser she was unrivalled, and her initiative was wonderful, for in considering some fresh project she had no precedent to help her; it was all pioneer work," Stringer said.

It was Miss Pearson's dedication that launched women's golf down an often treacherous path to the glory and riches that await today's best players.

It began early in 1893 when Issette and a few other Wimbledon ladies were interested in starting a national championship. They consulted Laidlaw Purves, a crack player, a golf architect, and a man wise in the ways of golf organization.

They were lucky in their choice because Purves behaved benevolently toward women and showed respect for their ideas. He proposed a meeting among representatives of all ladies' golf clubs for the purpose of setting up a national organization.

On April 19, 1893, representatives of ten ladies' golf clubs arrived at London's Grand Hotel on Trafalgar Square for the meeting.

An early gathering of female golfers pose before teeing off.

Purves felt that the women could profit from the mistakes of male golfers, who suffered, he said, "from an oligarchy of each Local Club ruling over its own individual members, and a great oligarchy of an ancient and venerable club ruling over the golfing world." He felt the women's group should represent all ladies' clubs and that each club should have a say in legislating its rules.

The central group, representing all clubs, was crucial. It gave women strength through numbers, without which they probably would have been restricted to the putting courses for many years.

The name "Ladies Golf Union" was adopted, and Purves, Talbot Fair, H.S.C. Everard of Scotland, and T. Gilroy of Ireland were named vice-presidents. Blanche Martin Hulton was the honorary treasurer and Issette Pearson, honorary secretary.

With the men serving mostly in an advisory role, the LGU began the business of setting up the first championship.

That summer Royal Lytham and St. Anne's Golf Club, north of Liverpool on England's western coast, was chosen as a tournament site. Like most courses on the English coast, St. Anne's had been built quickly, designed on the spot by its architect, George Lowe. Like the Scottish links, St. Anne's followed the natural contours of the

Contestants in one of the first British Ladies golf championships around the turn of the century.

land, but by modern standards the holes on the ladies' course were short and easy:

Ladies Championship, Royal Lytham and St. Anne's Golf Course, 1893

Hole	Length
1	244 yards
2	221 yards
3	328 yards
4	182 yards
5	207 yards
6	337 yards
7	120 yards
8	272 yards
9	221 yards

And so the contestants were invited to gather in June for the first women's championship.

Imagine a player dressing for the first round of play. Stockings, carefully smoothed, went on first. Then, in her chemise, the woman would fit a heavily boned corset around her waist, for the admired wasplike middle, and anchor the stockings to the garters. Drawers came next, then two petticoats would be spread in a ring on the floor and the player, now wearing thick-soled shoes with nails or heavy boots with heel guards resembling horseshoes, would step into the petticoats. Next she would put on a long-sleeved white blouse with puffy leg-of-mutton sleeves.

The sleeves were so voluminous that someone had the good sense to put an elastic strap around the left arm, "or we should never have seen the ball at all," said one player. Players who wore a highly glazed double collar rubbed their necks raw in the course of a round.

Next the lady golfer stepped into her long skirt. Skirts were lighter weight in summer, and in winter they were bound with leather so that mud could be sponged off easily.

"But oh, the weight of the petticoats, the skirt with its collection of mud, and the unhealthiness of the whole thing," said one player.

The only satisfactory method of removing mud stains from a skirt, it was said, was to dye the skirt the same color as the mud.

The golfer topped off her attire with a stiff Petersham belt, a necktie, a boater-type straw hat, and chamois gloves.

Finally, more or less dressed for battle, the women prepared to tee off in their first Ladies' Championship.

Beauty and the Best

Lady Margaret Scott was a slender, graceful woman of eighteen blessed with luminous eyes and long dark hair that she wore in a soft chignon under her straw boater. Her skill as a golfer was undenied; she was easily the best woman player in the land. Yet there was some feeling that Lady Margaret did not take her game seriously and was inclined to be frivolous, as evidenced by that carnation that she always wore for luck.

Lady Margaret and her family were members of Minchinhampton, a course built in 1889 in the town of Stroud in Gloucestershire.

Minchinhampton members were very proud of the girl's skill but felt that without the steadying influence of her father, Lord Eldon, Lady Margaret would not reach her full potential as a golfer.

A father's presence at tournaments was tolerated. Papa was a forceful figure in the Victorian family, and it was he who laid down certain guildelines for a proper Victorian daughter. Her first protector would be her father, and when she married, the woman would find her fulfillment in doing the bidding of her husband.

It isn't so remarkable that Lady Margaret and her sister, Lady

The first champion, Lady Margaret Scott.

*Lady Margaret **(seated second from left)** with cup, caddies, and contestants from the British Women's Amateur Championship, which she won three times in a row.*

Louisa, a lesser player, were allowed to play golf. Golf was considered an accomplishment, like embroidery or playing the piano.

While boys were taught by tutors, then sent away to barbaric public schools, girls often had governesses until they exchanged the schoolroom for the drawing room. A few were sent to young ladies' academies, where they acquired little education but many accomplishments.

By the late 1880s the marriage market was still overcrowded with females, and Victorian literature shows parents who were deeply preoccupied with the problem of finding husbands for their daughters.

The number of male births slightly exceeded female births, but more boys died young. War took the lives of many men, and the imbalance was increased when the empire dispatched eligible young men to govern the colonies. A few determined women struck off for Asia and Africa, where husband-hunting was good. The majority stayed home, and there was desperate competition for husbands while their youth lasted, which in Victorian times was not very long. The tags "old maid" and "spinster" haunted the average young woman who reached her middle twenties without finding a mate. Her future was bleak. In the eyes of the world and her family, she was a failure, doomed to stay at home, gradually taking over the housekeeping as her mother aged.

A great deal of talent and energy were frittered away in those claustrophobic homes. Hundreds of able women were doomed to inaction. Some took refuge in ill health, a classic escape mechanism best exemplified by Elizabeth Barrett Browning. Browning suffered a slight accident in her youth and took to her sofa. She lay on it, or in her bed, for thirty years, enveloped in the domineering affection of a stern father. Luckily, her poems attracted the attention of another poet, Robert Browning, and with his inspiration she found the strength to leave her sofa, make a runaway marriage at the age of forty, go to Italy, bear a child, and live another fifteen years.

In this stifling atmosphere, the development of competitive golf for women was a bold stroke. The privileged classes were perhaps blinded to the social ramifications of allowing a woman to choose a weapon, make a mighty swipe at an object, and then chase that object at a brisk pace.

Such activities hardly encouraged a female's more submissive nature.

However, men like Lord Eldon were very proud when their young daughters showed talent for this lively new fad.

And so, Lady Margaret Scott and Lady Louisa prepared for their trip to the first national championship, aflutter with the excitement of the upcoming competition.

A trip without their father was unthinkable, and the other contestants were relieved that Lord Eldon was not a man to inflict listen-

14

ers with a rambling diatribe on his daughters' achievements.

That sort of interference could be intolerable.

One player of the 1890s recalled the mother of a famous woman golfer who held forth on a journey to a tournament. As the traveling party left Larne, the mother launched into a monologue of praise for her daughter, prompting the player to settle down for a nap. When the player awoke at Stranraer, the proud mother was still rattling on about her daughter's skill.

"I almost thanked the stars that my parents did not patronize championships," the player wrote. "Since then people have been known to express the opinion that all golfers should be orphans."

Lady Margaret already enjoyed a reputation as a great player. She had played in a men's tournament at the Cheltenham club the previous year, and to the utter dismay of the other contestants, she had won. A field of her peers was not expected to give her much trouble.

Lady Margaret Scott was a charming girl, in a class by herself as a player, and she could have given Joyce Wethered a good match in later years, wrote Mabel Stringer, a magazine correspondent.

A Lucien Davis drawing from 1890, "Golfing on Minchin-hampton Common: A Hazard on the Ladies' Course," is a sly joke. In the picture the woman swinging the club is reputedly Lady Margaret, the "hazard" of which other players had to beware.

The ladies' course at Royal Lytham and St. Anne's was a tame setting for the first championship. It was built in a city neighborhood and, at dusk, one could stand on a fairway and see the twinkle of gas lights in the Tudor-style brick houses that surrounded the course.

While St. Anne's was a fine course, it had none of the high drama of the seaside links. In this urban atmosphere, the players wouldn't contend with ocean breezes. This was no small matter. High winds threatened not only the player's shotmaking but her wardrobe, and a good stiff gust into her billowing skirts could literally knock her to the ground. Most players prepared for a blustery day by including a "Miss Higgins" in their costume, an elastic band slipped around the knees when the player was addressing the ball. It was an unsightly contraption but served the very practical purpose of holding the skirt in place.

Other than Lady Margaret, the best player in the field was Issette Pearson, the tall, solid, LGU secretary whose friends affectionately dubbed her "the retriever pup" because she had boldly cropped her black hair in a short, curly coif. Miss Pearson was an intelligent player and for a time was the only woman with a scratch handicap. Unfortunately, she was one of those women who performed beautifully in a light-hearted round with friends but became nervous in competition and seldom played to her capabilities.

In this first championship, Miss Pearson easily could have been distracted by her duties—the tee times, scoring procedures, and administrative headaches that were part of the competition.

Like other women who have been weighted down with the burdens of being the first of their sex to achieve a highly sought goal, Miss Pearson surely knew that if there were any controversies or unpleasant battles, there would be no second championship, at least not for several years. To her credit, the tournament went smoothly, but she paid a price with her game and in the end was no match for Lady Margaret.

The two met in the final, a match scheduled for 18 holes, which meant they would go around the nine-hole ladies' course twice.

Both players used the old St. Andrews swing, winding up very much like a corkscrew on the backswing, both elbows bent, the club nearly bouncing off the player's neck.

In later years Lady Margaret modernized her swing to a degree by shortening it to an almost horizontal position at the top of her backswing. But in this early championship she was still using the long swing, which was felt to be more effective with the solid gutta-percha golf ball.

On the day of the final match, Lady Margaret, wearing her carnation and with her father in tow, used her woods to great advantage. She was particularly adept at banging shots out of tight fairway lies with a brassie, a club resembling the modern 2-wood, and she fired a 41 on the first nine. The score completely discouraged Issette Pearson, who was trounced, 7 and 5.

The 41 was a very fine score for the times, even over the shortened ladies' course. That same year William Auchterlonie won the British Open with a 72-hole score of 322, an average of 80.5 per round.

Following Lady Margaret's win, her father made her victory speech for her.

In 1894 Issette Pearson was revenged when she beat Lady Margaret, 2-up, in a club match at Wimbledon, but Lady Margaret Scott would dominate the national championship for three years. She defended her title in 1894, when the championship was played at the Littlestone Golf Club in Kent.

The club had a separate clubhouse for ladies, a building that Mabel Stringer called "our wretched little tin tabernacle."

The men of the club had provided a dismally small sum for furnishing the building, so the women decorated it with furniture they hauled by carriage from their own homes. In winter the cold, drafty little clubhouse was heated with an oil stove that belched smelly black smoke. In summer the tin building was like an oven, so unbearably hot that it was totally unusable.

Fortunately, the second championship was held in May and drew sixty-three contestants. The draw for match play pairings was made in London and, with an odd number of entries, it appeared a bye would be necessary in the first round. However, one of the LGU vice presidents saved the day by entering the name of his wife to even out the field.

In the field this year was Lottie Dod, one of the era's greatest sportswomen who, having conquered tennis, skating, and alpine climbing, had recently taken up golf. Miss Dod had won the Lawn Tennis Championship in 1887 and was a five-time champion. She was also national skating champion. In 1904 she would win the Open Golf Championship. Her very presence in the 1894 tournament acknowledged the growing stature of women's golf.

Mabel Stringer vividly recalled the merry spring morning of the opening round.

"The little crowd, mostly players waiting their turn to go off, the brilliant sunshine, the red coats of those who had already won their spurs . . . There were no reporters, no photographers, and no referees. . . . But the whole meeting was just like an ordinary everyday friendly match. Following some of the matches were a few spectators, curious to see how women could play. Lady Margaret Scott and the northern crack [player], Mrs. Ernest Catterall, had about a dozen or so round with them, for both enjoyed quite a big reputation."

Before the event, an unknown poet had scrawled a verse on the floor of the humble clubhouse.

> *E. Catterall would scatter all,*
> *If in the fateful draw*
> *She had not got the champion Scott*
> *Who is a gowfer braw.*

The clubhouse prophet was right. Lady Margaret easily beat Mrs. Catterall that day, 6 and 5, and went on to win the championship. Once again, she met Issette Pearson in the final, defeating her, 3 and 2.

By 1895 it was nearly a foregone conclusion that no one could beat the "gowfer braw." The tournament was to be held in Ireland, at the Royal Portrush Club. The trip was a festive one. The players took a night boat to Belfast, and under the star-filled sky, the moon shimmering on the sea, the upper deck resounded with the merry tinkling of champagne glasses as the ladies bounteously celebrated their third great get-together.

Today the course at Royal Portrush is much different from the original layout, which was built in 1888, but the historic landmarks of the area are as hauntingly lovely as when the players arrived from Belfast. One can imagine the excitement of the contestants as they came ashore. In carriages and coaches they followed the Antrim coast road, one of the most beautiful in all of Ireland, passing the ancient ruins of Dunluce Castle. As they passed the castle and rounded a bend, they abruptly came upon a breathtaking sight; all the green glory of Royal Portrush was spread below them from the inland holes to the sea, with a profusion of spring flowers—primrose, bluebells and dog-rose—scattered madcap like confetti along the tumbling dunes of the fairways and rough.

Members of Royal Portrush took the competitors sightseeing to Dunluce Castle, where the Spanish Armada reputedly met its demise. It was a cold, windy day, and the castle was perched high above the rocky coast. As the players and their hosts playfully leaped across a small fissure in the rocks, below which pounded the sea, a sudden gust shot up through the crack, scattering hair combs and men's hats and blowing the contestants' billowing skirts up over their heads.

Naturally, as on any embarrassing occasion, someone had a camera and "a libellous and exaggerated picture" was later presented to a gallery.

There was more frivolity before the tournament began. A calcutta, then called an "auction," was held and, to no one's surprise, the highest bid, thirty pounds, was for Lady Margaret Scott. She did not disappoint her bidder. Lady Margaret safety navigated the breezy seaside Irish links and captured her third and final championship, defeating Miss E. Lythgoe in the final, 5 and 4.

She had enjoyed a remarkable reign as a champion. In three years she was carried as far as the 17th hole only twice, against Miss M.E. Phillips and against Mrs. Ryder Richardson.

Lady Margaret Scott later married and became Lady Hamilton Russell, winning three consecutive Swiss Ladies' Championships under that name. She died in 1938 at the age of sixty-three.

Issette Pearson continued to work on behalf of the LGU, holing up in the small office over a shop in Regent Place to do the clerical work and correspondence with the help of willing friends. She eventually neglected her golf in order to concentrate on the numerous tasks of the budding organization.

"I do not think any one of us will ever rightly realise what Issette Pearson stood for in the early days of the LGU. : . ." wrote Mable Stringer. "Nor, I think, has it occurred to the majority of us how extremely fortunate we were in having the integrity, the brains and the personality of such a woman to lay the foundations."

Miss Pearson married T.H. Miller in 1911. Her husband died in 1916, and she continued as honorary secretary of the LGU until after World War I, when she retired to her home in the north of England, joining old golfing friends only on special occasions. She died in 1941, some forty-eight years after that first women's championship.

And so the first three championships had been played, Lady Margaret had proved herself the superior player, and that was that. For fun, the women could look back at the merry champagne party on the night boat from Belfast and the thrilling view of Royal Portrush as they had rounded the curve on the Antrim coast road. The draw for match play had been exciting, and there were happy memories of the night of the calcutta and the comical blustery day when the wind had compromised their modesty by blowing their skirts above their heads. They had paid no price for any of this and had enjoyed the hospitality and merriment with no effort.

It had been like a party, in other words, worth little more than a memory. Scorecards were saved as one might save a faded dance card from some splendid and glorious night—except that something had changed, and there was now a vague premonition of what ladies' golf might become.

Women had played golf for a title that meant something. They had played a national golf championship a full fifteen years before they were allowed to compete in the Olympic games. And golf's great appeal, its singular test of nerve and intellect and strength, now intoxicated women too. They had discovered an earnest personal test, one waged between a woman's own good mind and body and the elements and the land. She would win or lose, play badly or well, but the responsibility of it, and the rewards, would be her own.

When the competitors departed the 1895 championship at Royal Portrush, their final night had been a festive one. Members of the club had wined and dined the players at a party in Belfast, then the men escorted the ladies to the Fleetwood boat and wished them well. Their boat sailed down Belfast Lough in the night, and the little band of women watched from the deck as the men, in a final farewell gesture, lit a bonfire on the grounds of Carnalea House.

The ship glided toward England on the silent black sea, and the women stood at the rail and watched the roaring bonfire until it faded to a distant glow in the dark. But another fire had been lit in those championships, one that would never go out.

2

The Suffragettes

It's curious that distaff golf has never really paralleled women's political advances. Instead, women's golf advanced through the decades at its own leisurely pace, often providing far more complex challenges than women could find in the outside world, but more often lagging behind the latest feminist attitudes. On one hand women's golf was of the world, and yet, at the same time, a little removed.

In 1893, when English women gathered at the Grand Hotel to form the LGU, it would be a full twenty-one years before they were entitled to vote on an equal level with men. But the wealthy Victorian women who were playing golf were highly publicized in the media of the time. A dazzled Victorian-era newspaper reporter wrote:

> For the fashionable beauty, life is an endless carnival, and dress a round of disguises. She does everything and the wings of Mercury might be attached to her tiny bottines, so rapid are her changes of scene and character. She is a sportswoman, a huntress, a bold and skillful swimmer; she drives a pair of horses like a charioteer, mounts the roof of a four-in-hand, plays lawn tennis, is at home on a race course or the deck of a fast yacht. She is aware of the

refinements of dining and has a pretty taste in vintages. . . . She is a power at the theater or the Opera and none is more brilliant at a supper party. Of the modern young lady a la mode, who wields alike the fiddle-bow, the billiard-cue, and the etching-needle, who climbs mountains and knows the gymnasium, none but herself can be the prototype.

Well, clearly this beguiling creature could do anything, even play golf. The time was ripe for change, but golfers had to organize carefully and with a nod toward public relations because the more strident suffragettes were upsetting the whole nation.

British suffragettes were militant, using acid to burn slogans like "Votes for Women" into golf course greens at Birmingham, a practice that spread to other areas. At Balmoral suffragists removed the red-and-white flags and replaced them with purple flags emblazoned with equality slogans.

They allegedly burned down a clubhouse and once dared to interrupt a match between two men. A detective intervened but had so much trouble controlling the situation that he asked the caddies to help. The caddies stonewalled; the suffragettes had enlisted the Caddies' Union in their cause.

In 1910 former Open Champion Harold Hilton and Miss Cecil Leitch squared off against each other in a match, which the suffragettes adopted as a *cause célèbre*, although the man-versus-woman battle was more or less the natural outgrowth of various contests between teams of men and women, where women were given strokes.

Playing conditions for the Hilton-Leitch match were severe: 72 holes, the first 36 on the old course at Walton Heath and the other 36 at Sunningdale. The match was to be played from the men's tees. In retrospect, it wasn't the challenge that it was cracked up to be because Hilton gave Miss Leitch one-half stroke per hole.

However, on October 11, 1910, hundreds of cars lined up along the course at Walton Heath, and the passengers craned to see their heroine, Cecil Leitch.

The 1908 British Amateur Championship was played at St. Andrews and marked the emergence of a new player who would attract the attention of the nation. On a misty morning in May, the girl stepped up to the first tee on the Old Course and elevated women's golf to its next level.

Charlotte Cecilia Pitcairn Leitch changed the way women golfers swung, the way they dressed, and the way in which they approached competition. There are those who argue that she is the finest female player Britain ever produced.

One of five Leitch sisters who grew up in Silloth, in Cumbria, Cecil was destined for stardom. As a child she mimicked male golfers at her club, adopting their strong grip and copying their forceful way

Cecil Leitch, three-time British Ladies Open Amateur Champion.

of swinging at the ball. It was this hard *hit* that set Leitch apart.

"She swung as gracefully and with as perfect rhythm as any of the old timers, who swung and did nothing else," said Eleanor Helme, "but into it all she put a hit, a perfect forcity of hitting, and what is more, she showed the world of ladies' golf that with the iron clubs they MUST hit, and hit hard, and hit only."

If it sounds ferocious, it was. Miss Leitch believed you must look upon a golf ball as your worst enemy and treat it as such. She used a very wide stance, and her swing was short, unlike the old looping St. Andrews swing. Leitch made a short, quick backswing and drove her irons low and with great force.

At the 1908 championship she was the subject of most of the pretournament speculation, although, as a young player in her first championship, she should have been an unknown quantity. But her swing and shots were distinctly different from the other players' and so impressive that she attracted a great deal of attention. Cecil thrived on it.

In the first round she fulfilled every expectation, walloping an American player, Miss M. Phelps, 9 and 8. At seventeen, too young for the English international team, which required players to have "twenty years' residence in a country," Cecil had remarkable poise.

In her second-round match with Maud Titterton, she was 2-down at the 17th. Here, on the famous Road Hole with its rolling,

23

tiered green, Cecil holed a snaking putt. The crowd went completely out of control, breaking into a burst of applause and loud cheering that so frightened a young horse, harnessed to a two-wheeled cart, that the horse bolted and stampeded through the gallery.

Shaken, Titterton missed her short putt for a half but fired back at the final hole. Her tee shot hit the tiny stone bridge crossing Swilcan burn and bounded over, and she won the hole and the match.

But no one was going to forget Cecil Leitch. Galleries have always loved young players and big hitters. Cecil was both. Charismatic, with her round and resolute jaw, piercing eyes, and long brown curls that were fastened on top of her head with a large bow, she played with such intensity that she attracted throngs of followers. Almost frightening in their devotion, they trailed her across the country and cheered loudly at her every success.

Issette Pearson Miller, perhaps recognizing something of her own forceful personality in the girl, took Cecil under her wing and made sure that she got the right tournament experience. Miss Leitch became a golfer to emulate, and her hard-hitting style inspired changes in women's swings.

"For a time there followed a wild orgy of 'slogging.' Every young player tried to hit the ball harder than the last, and a great deal harder than was possible for any of them, and the short game was left neglected in the corner," Eleanor Helme said.

The 1910 match between Cecil Leitch and Harold Hilton was like a carnival. Large bets changed hands, and the crowd applauded wildly as Cecil strode onto the tee in a cream serge skirt, white blouse, green tie, blue stockings, and tan shoes, a costume dutifully described in newspapers the following morning.

But even Cecil could be intimidated by the huge crowd. She played shakily at first, pulling her first shot and hitting a baby carriage as the gallery yelled "Fore" at two gurgling baby boys in the carriage. The children were unharmed, but Miss Leitch was rattled. At the third hole she hit a dog. At the 15th she struck an umbrella, then a walking stick. The crowd was nearly out of control, and on one hole Hilton had no room in which to swing his club. The two staggered along, and at the end of the day Hilton was 1-up.

Two days later Cecil won the match, finishing off Hilton on Sunningdale's 17th green. Her win prompted some suffragette cartoons in the newspapers, but the match was played in honest good humor between the two golfers.

With the suffragettes on the march, the balance could have been tipped against any developing British women's organization. Luckily, the LGU generated mostly favorable publicity and grew in strength. By 1912 the LGU had more than five hundred affiliated clubs and had successfully set up a handicapping system used by women throughout England.

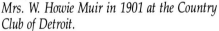

Gladys Ravenscroft, 1912 British Ladies Champion and 1913 U.S. Women's Amateur Champion.

Mrs. W. Howie Muir in 1901 at the Country Club of Detroit.

Yankee Doodle Dames

In America, women's golf lurched off to a shaky start in the 1890s. Powerful new economic and social forces were at work, and the timing was right. This was the robust new era of can-do America; the nation was full of hope and energy. The wounds of the Civil War were healing, and America was rebounding with the excitement of the industrial age. An entire new generation of American aristocrats appeared, men who made fortunes in steel, finance, railroads, and oil. As the turn of the century approached, the fortunes of such men as Andrew Carnegie, J.P. Morgan, Henry Flagler, and John D. Rockefeller were new. The American millionaire was at his zenith and, in search of pleasant weather and new diversions, these golden barons and their friends flocked to the fashionable seashore colonies in summer. In winter they sailed to France. Georgia's Jekyll Island was a springtime resort for millionaires, where Morgan, Rockefeller, and Vanderbilt owned so-called "cottages," rambling Victorian castles that huddled together like so many giant wedding cakes. And at each new spa, the growing leisure class sought new amusements.

In 1899 economist Thorstein Veblen characterized a lady as one whose function it was to display her husband's wealth by spending. The leisured lady herself had become a status symbol, said Veblen, "a means of conspicuously unproductive expenditure."

In fact, the role of all American wives was changing.

In pre-industrial America, the housewife's work was a major economic force in the family. Men and women worked side by side on farms and plantations, earning support and a little cash. Women always had their egg money, for example. They were respected for such skills as making candles, churning butter, spinning thread, weaving, and carding wool.

The pre-industrial housewife had an important family role as teacher and nurse of the sick and the old. She was a respected force in the church and community. As the family evolved from a production unit to a consumption unit, she became a shopper and maintainer of goods rather than a producer of goods. Skills and work satisfaction began to disappear. Education, welfare, and health services no longer belonged to the housewife. These most satisfying and challenging tasks were taken over by workers on the public payroll, leaving her with the unskilled drudge jobs.

Families changed. Women in the nineteenth century had fewer children and spent less of their lifetime in child-rearing. In suburban households and city apartments, housewives were now isolated from relatives and close neighbors and were, for much of the day, without children. Their work was lighter but their function lessened. Women had time on their hands.

Wealthier women might be exempt from doing housework at all, replaced by other woman to do the labor for them. They could pursue community and volunteer activities, recreation, and self-improvement.

Meanwhile, American men were enjoying golf.

Men with money were building golf courses for their own use, and courses were springing up near fashionable colonies and resorts—the most notable at Yonkers, New York; Shinnecock Hills on Long Island; and at Newport.

In 1894 the *Ladies Home Journal* threw its weight behind the game and urged American women to take up golf. An article by John Gilmer Speed said men and women could easily learn to play "in middle life."

"With golf links in every neighborhood there is no reason why the middle-aged woman should fasten herself in a rocking chair and consent to be regarded by the youngsters around her as antiquated at forty-five. Instead of that, she can, with her golfing club, follow her ball from link to link, renewing her beauty and her youth by exercise in the open air," wrote Speed.

This is what newly leisured women were reading, and none took golf more seriously than the ladies of Morristown, New Jersey.

Morristown was a quiet little village inhabited by the very rich. Many residents were learning to play golf, and when a few got together to plan a golf course there would have been no stir, except that the group was made up entirely of women.

A small group yearning for an 18-hole course of their own met at the home of Mrs. Henry Hopkins.

(Except for a rare mixed-foursomes event, women had been restricted to the putting course. In 1892 Shinnecock Hills Golf Club had built a course for women, but it had only 12 holes.)

At Mrs. Hopkins's house, the women decided to undertake a huge task—they would commission the design and building of their own 18-hole course. For women only. Honorary memberships were granted to the clergy, and two hundred men were allowed to join as "associate members."

Miss Cornelia Howland was elected president of the new club, which was called Morris County Golf Club.

A course of 6,030 yards was laid out, extremely long for women at that time. Six holes were over 400 yards. The 545-yard 13th, for example, played to a par of 7 and a "bogey" of 8.

It was fashionable to attach a name to each hole, and the Morris County members had charming orginality; the Hoodoo, Devil's Punch Bowl, Blasted Hopes, and Setting Sun were some of their favorites.

When nine holes were ready, the members organized a festive opening day. Golf was a novelty but very much in vogue, and the Morristown ladies managed to snare the international set for their festivities, along with the scions of the wealthy colonies around the Hudson River and Westchester County, New York. Among the guests were the Marquise de Talleyrand-Perigord of Paris; Prince Rospoli, the mayor of Rome; and Princess Rospoli.

The afternoon golf exhibition was, at best, quaint.

Mrs. Arthur C. James was given the honor of hitting the first ball. Intimidated perhaps by the historical significance, she drew back the club, swung, and whiffed the shot. Poor Mrs. James took 12 strokes to reach the green, just 238 yards away.

Lois Raymond, another player who managed to make contact but moved the ball only a couple of inches, stamped her foot and cried, "Isn't that too mean for anything!" The gallery trailed after the players, wagering candy on the outcome.

The excitement didn't last long. Soon an ominous shadow loomed over Morris County Golf Club—the male associate members. Husbands became a disquieting presence. They insisted the club should be incorporated and should own the grounds, making the club a business. A woman simply didn't have a head for business, they claimed, so men should take over.

Gertrude Fiske losing in the first round of the 1902 Women's Amateur at the Country Club, Brookline, Massachusetts.

In January 1895 the members held a meeting and elected Paul Revere of Morristown as president. All officers were now males.

No one was sure exactly how the men wedged their way into the club's leadership, but many residents believed the men had pressured their wives to vote their way.

After the takeover, Revere called formally on Cornelia Howland to tell her of the change. He returned a shaken man, pale and mopping his brow. Miss Howland had refused his offer of the post of honorary president and never again played at Morris County Golf Club.

The all-women golf club was an experiment that failed, but Morris County left an ironic brand on women's golf: In 1896 the club hosted the second U.S. Women's Amateur Championship, won by Beatrix Hoyt. The championship cup was donated by Robert Cox, of Edinburgh, Scotland. Cox had donated the trophy the previous year with the stipulation that the 1896 Championship be played at Morris County—he had helped lay out the course in 1894.

While Cox's golf course is no longer a women-only preserve, the Robert Cox Cup remains one of the most beautiful in the game, with its delicately tinted golf scenes and ornate silver trim, and continues to be the prize for the U.S. Women's Amateur Championship.

Around 1897 Morris County Golf Club was expanded to 18 holes. The present clubhouse is the club's third. In 1902, just seven years after men took over the club's operation, the original clubhouse burned—only a section of the ladies' locker room was left standing.

*Semifinalists in the 1914 North and South Women's Amateur (from left):
Mrs. J.R. Price, 1912 Champion; Nonna Barlow, runner-up in the U.S.
Women's Amateur in 1909 and 1912; Louise Elkins, 1911 Champion; Miss
F.J. Harvey, 1903 Canadian Amateur Champion.*

An Escape from Croquet

Nearly every stylish American household of the late 1800s subscribed
to *Frank Leslie's Popular Monthly,* and in 1877 the magazine offered its
readers a preview of a new vogue.

The magazine's June issue told readers about golf, long the rage
in England and Scotland. What is remarkable about the article is that
the author nudged women toward the game, although men were
barely catching on to golf's rudiments.

In a story entitled "The Game of 'Golf,'" the magazine urged
ladies to give the game a try. "It would certainly be a welcome addition to our meagre list of outdoor sports if 'Golf' could be introduced
and acclimatized," said the article, "and the opportunity it would offer to the fair sex to escape from the wearisome monotony of croquet
would doubtless make it a favorite game, not only with 'ladyes fair,'
but with their attendant knights and squires."

Golf's exposure in *Frank Leslie's Popular Monthly* created little
sensation in the summer of 1877. In fact, an adjacent story about a
haunted house and the ghost of a young woman "with disheveled
tresses and black cloak, and the blood scar across her throat," probably caused more of a stir. But Americans were on the threshold of
discovery.

A Canadian golf course, the Royal Montreal Golf Club, had
been organized in 1873. Much earlier, in about 1791, Americans had

founded the South Carolina Golf Club in Charleston, and in about 1795 had organized the Savannah Golf Club in Georgia. These first two United States golf clubs were founded by merchants, mostly Scottish-born, and, curiously, the game in those years was considered bourgeois. Nearly one hundred years later it would become a game for the wealthy.

In 1888 John Reid, a transplanted Scot, organized and financed the St. Andrews Golf Club at Yonkers, New York, with a handful of friends.

The first mixed-foursome event was played on St. Andrews' six-hole course in 1889. Reid and Miss Carrie Low defeated the team of Mrs. Reid and Henry Upham in a close match.

At Newport, Rhode Island, summer mecca for the wealthy, "The Sugar King," Theodore A. Havemeyer, and his friends, Cornelius Vanderbilt, John Jacob Astor, Oliver Belmont, and others, financed the construction of Newport Country Club. The Southampton set chipped in to build Shinnecock Hills.

In the summer of 1892, Miss Florence Boit returned to the United States after a visit on the Continent. Miss Boit had visited the French resort of Pau, where the Duke of Hamilton and a few friends had built the first golf course on the continental mainland in 1856. Miss Boit came to the United States to visit her aunt and uncle, the Arthur Hunnewells of Wellesley, Masachusetts. She had learned the game at Pau and, assuming there would be several courses around Boston, brought her golf clubs with her.

Of course, there was no golf layout in the area, but Florence's charming descriptions of her golf exploits in France tempted Arthur Hunnewell and his neighbors, who happened to be his brother-in-law and his nephew, to turn their three adjacent lawns into a rough golf courses with seven pitch-and-putt holes. Miss Boit added her touch by using flowerpots for the cups.

One visitor to the Hunnewell's lawn, Laurence Curtis, was so intrigued with this new game that he wrote a letter to the Country Club, in Brookline, and recommended that golf be given a trial. Curtis wrote that a course could be built for about fifty dollars, and the executive committee approved the project. The following spring, six holes were constructed. However indirectly, Florence Boit had kicked off the golf boom in Massachusetts.

Golf courses began popping up everywhere, and by the turn of the century there were over a thousand worldwide.

Society's favorite architect, Stanford White, designed a great rambling clubhouse for Shinnecock Hills, and after that every self-respecting club needed a clubhouse. The clubhouses enhanced golf's social charms, promoting the "club" aspects of the game. Wealthy members could pleasurably drink and dine even if they never set foot on the first tee.

Herbert Warren Wind's masterpiece, *The Story of American Golf,*

Founders of the Morris County (New Jersey) Golf Club, 1893.

beautifully describes the beginnings of the game in the United States. Wind felt that the adoption of golf by college boys promoted the game as one that athletic men could enjoy.

Golf has always been romantic—a graceful game pursued among gentle hills, bubbling brooks, and tree-lined fairways—but men noticed the obvious absence of pretty women lounging around their clubhouses. While they might be less inclined to enjoy females frolicking on their fairways, in order to attract them to a golf club's social occasions, men were going to have to let women play golf.

Well, that was the beginning, and there was no stopping the game's enchantment for women as well as men. The New Jersey ladies organized their Morris County Golf Club in 1893.

Two years later, the infant United States Golf Association sponsored the first United States Women's Amateur Championship at the Meadow Brook club on Long Island. On November 9, 1895, eleven women teed off in the 18-hole Championship. Four contestants were from Morris County Golf Club, three from Shinnecock Hills, two from Essex County, one from Newport, and one, Miss May Bird, from the host Meadow Brook club.

The field played nine holes before lunch and nine holes after. In the end, Mrs. Charles S. Brown, of Shinnecock Hills, won with a

Mrs. Charles S. Brown, 1895 U.S. Women's Amateur Champion.

nifty 69-63—132 to become America's first women's national champion. Miss N.C. Sargent, of the Essex County club, was runner-up at 134. A silver pitcher, donated by R.D. Winthrop and W.H. Sands, was the prize. The trophy is today in the museum at Golf House.

And so, women's competitive golf was finally launched in the United States. The very next year the first of a long line of great American players emerged, Beatrix Hoyt, a sixteen-year-old whiz from Shinnecock Hills.

An Aristocratic Game

The golf boom mattered very little to the masses. In the 1890s working Americans had some disdain for golfers. Baseball was the national pastime, and college football was catching the American imagination.

Women, meanwhile, were making moves on several fronts as they sowed the seeds of social activism and sought the right to vote. Elizabeth Cady Stanton and Susan B. Anthony had been promoting suffrage for years. Jane Addams, an ardent pacifist who would win the Nobel Peace Prize in 1931, was deeply involved in helping the poor at Chicago's Hull House, which she had founded in 1889. The American Impressionist painter, Mary Cassatt, was studying in Paris and, across that magical city, Marie Curie was bending over the laboratory table where she would discover radium in 1898.

But they were the rare few who would receive international acclaim. In the 1890s most women were relegated to the roles of wife,

32

mother, and homemaker. On one end of this spectrum were servants and factory workers, and on the other end, grand ladies of society.

One society girl, young Beatrix Hoyt of Shinnecock Hills Golf Club, emerged as the first truly good American player. Although Miss Hoyt never reached the caliber of Britain's Lady Margaret Scott, she was good enough to dominate the budding American women's golf scene for three years.

A reporter for the *New York Sun* called Miss Hoyt a brilliant player. "So far as our home-bred golfers are concerned, she is not only in a class by herself, but also superior in the quality of her game to any of our men," the unknown reporter wrote in 1898.

Beatrix won three U.S. Women's Amateur championships in a row, from 1896 through 1898, and was the best player of her day. However, her scores in competition hovered around the 90s, while Lady Margaret had several times shot in the 70s in tournaments. The Americans were just learning the game, while the British thoroughly dominated women's golf.

At sixteen Beatrix Hoyt won the 1896 U.S. Women's Amateur at Morris County Golf Club. Twenty-nine women competed, and Miss Hoyt won the qualifying medal with a 95. In 1897 she repeated, winning at the Essex County club, where she was medalist in a pouring rain with 108.

The following year was a banner one. The championship was played in October at the Ardsley Club at Ardsley-on-Hudson, New York, and sixty-one contestants showed up. Golf was now attracting so much attention that a large crowd watched the play. Several hundred came from their towering homes along the Hudson River, and many more arrived from New York City by train.

"The glittering array of vehicles that unloaded their passengers at the clubhouse door included every type from four-in-hand drags to pony phaetons, and also a horseless carriage with thick pneumatic-tired wheels that conveyed Amzi L. Barber and his family," wrote the *Sun* reporter. "The day was charming. . . ."

Playing "coolly," Beatrix Hoyt, her long black tresses blowing in the breeze, broke the women's course record by four strokes with a 92 in qualifying. Her shots were machinelike. Not a topped or "foozled" (shanked) shot in the bunch.

She was fortunate in her choice of a caddie, W.H. Sands, a member who gave her tips throughout the round.

"No player ever followed instructions more implicitly, for whenever Sands would mark out the line to be followed Miss Hoyt would obey him with the most perfect accuracy. She buried her own individuality completely, and the two made a splendid team," said the *Sun*.

American women's golf was still little more than a social occasion. Members of the gallery, which included Mrs. John Jacob Astor, were listed in news accounts along with the players. Fashions were described in detail. Golf costumes were somewhat more practical

Beatrix Hoyt, the first truly good American player, demonstrating her long swing.

than in the past, but one critic hinted that "the scores . . . were in the inverse ratio to the newness of the gowns."

The best players looked for less formal clothes, and the press dutifully described Miss Hoyt's choice of outfits, "a dark brown tailor-made cloth skirt and a pink silk waist, white cravat and low cut tan shoes."

A gallery of social arbiters trooped over Ardsley to follow Beatrix in her qualifying round. In the bright sunshine, "the vivid red of golfing coats added life and contrast to the latest autumnal creations of milliners and modistes."

Miss Hoyt didn't disappoint her fans, firing a 92 and getting off several long wallops with her long swing and full follow-through.

The *Sun* gave lengthy coverage to the qualifying round.

> A great player at golf is one who can make up quickly for any mistakes, and on the fourteenth hole Miss Hoyt proved her right to be in this category. She nearly made the 235-yard green on the up-hill drive and played a mashie on the second. There was some rough ground before the green. "You must pitch high, Beatrix: don't try to run up!" ordered Sands. Miss Hoyt followed his advice, getting within fifteen feet of the hole. The putt ran down, the ball going so slowly as it neared the hole that everyone thought it would stop. Both Miss Hoyt and Sands, in the way golfers have, clucked at it like a horseman to his trotter on the speedway. It was an exciting moment, but the ball had just life enough to reach the hole, into which it toppled like a squirrel darting into a hollow limb.

The newspaper devoted a full forty-eight inches of copy to the

Ruth Underhill, 1899 U.S. Champion.

Georgianna Bishop, 1904 U.S. Champion, and Mrs. Charles T. Stout in 1907.

qualifying round of the 1898 championship, under the headline WOMEN STARS AT GOLF, lauding the golfers for "a sweet run-up shot," or "cracking drives."

In 1900, at twenty, Beatrix Hoyt made her last tournament appearance. Shinnecock Hills, her home club, hosted the championship, and the members eagerly awaited another victory by their Beatrix. Golf, however, had attracted new young players who wanted glory of their own, and the Boston papers accurately predicted that Miss Hoyt might run into rough going after qualifying. Beatrix was medalist with 94, followed by Frances Griscom of Philadelphia at 96. In third spot was Margaret "Peg" Curtis of the Essex County club with a sporty 101.

The women were hitting the ball quite long for that day. Louise Maxwell won a driving contest during the championship with a drive of 189 yards five inches. Six golfers drove over 180 yards.

Beatrix made it to the semifinals with what the papers described as "feeble" play. On the eve of Miss Hoyt's semifinal match with Margaret Curtis, one newspaper correctly predicted a very good contest.

Margaret was only sixteen. The daughter of the late businessman Greely S. Curtis, she had been raised around golf and had played since she was old enough to swing a club.

Generally fond of sports and a good horsewoman, she took to the game well. Margaret was a good putter and hit a long ball. As she marched through the 1900 championship, golf fans scrambled to learn more about her. (This was only the beginning of her lifelong tie to the game, one that would one day have international impact when, with her sister Harriot, she founded the competition between America and Great Britain and Ireland, called the Curtis Cup Match.)

The Shinnecock Hills members who trailed after the Hoyt-Curtis match had worked hard to bring the championship to their club. It was thought that Miss Hoyt, who had won three straight and been medalist in four, could easily trounce the field on her home course. The gallery "had the utmost confidence in their favorite's ability vanquish all comers" that August day.

But little Peg marched to an early lead, dampening the gallery's spirit by sweeping four straight holes and keeping her lead through the turn. "This brought Miss Hoyt to her senses, and the golf she played on her homeward journey was the finest exhibition of skill that has been seen upon the links this season."

Beatrix managed a sparkling 43 on the home nine and squared the match at the 18th, to the great joy of the crowd. But Peg was too sure, too steady, while Miss Hoyt seemed nervous throughout the match, a common ailment when a golfer performs before her friends and family on her home course.

In sudden death, the two halved the 19th but, on the second extra hole, Miss Hoyt hit into a bunker and made 6 while Miss Curtis managed a 5 and won the match.

It was a great upset, and Beatrix Hoyt, at the age of twenty, retired from tournament golf on the spot.

Peg lost in the finals to Frances Griscom, a brilliant putter from the Merion Cricket Club, 6 and 5, but the Curtis sisters were in women's golf to stay.

Before the 1901 Women's Amateur, a zealous reporter for the *Boston Evening Record* called Margaret a most expert golfer, "just as she has charming personality, by gift divine."

A Margaret Curtis victory in the 1901 Amateur was "the cherished hope of Boston golfers" after her near-win in 1900. Peg slipped by her first opponent, 2-up, but Harriot lost to Mrs. N.P. Rogers, 1-up.

Their brother Greeley wired his wife:

"PEG 2 UP HIGH [Harriot (presumably)] ONE DOWN GREAT SPORT. CURTIS."

However, Genevieve Hecker, who was called "a natural," won the championship. Margaret redeemed herself by winning the driving contest with a poke of 204 yards. She was considered a rare talent. "Her forceful play suggests possibilities beyond what any American girl has yet accomplished, but, like most of the brilliant young golfers who had come to the fore within the past few years, she had not yet acquired the qualities which inspire confidence," one newspaper reported.

The Curtis sisters went on to become national champions. Harriot would win the 1906 U.S. Women's Amateur. The following year the two sisters met in the finals and Margaret was the winner, 7 and

Genevieve Hecker, 1901–02 U.S.
Champion.

Rhona Adair brought her enthusiasm for
the game to the United States.

American women golfers were
. . the kindest and best-natured set
of people," said Rhona Adair during
her 1903 U.S. tour. These Wellesley
College women played golf as part of
their studies.

6. Margaret would capture a total of three U.S. Women's Amateur
championships, also winning in 1911 and 1912.

Their greatest role in the game, however, was yet to come.

The Irish Lass

Across the Atlantic, a lovely young Irish woman, Rhona K. Adair, was
romping through tournament fields that included the best players in
the world. Miss Adair was the next great star. A lithe girl with a milky
complexion and rich red hair, she came from Portrush to capture the
1900 and 1903 Ladies' British Amateur and won the Irish champion-

ship four consecutive times, from 1900 through 1903.

In 1903 she sailed for the United States. The *Illustrated Sporting News* called Miss Adair "the foremost woman golfer in the world," and hired her to write an exclusive copyrighted article, "the only one she will write for any American publication, [in which] she gives her impressions of America's leading women players and best courses, and tells of the advantages of the game as an important aid to good health."

Rhona Adair played several American courses, including Merion and Baltusrol, and was particularly impressed with the latter, an A.W. Tillinghast design.

"The holes are perfectly laid out, while the scenery is magnificent," Miss Adair said. "They compare favorably with the leading inland courses in Great Britain."

She easily won an invitational at Merion, which featured all of the best American players with the exception of Bessie Anthony, the reigning Women's Amateur champion.

Rhona, who had played the game since childhood, had a wide arc, and her finish was high and beautifully balanced. She hit the ball hard and practiced a great deal. She had, she said, "made a life-long study of the second shot." She frequently used a half-swing, or punch shot, in windy weather, certainly a finesse shot for that time.

"While I think putting is my strong point, I have tried to bring all other shots up to a certain standard by long practice to maintain a good average all the time," she wrote.

During one of her rounds in America she faced a tee shot of about 170 yards across a river. Her first two hit the bank and rolled into the water. Miss Adair asked the gallery if there was an easier crossing. Someone pointed to a spot five yards from her first failed attempts. She aimed at the spot, swung, and hit her ball across the river.

Rhona Adair used medium-weight clubs with stiff shafts, and her putter was a gooseneck design, all of which was revealed to a breathless public by the *Illustrated Sporting News*.

But she was a gracious woman and careful to praise American women golfers, noting that "the army of women golfers has reached enormous proportions and is increasing every year."

She called them "the kindest and best natured set of people. . . . They seem above the petty squabbles and jealousies which are frequently met with at large gatherings of women . . . the majority are always ready and willing to help on beginners and encourage them with stories of their own struggles when novices."

Her visit was a great success, and Miss Adair urged American women to meet their counterparts in Great Britain "at regular intervals." She particularly singled out Margaret Curtis as a skilled player, saying, "with more experience in match play, I think she could hold her own with anybody."

And she complimented American women for their "rapid strides" in improving their style of play and for their "pluck [and] cheerful manner of playing all kinds of weather and their universal heartiness."

Upon her return to Ireland, she married and became Mrs. Cuthell. In 1930 she was elected president of the Ladies Golf Union. Rhona Adair died in 1961 at the age of eighty-three.

Perhaps unwittingly, she had planted the seed of competition between American and British players. In her visit to the United States she predicted that a team of the best British players would trounce an American team. She phrased it graciously, but her comments may have struck the fancy of the Curtis sisters.

Miss Adair's innocent comparisons of American and British women golfers probably came at the urging of the editors of *Illustrated Sporting News* who, no doubt, wanted a good story. Less than a challenge, it was only an idea, but it's likely that Rhona Adair helped inspire what would one day be the greatest dream of American and British amateurs—a spot on the teams that played the Curtis Cup Match.

*Margaret Curtis, winner of the
U.S. Women's Amateur in
1907, 1911, and 1912.*

3

The
Curtis
Cup
Begins

The Curtis Cup matches
grew out of what was little more than an impromptu pickup match.

In the summer of 1905, sisters Margaret and Harriot Curtis of
Boston sailed for England to play in the British Ladies' Championship
at Cromer. Several other good American golfers also made the long
transatlantic crossing to enter the field, including Georgiana "Georgie"
Bishop, the 1904 U.S. Women's Amateur champion; Mary B. Adams,
who was steadily shooting scores in the 90s in national competition;
and Frances C. Griscom.

Miss Griscom was an adventuress. Born in Philadelphia, she
was an expert trapshooter, an avid fisherman, and a woman who loved
to drive her coach and four at full gallop. Frances was the first woman
in her hometown to own and drive a car, and during World War I she
would drive a Red Cross ambulance. She would also become a part of
the first international team matches.

The exciting prospect of an international match between American and British women had captured the interest of Ladies Golf Union
secretary Issette Pearson Miller as early as 1898. Now, seven years later,
the presence of a strong American contingent led to a match appropri-

Frances Griscom, 1900 U.S. Champion.

ately entitled "America versus England." A crew of English, Scottish, and Irish players, including Dorothy Campbell, Lottie Dod, Alexa Glover, Mary Graham, the sisters May and Florence Hezlet, and Elinor Neville, walloped the Americans, 6 points to 1. Though they had lost, the excitement of the match spurred the sisters Curtis to see what could be done to establish a true international competition.

Margaret and Harriot returned to England two years later in 1907. On arriving, "Miss Harriot," as she was ever referred to in the newspapers, strolled down the ship's gangplank sporting a hat with a huge ostrich feather. The effect impressed English golf writer Mabel Stringer, but England's adverse weather discouraged such finery.

"Feathers and such gear were no manner of use at Newcastle with the awful gales and drenching rain we had during our stay," wrote Miss Stringer.

The Curtis sisters competed in the British tournaments, improving their play through lively matches with superior players. More important, they reestablished their international ties, strong bonds with British and European golfers that would eventually prompt them to spearhead the Curtis Cup Match, one of the most esteemed of amateur competitions.

Over the coming decades there were many attempts at organizing a team match between American and British players. In 1909 the USGA offered to donate a cup for such a match, but the LGU turned it down, believing it would be difficult to select an official English team.

A few informal competitions did take place. In 1911 a match was staged after the British Ladies' Championship at Portrush, called "American and Colonial versus Great Britain." The British won again, this time by a margin of 7 to 2.

Margaret Curtis was also a crack tennis player.

The U.S. group at the 1905 British Ladies' Championship. Harriet Curtis is in the rear, and her sister Margaret is at the right.

Meanwhile, the Curtis sisters continued to compete and win, and in 1912 Margaret Curtis showed some grit in winning her third U.S. Women's Amateur: The day before the final match, she had cut her right hand very badly on a French door. All but two fingers of her hand were bandaged, and blood appeared on the bandage throughout the round.

Local newspapers casually mentioned that cocaine was used to deaden the pain.

Nevertheless, in a courageous performance, Margaret defeated Nonna Barlow in the finals, 3 and 2.

The 1912 Women's Amateur was also notable in that it may have been the first time golfers were "buzzed" by an airplane. Margaret's brother Greeley flew to the championship from Marblehead, Massachusetts, in a "hydro-aeroplane," covering the seven miles in seven minutes. From the air Greeley watched his sister play the fourth hole, then flew home.

Coming from a socially prominent family in Boston, the Curtis sisters had great golf bloodlines. Their uncle Laurence Curtis was the second president of the United States Golf Association, and their brother James was captain of Harvard's golf team and intercollegiate champion in 1898.

Margaret and Harriot would be key forces in the growth of women's golf, but they were extraordinary women, and golf was only one of many interests. Throughout their lives, the Curtis sisters threw their energies into a number of causes.

At the time of their 1905 voyage to Cromer, Margaret was a member of the first class at Boston's Simmons College School of Social Work. Her early assignments included relief work with victims of the great Chelsea fire. A crack tennis player, she captured the 1908 national grass court doubles title with Evilynn Sears.

In 1913 the Curtis sisters renewed efforts to promote an international women's golf match. They helped promote a competition between the United States and a team of British and Canadian golfers. The match, in Wilmington, Delaware, site of that year's U.S. Women's Amateur, was informal, but it made the newspapers.

The British-Canadian team included Gladys Ravenscroft, who would win the national women's titles of England and the United States; England's Muriel Dodd; Ireland's Mabel Harrison; Canadian players Violet Pooley, Florence Harvey, and F.B. Scott; and a Miss Chrysler. The American team was made up of Margaret and Harriot, Lillian Hyde, Marion Hollins, Nonna Barlow, Georgiana Bishop, and Katherine Harley. The British won narrowly, 5 to 4.

Over the new few years, other attempts to organize an official match between the two countries were in vain. Glenna Collett approached the Metropolitan Women's Golf Association to sponsor a match but was turned down.

Meanwhile, Margaret's golf was suspended until 1924. She jumped into the thick of World War I as chief of the American Red Cross's Paris bureau for refugees, dashing around the French capital in her Model T Ford or taking the wheel of an ambulance.

Margaret remained in Europe after the cease-fire, helping a Quaker organization resettle French villages destroyed by enemy guns, establishing child health-care clinics, and working with displaced families in France, Austria, Poland, Greece, and Czechoslovakia. At the conclusion of her work in Europe, the French government awarded her the Legion D'Honneur, one of its highest civilian honors.

44

Following the war, efforts to establish an international women's golf match continued. In 1924 and 1927 the Women's Eastern Golf Association met with the LGU and the French Golf Union to try to work out details, but financing the teams was considered too expensive.

In 1927 Margaret headed an informal committee for which she had drafted two other powerful women—Fanny Osgood, three-time Eastern champion and a noted American women's golf executive, and socialite Eleanor W. Allen of Boston's Oakley Country Club—to try to get the match off the ground.

"Canada is enthusiastic. . . . France is eager. . . . Conservative England is very favorably disposed," said one Boston newspaper, reporting the offer. The committee had ironed out numerous details. "No [team] member will be permitted to pay her own expenses," said the article. "If a wealthy woman happens to be selected for the team and is anxious to ameliorate the burden of financing, she will be permitted to contribute a sum of money to the general fund."

The Curtis sisters took the initiative by donating a simple Revere bowl as a trophy.

"We were not impressed by either the size or quality of the cup," Margaret recalled some years later, "yet it was the best that could be obtained in Boston, at the time. Our chief aim was to do something to accelerate the start of matches with the girls overseas."

But the biggest stumbling block was still money, prompting Margaret to mail her pledge to England's Cecil Leitch, four-time British Ladies' Amateur champion, to take care of expenses.

28 July, 1928

I will give a guaranty of $5000 per match for the first ten matches played, to be used in defraying the expenses of the members of such team or teams as cross the Atlantic Ocean to compete.

This will help out Canadian, British, French teams, etc., as well as American. . . .

There is only one condition attached . . . complete anonymity.

Margaret's pledge was not made public, and her request for anonymity was honored so well that neither USGA nor LGU officials have any record of her pledge. But Margaret's gesture may very well have been the offer that eventually kicked off the competition.

A 1929 meeting among leaders of women's golf, however, was again futile.

In 1930 Glenna Collett arranged an informal match between America and Great Britain. Again arrangements were unofficial, but in a 1985 interview Glenna, now Mrs. Edwin H. Vare, recalled that a travel agency financed the competition.

It would be a wealthy Frenchman who initiated the first international match. In 1931 Andre Vagliano presented a silver trophy, the

Joyce Wethered tees off in the first Curtis Cup Match (1932) as Glenna Collett Vare, Marion Hollins, and Molly Gourlay watch.

Vagliano Cup, for annual competition between Britain and France.

That same year the LGU finally agreed to matches with the United States and a team from France. When former British Amateur champion Sir Ernest Holderness heard of the plan, he warned the group of impending financial strain. Such matches, Holderness wrote, "tend to create professional amateurs." He believed the competition would take the fun out of amateur golf. (In a brutal epilogue, he added, "No one could expect a married woman with young children to win championships. That is a shocking thought. It would be enough ground for a divorce.")

The concentration of effort was bound to eventually achieve success, and finally, in 1931, the USGA and the LGU agreed to stage what would become the Curtis Cup Match. The teams would compete every two years, alternating sites in America and Great Britain. The initial proposal included France, which could field a team whenever it chose.

The first Curtis Cup Match was staged in May 1932 at England's Wentworth Golf Club and drew fifteen thousand spectators. The British team included the great Joyce Wethered (who was also captain), Wanda Morgan, Enid Wilson, Mrs. J.B. Watson, Molly Gourlay, Doris Park, Diana Fishwick, and Elsie Corlett. The Americans, headed by captain Marion Hollins, fielded a team of Glenna Collett Vare, Opal Hill, Virginia Van Wie, Helen Hicks, Maureen Orcutt, Leona Cheney, and reserve (alternate) Dorothy Higbie.

Led by the Glenna Vare–Opal Hill defeat of the Wethered-Morgan team, the Americans swept the foursomes. But Miss Wethered defeated Mrs. Vare in the singles matches, and the British

The 1934 Curtis Cup Match.

managed a few points in the afternoon. When the dust had settled, the Americans had won, 5½ to 3½, and the silver Revere bowl, the Curtis Cup, was brought home to the United States.

The Americans successfully defended the cup in 1934. Glenna Collett Vare's account of the 1936 match in England enables us to share the true flavor of this sporting tradition.

> The team set sail on the *Hansa* at midnight, April 15th. We had eight pleasant days on board. The boat was small, the passengers mostly were quite genial and the weather bright. Patty [Berg] was the only one of us to feel the slight motion of the boat but we decided that maybe the pastry chef and his concoctions had something to do with it.
>
> . . . At the Savoy Hotel we were surrounded by more friends and flowers and there was a stack of invitations from golf clubs offering their courses for practice, besides invitations from the Ladies Golf Union and the Ladies Golfers Club to dine.

After several days of lunching with royalty and enjoying the hospitality of several fine courses, like Maidstone, the Americans journeyed to Gleneagles in Scotland to attempt to hold the cup. The Scottish Ladies Golf Union gave each American a gold pin in a heather design for a good luck charm.

". . . May 6 dawned bleak and cold with a strong wind and a heavy Scotch mist, of which we had heard but not seen," wrote Mrs. Vare. "So we bundled in our warmest clothes, gloves, scarfs, and umbrellas, and set off for the first tee. Patty drove the first ball and we were off. By noon, we were just where we started—even, except

Molly Gourlay, British Curtis Cup player and French Amateur Champion.

colder and wetter. Leona Cheney wore a heavy tweed coat between shots and looked more like a galleryite than a golfer, except when she took it off to play."

(Many matches were played before golfers discovered winter underwear. Polly Riley recalled that she once played a Curtis Cup Match wearing her silk pajamas under her golf clothes. Miss Riley also noted that early Curtis Cup players had to buy their own uniforms and pay their own transportation to New York, from which they sailed to England.)

For the first time the match ended in a tie, 4½ to 4½. The deadlock meant that the American team, as the holder, retained the cup; nonetheless, the match had been a triumph of goodwill. "The presentation in the big ballroom was very cheery," said Glenna. "The cup was filled with champagne and passed freely around. The British Team sang 'Auld Lang Syne' and we surprisingly complied with 'The Gang's All Here.' Everyone was satisfied with a half because on such a day no one was equal to her best golf."

The Americans then drove to Southport for the British Ladies' Amateur, which was won by the great English player, Pam Barton. Marion Miley of Kentucky best represented the Americans, getting to the quarter-finals. The team sailed for France, played several informal games with French golfers, and was presented a charming trophy by the daughter-in-law of the American ambassador. The trophy has since disappeared.

Margaret and Harriot Curtis in their later years.

The 1938 Curtis Cup Match was the last until 1948. Americans Estelle Lawson Page and Maureen Orcutt are here flanked by British opponents.

The Americans sailed home on the *Queen Mary,* "the stir and excitement of her maiden voyage a fitting climax to a very enjoyable trip," wrote Glenna.

Outside the small circle of women amateur golfers, the match was little noted on this side of the Atlantic. No celebrations greeted the Americans dockside, and there were no ticker-tape parades down Broadway. For decades the competition continued in relative obscurity.

"The Curtis Cup Match was the best-kept secret in golf," said Judy Bell, a two-time participant in the 1960s and twice captain of the American team.

Margaret and Harriot Curtis, however, had done what they had set out to do. The Curtis Cup Match was a reality, and the sisters went on about their lives. Harriot was a civil-rights activist. For a time she was dean of women at Hampton Institute, a predominantly black college in Hampton, Virginia, and for many years Harriot served as secretary of the United Negro College Fund campaign in New England.

Margaret remained active in Boston charities. During World War II she oversaw waste reclamation and recycling as the War Production Board's Massachusetts chief of salvage. Golf, however, remained one of her fondest pursuits.

In 1958 Margaret was honored as the recipient of the Bob Jones Award, the highest honor bestowed by the United States Golf Association.

Accepting the award, the driving force behind the Curtis Cup Match summed up her great affection for the game. "Golf is my life and I love it," Margaret said. "I'd play it with rocks if I had to."

Through the years, appointment to the Curtis Cup team became the goal of every woman amateur golfer on both sides of the Atlantic. Golfers planned their competitive schedules with the Curtis Cup selection as their impetus to play in certain tournaments. For many women, selection to the Curtis Cup team has been a lifelong quest.

Sooner or later this focus was bound to rally public enthusiasm. At the Prairie Dunes Country Club in Kansas in 1986, after an unbroken string of thirteen American victories, the team from Great Britain and Ireland upset the Americans, triggering new excitement in what was now a truly competitive match. In 1988 Great Britain and Ireland successfully defended at the Royal St. George's Golf Club in Sandwich, England, putting the Americans in the unfamiliar position of underdog for the 1990 match.

At last the rivalry had reached competitive stature, and public interest grew. The 1990 Curtis Cup Match was televised in the United States and Great Britain. At lovely old Somerset Hills Country Club in New Jersey, thousands of fans, sporting the Stars and Stripes or the Union Jack, trooped after the matches. In a tense battle, America's top amateurs won the cup for the twentieth time. The match was once again truly competitive and the Curtis Cup's popularity at a higher level than ever.

"The game," said Judy Bell after the thrilling victory, "is on."

The Great Scot

There could be some argument that Dorothy Campbell Hurd Howe was the best international player of all, winning in every country in which important championships were played.

In 1909 she became the first player to capture the British, the U.S., and the Canadian championships in the same year. She won the British Ladies' in 1911 and the U.S. Women's Amateur Championship in 1909, 1910, and 1924. She won the Canadian Championship three years in a row and the Scottish Championship in 1905, 1906, and 1908. She even won in Bermuda.

Born in North Berwick, Scotland, Miss Campbell was a slender woman, her good plain Scottish face softened by a perfect little cupid's bow mouth. Her carriage and grace on the course inspired an accolade to her and her opponent by George Harold, following Dorothy's victory over Florence Hezlet in the final of the 1909 British Ladies' Championship at Royal Birkdale.

> *Shrieking stewards, rushing madly*
> *Over all the course,*
> *In excitement tripping gladly*
> *Into sand or gorse,*
> *Mighty crowds, the bunkers swarming,*
> *Rushing on ahead,*
> *While the green-men, loudly storming,*
> *Scorching language spread.*
>
> *Engulf'd and swallowed in the turmoil*
> *'Cause of this array,*
> *While the rushing crowd their clothes soil*
> *Cooly do they play—*
> *Two fair ladies bravely striving,*
> *Each with mighty heart:*
> *Now they're putting! Now they're driving!*
> *With consummate art.*
>
> *Two fair ladies, dainty, graceful—*
> *Nervous?—not at all;*
> *Of the thronging crowd unmindful,*
> *Philosophical;*
> *Though a fate, unkind and cruel,*
> *Hang o'er all they do,*
> *Yet how well they take their 'gruel'*
> *'Sportsmen' through and through.*

Dorothy Campbell played a primary role in one of those moments that, on reflection, carried women's golf to the next, higher, level, giving women a heady view of what they might become. The 1908 British Ladies' Amateur was one such moment. For the first time in three hundred years, women were allowed to stage their championship at the Royal and Ancient Golf Club of St. Andrews.

Dorothy Campbell Hurd Howe,
one of the greatest international
players ever.

Dorothy Campbell Hurd Howe with
her son at Pinehurst.

The Old Course was mecca, said Mabel Stringer. "Not only did our presence there indicate that any prejudices against women's intrusion on men's rights had been overcome, but the subsequent happenings of the week clearly showed that we had justified our rights to play over the ground where other women had played three hundred years before."

Stringer was on her way to lunch at the Grand Hotel when she met Old Tom Morris, the Scottish professional who helped key the evolution of the early game.

"He took the greatest interest in the play all that week," Stringer said. "He said that he had always hoped to live to see a ladies' championship at St. Andrews."

The finalists had been decided on Friday. Maud Titterton had barely edged the young crack, Cecil Leitch, in the semifinals. Mrs. Campbell beat Hilday Mather on the 22nd hole and Old Tom felt that she might capture her first championship that afternoon. Miss Campbell's long semifinal struggle delayed the final until three o'clock. A blanket of mist gave the Old Course an ethereal quality, while the gray old town of St. Andrews was nearly hidden in the fog. The town had virtually closed down; shops were shut for the day, and school children were given a holiday so that everyone might watch the Titterton-Campbell match.

By one conservative estimate, nine thousand people surrounded the first tee, lined both sides of the first fairway, and circled the green. It was a record turnout for the Old Course.

The weather worsened. On the 11th, a terrible storm descended, peppering the players with hail, sheets of rain, and blasts of wind. Bravely, the Titterton-Campbell match staggered on, although some greens were converted into small ponds.

The course, maddening in its ability to send seemingly perfect shots careening off into the heather and gorse, was whimsical in its treatment of the whole affair. Titterton watched her ball bound through the Swilcan burn on the final hole, enabling her to square the match. Such bounces decide championships, and when the two returned to the first extra hole, Maud made an easy four and beat Dorothy Campbell, 1-up.

The championship ended on a sad note. Old Tom Morris, who had spent most of the week sitting outside his shop giving a cheery greeting to all, died two days later.

Dorothy Campbell was revenged, winning the 1910 championship and again in 1911. (Maud Titterton moved to South Africa and won the South African Championship in 1912 and 1913.)

Miss Campbell, self-taught, had mastered an almost mystical run-up shot that she used at distances of up to 50 yards from the hole. After beating Chicago's Mrs. F.E. Letts in the finals of the North and South Championship by holing two such shots from 40 yards out, she wrote of a funny little aftermath to the match.

"In the gallery was an American lady who came under the categorical definition of 'recently fortunate' and who was smitten with a craze for golf. She determined to add my type of stroke to the rest of her lately acquired possessions and characteristically went to the local professional and said, 'I want you to teach me her chip shot,' to which the Scot with equally characteristic brusqueness and brevity replied, 'I'll no; yon's a freak shot.'"

She hit a sort of dragging shot, attributing the effect to a highly unorthodox grip, where she firmly grasped a mashie or midiron in the palm of her left hand with her thumb around the shaft. She then placed her right hand under the shaft, holding the club in her right palm. Closing the clubface slightly, she made a slow rhythmical swing, striking the ball on the downswing and hitting a low, running shot. It was her most effective weapon and won many a match.

Dorothy Campbell had such affinity for the club she used for run-up shots that she gave it a name: "Thomas." Thomas was a goose-neck mashie, or 5-iron, with a small face.

She named her putter "Stella" and once used Thomas and Stella to great advantage in a round at Augusta Country Club, holing two chip shots and recording only 19 putts in 18 holes, which bettered Walter Travis's record of 21 putts.

Dorothy was the first woman to win "the double," in 1909 winning the British at Royal Birkdale and the U.S. Amateur at Merion Cricket Club.

In 1910 she moved to Hamilton, Ontario, Canada, then won the U.S. Women's Amateur for a second time, beating Mrs. G.M. Martin, an Englishwoman, in the final. Dorothy married J.B. Hurd of Pittsburgh in 1913 and went into semiretirement.

When she returned to tournament play in the 1920s, she recognized that her old-fashioned sweeping swing wouldn't do the job. With the help of George Sayers, another native of North Berwick who gave lessons in Philadelphia, Mrs. Hurd changed to the Vardon grip and a version of the modern swing. Soon, she was back in the thick of it.

By 1924 she was forty-three and presumably over the hill, a player who gets a big hand on the first tee for nostalgia's sake. The favorite in the U.S. Women's Amateur was a striking young socialite, Glenna Collett, the 1922 champion who was now playing on her home course, Rhode Island Country Club.

Predictably, Glenna was sensational in the early rounds. Her classic swing took her to a record 79 in qualifying, the first time a woman had broken 80 in national competition in the United States.

Glenna was upset in the semifinals by Mary K. Browne of Los Angeles. Miss Browne, U.S. lawn tennis champion in 1912 and 1913, was virtually unknown as a golfer, but her 19th-hole defeat of Glenna gave her an immediate reputation.

Miss Browne's triumph was short-lived. She met Mrs. Hurd in

54

By the 1920s, women's golf tournaments were attracting large galleries.

the finals and, while Browne was a long hitter, she couldn't upset the veteran with the hot putter.

"When Miss Browne seemed to have an opportunity to get uncomfortably close in the way of holes won, Mrs. Hurd would usually sink a long putt or lay up a chip dead for a halve," said a newspaper account.

The matronly Mrs. Hurd, after beating such stalwarts as Maureen Orcutt in the early rounds, trounced Miss Browne, 7 and 6. It was her last national title, one of 750 victories in her brilliant international career. She continued to play occasional tournaments but enjoyed mostly casual rounds.

Dorothy Campbell died in 1963 when she was struck by an onrushing engine while changing trains in Yemassee, South Carolina. She was eighty-two.

The Girl Who Beat Bobby Jones

Alexa Stirling, a slip of a girl with red hair, freckles, and a wide bright smile, was the only female to defeat Bobby Jones in serious competition. Admittedly, it was early in Jones's career, and Alexa had the distinct advantage of maturity and advanced skills—she was twelve, he was six.

Like Jones, Alexa grew up in the well-to-do summer colony around the old East Lake Golf Club near Atlanta. She was the daughter of Dr. and Mrs. Alexander Stirling, both of whom were Scots and

Robert T. "Bobby" Jones Jr. and Alexa Stirling, 1921.

golfers. Dr. Stirling was the acting British Consul in Atlanta. Alexa was a frail child and he felt she would benefit from a rural setting, so he moved his family to an English-style cottage across from East Lake's 10th tee.

Alexa took her first lessons from Stewart Maiden, a Scottish professional who barked out simple instructions and taught her what was known as the Carnoustie swing. Maiden's other protégé was Jones.

Maiden was a man of few words, but each phrase was meaningful.

Jones recalled his first lesson with Maiden, when the sole instructions were, "Square yourself around a bit."

Which Jones did.

Then, "Move that right foot and shoulder back a bit."

Which Jones did.

"Now what do I do?" Jones asked.

"Knock hell out of it!" Maiden barked.

In 1908 young Bob and Alexa were invited to a neighborhood children's party, where the entertainment was to be a six-hole golf competition. Alexa made a lower score, but Jones somehow wound up with the trophy. Throughout his unequaled career, that little three-inch cup remained his most treasured prize.

Alexa Stirling won the U.S. Women's Amateur three times.

"I'll always believe Alexa won that cup," Jones wrote, ". . . [but] I took it to bed with me that night. . . . I've a hundred and twenty cups and vases now, and thirty medals, but there's one little cup that never fails of being kept well polished. And I never slept with another one."

Alexa remained modest about that occasion.

"I had an advantage over Bob in those days," she said later. "I was twelve and he was only six. And I have to be honest; it wasn't very long until he was defeating me."

Alexa's game improved rapidly. At nineteen she won the 1915 Southern Amateur Championship and played well in the U.S. Women's Amateur, reaching the semifinals. It soon became clear that she had what it takes to win.

Another great redhead, Miss Patty Berg, has given speeches on the theme, "what it takes to become a champion." When she lists dedication, inspiration, and the will to win, Miss Berg is right on the mark. But there must be more, some explanation as to how a wild array of personalities and temperaments can hone themselves into the common mold of a champion. In no way did the flamboyant Babe Zaharias resemble the reserved perfection of Mickey Wright, nor did the dramatic Miss Berg align with the personality of shy Joyce Wethered. And yet this diverse group rose to great performances. If there is one shared quality that Miss Berg might have neglected to mention, it may be a common ability to sublimate emotions in the heat of battle. No matter how high JoAnne Carner and Mrs. Zaharias might kick a leg after making a long putt, you can bet they weren't out of control, and most probably they were already thinking of the next tee shot. And, no matter how frazzled the sensitive Miss Wright might have been during her glory years, on the golf course she was the picture of serious concentration. The champion, no matter how colorful outwardly, seemed to have an inner core of cool reserve.

Alexa Stirling was like that. She was also a golfer of great grace. Not only did she boast the smooth Carnoustie swing taught her by Maiden, she played with an aura of deliberate calm, accepting bad and good shots with equanimity.

"The player who is going to win most often is not the one who is superior in strength of distance," she once wrote, "but the one who can make the fewest mistakes and keep out of as much trouble as possible, but when once in trouble can cope with any situation."

Miss Stirling captured her first U.S. Women's Amateur in 1916 at Belmont Springs Country Club in Waverly, Massachusetts, an achievement that some observers thought might be a chance happening. It would be three years before they discovered that Alexa Stirling was no flash in the pan.

In 1917 all games seemed frivolous, at best. The world was at war and championships were canceled for three years, but Alexa and Bob Jones became members of a famous little wartime pairing. With Atlanta teenager Perry Adair and Elaine Rosenthal of Chicago, Bob and Alexa barnstormed the United States in a series of exhibition matches benefitting the Red Cross.

Jones remembered it as having "the time of our lives, traveling all over the eastern part of the United States, playing golf almost every day, and being acclaimed as fine young patriots—a phase of the tour which never seemed to register with me. I couldn't see that we were doing anything for our country. Simply playing golf, which was what we would rather be doing than anything else; visiting new golf courses—having a grand time."

One day Alexa would be paired with Jones, the next with Adair. Chaperoned by Elaine's mother, they rolled along on a merry tour of golf courses: New London, Boston, Holyoke, Maplewood, Poland Spring, Essex, and the Wannamoisett Club in Providence, Rhode Island. Their tour was one of the first times that admission was charged, and the youngsters raised a then-staggering $150,000 for the Red Cross.

At the Wannamoisett Club in Rhode Island, there was one of those totally unpredictable encounters of legend; Alexa Stirling launched the dreams of a girl who would soon become the nation's finest woman player.

"I owe much to having seen her play when I was just coming to

Mrs. G. Henry Stetson, 1926.

understand golf a little," Glenna Collett said. "She put the kindling in the fire that was just beginning to burn."

Miss Collett's interest in golf was sparked when the four famous teenagers played at Wannamoisett. Most of the attention during the tour had focused on Jones. He was a bona fide prodigy; the previous year, at fourteen, he had reached the quarter-finals of the U.S. Amateur. But the women and girls in the gallery came to see Alexa Stirling, and they watched her every move.

Miss Stirling was a natural heroine; a lovely girl with a delicate, wholesome prettiness and a wide flashing smile, she was one of those women of whom other women can't manage to be jealous. She was a good dresser, wearing gored skirts of fashionable length, the hemline stopping at the bottom of a well-turned calf. She sometimes wore rich belted sweaters, usually a tie of some sort, and often a soft, wide-brimmed cloche hat.

Alexa was reserved and wonderfully poised, Glenna noticed, and she played in an unhurried manner, unflustered and seemingly sure of herself at all times.

Young Glenna was inspired.

"Except the players, I was the busiest person on the links that day," she said. "I followed eagerly on the footsteps of the girls and had a close-up of every shot played. I gazed in wonder at every kind of shot both girls made, but what impressed me most was their driving and putting. I had never seen any woman play golf in the manner they played it."

Thrilled by Alexa and Elaine, the following day Glenna tried to mimmick the two as she swung her own small clubs. She shot a 49 for nine holes, her best score by several strokes.

"I was pleased beyond measure," Glenna said.

Alexa Stirling's career was just beginning. The U.S. Women's Amateur, discontinued during the war, resumed in the autumn of 1919 at Shawnee Country Club in Pennsylvania. In the first round Alexa faced Mrs. Caleb Fox, a sprightly woman in her sixties who had played in every Women's Amateur since 1899.

Strangely, Alexa had an erratic round. While Mrs. Fox regularly outdrove her, Alexa banged her tee shots into all sorts of trouble but pulled off magical recovery shots with her midiron and mashie and closed out Mrs. Fox, 3 and 1.

Other close matches followed: She beat Marion Hollins on the 17th; defeated Mrs. G. Henry Stetson, 3 and 2; and narrowly edged Mrs. C.H. Vanderbeck, a former champion, on the final hole. In the finals she would play Mrs. W.A. Gavin, who had tied Alexa for the qualifying medal with a score of 87.

Alexa had something to prove. In spite of her 1916 victory and the celebrity she gained from the Red Cross exhibitions, she wasn't recognized as a great player but was one of many favorites. She struck off in the championship's final round, determined to show she was more than Bob Jones's childhood friend.

Alexa closed out Gavin, 6 and 5, and convinced the reporter for *The New York Times*, that she was a deserving champion.

"There is positively no American woman golfer close enough to the champion to be called a dangerous rival," said the *Times*. "She plays as near a perfect game on the links as any woman golfer who ever addressed the ball. She has that deliberate nature, that championship quality over the course which is typical only of a great master of any game."

Alexa Stirling had something else—that little extra polish and sportsmanship that had inspired her to graciously concede the qualifying medal to her opponent, Mrs. Gavin, at the awards ceremony.

Miss Stirling won the U.S. Women's Amateur again in 1920, for three victories in a row. She also won the 1920 Canadian Championship. In 1921 she sailed for England, hoping to become the first American to win the British Women's Amateur (formerly known as the British Ladies' Amateur).

The war had taken its toll on the ranks of Britain's finest players: Stella Temple, runner-up in the 1912 Championship, did exhausting work for the Allies in France and, weakened by her wartime efforts, died in the 1918 flu epidemic at the age of twenty-eight. Madge Neill Fraser, a Scottish international player with many high tournament finishes, died in 1915 on active service in Serbia, where she was a volunteer nurse and driver.

By 1921 Britain's top players had returned to tournament golf. Even here were reminders of war. The 1921 British Championship was played at ancient Turnberry, which rambles over Scotland's rocky coast. During the war the course had been turned into an airfield, and many of its beautiful natural swells and dunes were mutilated, scraped level for runways and hangars.

The course looked flatter and easier, but nothing could defeat Turnberry's most awesome hazard, the weather. In the middle of the most idyllically peaceful day, the clouds can roll up over the sea, blowing in a storm and turning the course into a monster.

Alexa was an unknown factor in Britain, but her arrival attracted great interest. Players were housed in the old Turnberry Hotel, and she was assigned a room next to the writer Mabel Stringer.

Bad luck put Alexa in a first-round match with Cecil Leitch. That morning the chambermaid woke Mabel Stringer saying, "This is th' eventful day. I've told her [Alexa] she can have her breakfast in bed an' rest awhile!"

Americans Marion Hollins, Edith Cummings, and Louise Elkins were also in the field and "added enormously to the pleasure of the meeting," Stringer wrote.

"The presence of players from overseas imparts an international flavour to the championships of nowadays, which we never enjoyed in the early times, and makes them infinitely more interesting," she said.

Although train service to Scotland was limited and the price of a railroad ticket to Turnberry was high, the tournament field of competitors was large. The week started pleasantly enough. Days were long, and after dinner the players motored to scenic spots to watch the fading sun. But Turnberry suffered from postwar poverty, and the players saw firsthand the abject poverty of townspeople affected by a great coal strike.

"We were reminded of its existence ever and again by the appearance of sad, hungry-looking women down by the links, who rattled collecting boxes under our noses and asked in hoarse tones for money for food for the 'wee bairns,'" Stringer said.

Golf pales against such anguish, but Alexa's match with Leitch was a diversion of sorts. Striking miners followed the play, melding into the large gallery. A number of people owned automobiles and parked them in long lines along Turnberry's road holes for the first-round match between the American champion and their own beloved Cecil.

Rain and wind, quite unlike anything Alexa had experienced in the United States, pelted the players and the gallery. Cecil, raised on the storm-swept Cumberland coast, was in her element.

The golf was wonderful, considering the weather, but Alexa lost the match. Her long journey had been unsuccessful, but her very attempt to win the historic championship impressed the British, and the bonds between players from both sides of the Atlantic were strengthened.

The 1923 U.S. Women's Amateur. Edith Cummings (left), winner, and Alexa Stirling, runner-up.

"The American girl fought magnificently against the heavy odds and won all our hearts by her pluck and true sportsmanship," Stringer said.

In 1934 Alexa won the Canadian Amateur for the second time, as Mrs. W.G. Fraser. Alexa Stirling Fraser had also been the first Southerner to win the U.S. Women's Amateur, breaking the hold of Northern players, and won that championship three times in a row.

She died in 1977, having left an indelible mark of grace and sportsmanship.

The 1920s were golf's golden decade. In 1920 the United States Golf Association had 477 member golf clubs. By 1930 the game had exploded, and there were more than fifty-seven hundred golf courses in the United States, of which about forty-five hundred were private.

The women golfers who played these courses were hearty and high-spirited, but almost without exception they were members of America's elite whose families belonged to the nation's great old private clubs.

In 1925 F. Scott Fitzgerald wrote *The Great Gatsby,* the grand chronicle of that era and that social set. In it, he described a girl golfer he called Jordan Baker, a charming sophisticate who gave up cocktails when training for a tournament but seemed to spend a great deal of time reclining languidly on divans and making delicious small talk with the glorious Daisy.

Fitzgerald described her as slender, pointing out that her eyes were sun-strained and that she wore clothes, even dresses, as if wearing sports clothes. He noted her jauntiness and her walk, which she seemed to have learned by walking on golf courses on crisp mornings.

Fitzgerald based his character on Edith Cummings, a real-life beauty who far outshone the era's reigning stage beauties. Miss Cummings became prominent when she defeated Alexa Stirling for the 1923 U.S. Women's Amateur Championship. She also won the 1924 Western Amateur.

Girl golfers, in the 1920s, were very much in fashion.

4

Grace vs. Power

Joyce Wethered was born on November 17, 1901, into a family that was comfortably well-off. Her father, H. Newton Wethered, was a good player and at one time had a handicap of 6, a skill not shared by Joyce's mother, who played golf for exercise.

Joyce began to play on family holidays in northern Scotland, where her father had purchased a holiday house across the road from a golf course.

With her brother Roger, who was two years older, Joyce would cross the road and drop over a low wall to the course, which became their natural playground. At Dornoch the children hung charts on the wall and each day charted their scores, taking great pride in their progress.

Ironically, Joyce was a delicate child, and her parents kept her at home rather than sending her away to school. She was reserved by nature. Her isolation made her even shyer and she developed few close friendships, but the stately Miss Wethered had a wide smile and a reserved, gracious manner that would soon appeal to galleries.

As a child Joyce took only one formal lesson. She was a great mimic. When her father took her to watch Harry Vardon and J.H. Taylor, she returned to Dornoch and imitated various parts of their swings. Later she tried to emulate Bobby Jones. Her skill was honed by rounds she played with Roger, who was good enough to later win the British Amateur in 1923.

Joyce entered her first competition in 1920, the Surrey County championship. To her own surprise she advanced to the semifinals, and she would later say she had been swept into competition before she even knew what it was about. She was nineteen, and the Surrey event was the extent of her experience until her friend Molly Griffiths urged her to enter the national championship, mainly as a companion for Molly. When Joyce's parents had no objections, she agreed to go.

A large field assembled in mid-June for the English Ladies' Closed Amateur Golf Championship at Sheringham. The week shaped up strangely; defending champion Cecil Leitch was nearly knocked out by a junior player in the early rounds, and many of the favorites lost early. Joyce was just another unknown youngster.

By the later rounds, seasoned players were holding their own and the tournament took on a more familiar form. The little-known Miss Wethered hung on for round after round, attaining a certain mystique as other players began to study her swing.

Although Joyce was going through the agony of trying to change a naturally flat swing to a more upright one, her fundamentals were sound. Unlike most women of the time, she used the Vardon grip. She had a very wide arc, kept her head almost completely still during the swing, and was one of the first women to delay uncocking her wrists through the ball. Her rhythm and timing were superb.

Cecil Leitch, meanwhile, was blasting her way through her bracket with characteristic fury—flattening an opponent here, dashing from behind to edge out another with desperate fireworks on closing holes.

In contrast, Joyce rolled over her opponents with aplomb, oblivious to all but her own game. She had that rare ability to shut out the gallery, the weather, and her opponent. Wearing slim, heavy skirts that fell nearly to her ankles, long cardigans, and a small cloche hat or beret, Joyce attracted admirers with her sheer artistry with her hickory-shafted clubs.

Still, it was a great shock when she made the finals to play the famed Cecil Leitch. This one match was about to divide British women's golf into two distinct camps—those who favored Cecil, and those who would say that Joyce outclassed the veteran—and the division would last for decades.

Cecil took an early lead and seemed to be on her way to a rout. Joyce, 6-down after 20 holes, bounded back with three straight threes. In the homestretch, Joyce won five holes in a row and squared the match at the 15th with a magnificent blind shot that finished a foot from the hole.

66

Joyce Wethered driving in the 1924 British Women's Open at Portrush. Cecil Leitch looks on from under an umbrella.

At the 16th, Joyce went 1-up. At the 17th, Cecil bunkered her second shot with a brassie. Joyce had only to make a rather simple putt for a win.

A railroad runs along Sheringham's 17th. When Miss Wethered stood over her putt, a train rumbled by with a great clatter. Joyce, unperturbed, calmly stroked the ball into the cup. Hole. Match. Championship. She had dethroned golf's queen.

Reporters later asked her how she kept her concentration through the passing of the train.

"What train?" was Joyce's now-famous reply.

Cecil, bitterly disappointed, knew that Joyce had ended her domination of women's golf.

The stage was set for a rematch when the two faced each other in the finals of the British at Princes the following year. Emotions ran high, particularly among Cecil's staunch supporters, who claimed revenge was near.

Oddly, an Irishman named Mr. Summerville, one of Cecil's most ardent admirers, was chosen to referee the match.

Cecil and Joyce played superbly. The match remained square until the afternoon round, when Cecil began to falter. The crowd was emotional, unrestrained in loyalties to one player or the other and, as his heroine began to stumble, Mr. Summerville wept in anguish and had to leave the course.

Joyce always credited Cecil with having "generalship," that abil-

Glenna Collett Vare.

Glenna Collett Vare in 1929 with her second of six Women's Amateur cups.

ity to summon up the will to pull desperate matches out of the fire, but Cecil couldn't save the match and lost at the 29th hole. The defeat marked the end of Miss Leitch's competitive career.

Joyce Wethered went on to become the best player of her generation. Her record was unequalled: she won four British Open Amateurs and five English Championships, losing only two individual matches.

Cecil Leitch retired, sold commercial antiques, and appeared at future tournaments only as a spectator. She died in 1977, having left a fine legacy: she was the first woman to take a real cut at the ball, and her competitive spirit generated huge interest in women's golf. Cecil's matches with Joyce Wethered were national events, and battles between the two received front-page coverage, advancing women's golf in the public consciousness.

Glenna

While the 1920s certainly belonged to Joyce Wethered, the era also marked the emergence of Glenna Collett as the darling of the golden age of sport as well as America's greatest woman amateur.

Glenna was born in New Haven, Connecticut, June 20, 1903, and moved to Providence, Rhode Island, with her family when she was six years old. A fine-looking child, she was wonderfully coordinated and became a good diver and swimmer. For a while Glenna cherished an ambition to be a baseball player. To please her mother, she played tennis. At fourteen, she was exposed to golf by her father, an athletic man who had been 1899 national cycling champion.

Twice a week Glenna took golf lessons from professional Alex Smith, a Scot who tutored Jerry Travers to three U.S. Amateur titles. Under Smith's knowing eye, she honed a fine natural swing that caught everyone's attention.

Glenna's swing technique was a bit like the modern swing, in that she achieved a full turn on her backswing without taking the club much past horizontal. Like Joyce Wethered and Bob Jones, however, she was up on her toes through the hitting area.

As a youngster Glenna was an erratic player, one day looking like a worldbeater, the next day driving wildly, putting badly, and scoring worse. In her first tournament, the 1918 Rhode Island championship, she finished last with a round of 132.

In 1920 Miss Collett entered ten tournaments without showing much improvement. After losing a match, 9 and 8, she remembered fighting tears as she walked back to the clubhouse. She was a fighter, however, and the humiliating loss inspired her to work harder.

Over the course of her life, Glenna wrote several books, and they help us understand her early golf.

"My play improved under the tutelary care of Alex Smith," she wrote. "I concentrated on long drives and iron shots and was educated to a better understanding of the putter."

Alexa Stirling helped Glenna correct a fault of closing her clubface at the top of her swing, and the tip helped her overcome a tendency to drive wildly. She was a very long hitter and at eighteen, at five feet six inches and weighing 128 pounds, she hit a tee shot of 307 yards, at that time the longest measured drive by a woman.

Glenna improved dramatically. In the 1921 U.S. Women's Amateur, she qualified with an 85 and won the medal. A week later in the Berthellyn Cup in Philadelphia, she closed out the illustrious Cecil Leitch on the final hole and was on her way to setting records of her own. She won the 1922 North and South and won the Eastern Amateur with a record score of 246 for 54 holes.

"I had gained the much-needed confidence, my nerves were steadier, my shots bolder—no opponent held any terror for me now," she said.

When Glenna arrived in White Sulphur Springs for the 1922 U.S. Women's Amateur, she was frightened by the attention of newspaper reporters, who sang her praises. No less worrisome was the attention of her father, "my most enthusiastic supporter, who expected such extravagant things of me, secretly hiding his disappointment in my failure to win the year before at Deal, when I won the medal."

Glenna got a great lift when she shot a 75 during practice, two days before the championship began. The round inspired a little routine; she remembered having enjoyed a dinner the night before of lamb chops, creamed potatoes, and string beans, so she continued to have that same menu each night of the championship.

She also wore the same skirt, sweater, and hat that she had worn for her magical 75, "needing something to cling to," she wrote.

The day of the qualifying round dawned bright and lovely, the contestants "all chatting and laughing, perhaps just a little nervous, but looking mighty smart in bright sweaters and white skirts."

Glenna was paired with defending champion Marion Hollins and, although somewhat awed by Miss Hollins, she fired an 81 to Hollins's 83 and won the qualifying medal.

Match play can be torturous, Glenna noted, "waking up each morning to the fact that today is going to be a lot harder than yesterday." She managed to get through the early rounds to face Edith Cummings in the semifinal.

"While we are very good friends, we are great rivals, and I knew it would be nip and tuck all the way as we both had the same goal in mind," Glenna wrote.

A reporter described the match, saying Miss Cummings "swaggered along as jauntily as a bullfighter, ready to pounce on any mistakes her opponent made. She was a striking, up-and-coming figure.

Edith Cummings, winner of the 1923 U.S. Women's Amateur, was considered a great beauty of the time.

No handsomer girl ever graced an athletic contest. She has Marilyn Miller and Julia Sanderson beaten a mile for sheer beauty. She looked like a bewitching blonde."

At the turn Glenna was 3-down to Edith but pulled herself together and was 1-up going to the final green. Glenna paused on a bridge over a stream as she walked to the final green, wearied by the hard match.

"I looked down enviously at the trout sunning among the rocks, happily oblivious of the army of a gallery and two harassed girls labouring under the strain of a ding-dong match," she said.

Glenna then made the crucial putt on the final green to ease past Miss Cummings, 2-up.

The following day she would play in her first championship final, a 36-hole match against Mrs. William A. Gavin of England, who had played fine golf all week.

"I felt that she did not do herself justice in the morning round. . . ." Glenna said. "I was amazed, but breathed a little easier, especially when I found myself 6-up at noon. I shall never forget the afternoon match, when my one short putt on the fourteenth green trickled into the cup for a win!

". . . Even when it was over, and I had won the championship, I couldn't believe it. My eyes, which had been for days riveted on the little white ball sailing and rolling . . . were raised for the first time. I had accomplished what I wanted to, when I had only half dreamed that I could, and I suppose I was the happiest girl in the world!"

At nineteen Glenna took her role as national champion very seriously and fought to play up to her new reputation. She even tried to be the versatile, well-rounded girl that reporters claimed she was, to the point of taking up new hobbies. Remember, Glenna was rhapsodized in newspapers and attracted huge galleries.

"I did not have enough sense of humor to know that a girl merely won the title by being at the top of her game in the major event of the year."

She won the 1923 Palm Beach championship and the Canadian Open Amateur, and she repeated in the North and South and Eastern. But in the 1923 U.S. Women's Amateur (which would be won by Edith Cummings), Glenna lost in the third round. She was somewhat relieved, she noted, having a feeling "of relaxation and freedom that came with the sudden loss of my title."

Glenna also claimed that her first national championship taught her about sportsmanship. Her sporting attitude was a key element of her character, one for which she would be honored for the rest of her life.

"Most difficult of all is trying to be 'a good sport,'" she wrote. "Now, there are times when it is next to impossible . . . you are compelled to do many things you don't give two hoots about, to go on parties when you just long to be in bed, to be nice to all sorts of people, who ask all sorts of favours.

"The champion, unless she has the skill of a diplomat, has no way of expressing her gratitude and at the same time refusing. Sooner or later the champion begins to realize that she is supposed to do this and that, either from a desire to be agreeable or an honest wish to live up to the sweet things said about her in the sport columns. So the title-holder becomes a bit of an actress, creating a professional manner. That's the insidious thing about being a champion. You change inside, or outside. But you change, anyhow."

Glenna remained in great demand throughout her career. Victory followed victory. She swept through the Florida winter amateur tournaments and was nearly unbeatable. Most astounding is her record in the U.S. Women's Amateur Championship.

She won it in 1922, 1925, 1928, 1929, 1930, and 1935, a total of six times. No other player would win as many. Since most good modern amateurs turn to the professional tour, Glenna's U.S. Women's Amateur record is likely to endure. Her string was approached only by JoAnne Gunderson Carner, who won the Women's Amateur five times, then turned professional.

Kay Jackson, a member of the USGA Women's Committee and

Joyce Wethered and Glenna Collett Vare during the first Curtis Cup match in 1932.

Glenna's friend of many years, recalled an incident near the end of Glenna's life.

Glenna Collett Vare was asked to make a ceremonial appearance at the 1987 U.S. Women's Amateur, and Kay came across the great champion sitting in a chair with a morose look on her face.

"Well, you look happy," Mrs. Jackson said to her friend.

"You know what I was thinking?" Glenna said. "I was thinking that I wish JoAnne had won that last championship so that I wouldn't have to come to these damn things."

Publicly, Glenna accepted her esteemed position with grace. As Bobby Jones wrote in the forward to Glenna's 1929 book, *Ladies in the Rough*, "Miss Collett typifies all that the word 'sportsmanship' stands for."

When Mrs. Vare died, in 1989, Judy Bell spoke for all of women's golf when she remarked that Glenna Collett Vare was our Bobby Jones. In every way, Glenna set a standard of excellence, one that will no doubt last forever.

The Match of the Century

In golf, lofty titles fall somewhat flat. A player's excellence is relative; it depends upon the caliber of her era, the competition, the quality of equipment, and the standard of golf courses. Suffice it to say that Joyce Wethered was a great player and the best of her time. She lost only two matches in tournament competition and played with such grace and discipline that she brought golf into the realm of art.

In her own era, Miss Wethered's biggest threat came from

"As graceful as any F. Scott Fitzgerald heroine."

Glenna Collett, and they carried on a great and courteous rivalry for much of the 1920s.

Their last battle was a classic meeting; the somber, elegant Miss Wethered came out of retirement to face the lovely American, Miss Collett. The two best players of their era faced off for a final time in the historic arena of the Old Course at St. Andrews, a match that captured the fancy of the sporting world and sealed the women's fame.

For sixty years after, Glenna and Joyce paid the price of all fame, withstanding journalistic assaults as interviewers beat a path to their doors. And for a time they were tolerant. Dutifully, each described the other's swing. Graciously, each recalled the other's separate quirks.

Joyce called Glenna, "generous-minded" and "sporting."

Glenna said Joyce had "a wonderful temperament."

But as they approached the age of ninety, each woman grew quiet on the subject of the other. It was as if their final silence came from some unspoken current between them, private knowledge gained from having so often studied the rival's separate strengths, from having pondered her possible weak links, until each knew the other nearly as well as she knew herself. By 1985, fifty-six years after St. Andrews, each woman had separately decided that she had said as much as she was going to say about the other.

Driving along Florida's southeastern coast, heading south on Route A-1-A, I saw the ocean in quick thrilling glimpses. Little vignettes of sand and water flashed by between the houses of northern people who had paid millions for the privilege of spending winters on the shore. Bright pinpoints of sun danced on the Atlantic, and the sea rolled to shore in long topaz curls. The singular dank fragrance of seaweed was on the breeze, and the ocean's muted roar rumbled through the bright morning like a drummer's salute to March.

Gulfstream, a resort village, was so small that it had no post office of its own, and Glenna Collett Vare received her mail via Delray Beach. Mrs. Vare got a lot of mail. The sitting room of her neat white frame house was stacked with it, and precarious piles of envelopes threatened to spill over the edge of a card table in the center of the room. Notes from autograph seekers, interview requests, and banquet invitations lay in haphazard tribute.

The woman in the brightly patterned dress eyed the stacks dolefully.

"I nevah seem to get it done," she said. "I am so fah behind."

The broad *a* lingered from her Rhode Island childhood and lent a note of disarming elegance to her conversation, but she was not a frivolous woman. There was to be no nonsense from Mrs. Vare.

She could have talked at length of the great match with Joyce Wethered, but Mrs. Vare recalled her memories reluctantly, almost gruffly, all the while stroking a small blond dog named Jimmy that lay curled in her lap.

"I got a note from her, you know. She wrote to me before the Curtis Cup celebration and said she could not come. There would be just too many people, she said. She's very shy, you know."

Secretly, Glenna would have preferred to dispense with our conversation and leave immediately for her afternoon card game with her pals. The only golf that held any real interest was her own match at Gulfstream, set for the following day. She had made the game with a brief telephone call, chuckling as she lowered the receiver.

"The men are going off first tomorrow. The women after, as usual. I'll bet we'll be held up all the way around!"

Very recently Glenna had shot a 36 on Gulfstream's back nine, but she left the course angrily, having played the front nine in 42.

She watched golf on television, she said. She liked Jack Nicklaus, and Barbara, his wife, had been lovely to her when she traveled to Columbus, Ohio, in 1980 to become the first woman honored with a plaque in the Memorial Garden at Nicklaus's Memorial Tournament.

In 1984 she made a rare appearance when she flew to Scotland for the Curtis Cup Match at Muirfield. England's Molly Gourlay was one of the few members of the original team to attend. Miss Gourlay was eighty-five at the time. Glenna was eighty-three.

"Every time there was anything happening, they'd pull out two chairs for Molly and me," Glenna tsked, "and there we'd sit, these two old dames, to be pointed out to everybody."

Mrs. Vare was a reluctant legend.

A small framed photograph stood on her living room table, a picture used in her book, *Golf for Young Players,* which she wrote in 1926. In it Glenna posed at the finish of her swing. The girl in the picture looked impatient with the long-ago intrusion, staring at the camera lens with a steely glare, a gaze that had withered many an opponent during America's Golden Age of Sport.

In the 1920s Glenna Collett was the finest woman player America had produced. Her soft features set off by startling blue eyes, she was as graceful as an F. Scott Fitzgerald heroine.

Glenna won her first U.S. Women's Amateur in 1922. She would win the Women's Amateur six times, along with a slew of lesser titles, but the British championship eluded her over the years, a failure that irked her enormously.

"More than once I have visualized myself, gray-haired and stooped, wearily trudging over the windswept fairways of an English course seeking that elusive title," she said, after several years of vainly chasing the British cup.

Glenna played against Joyce Wethered for the first time in the 1925 British Women's Amateur Championship at Troon, on Scotland's Strathclyde coast. A rugged course, Troon did not bode well for Americans. Walter Hagen had lost the 1923 Open here by one stroke.

The course was playing long for the women's championship, and par was set at 79.

As luck would have it, Glenna and Joyce landed in the same bracket and worked their way through the draw to meet in the third round.

Early on, journalists sensed a hot story and ballyhooed the meeting, whipping the pro-British crowds into a frenzy.

Miss Wethered guessed that the wild publicity would accomplish one of two things; either both players would rise to the occasion, or one would fail under the strain of it. And Joyce felt that Glenna would be the more likely player to succumb to high emotions. While Glenna's best rounds were brilliant exhibitions of crashing drives and pinpoint irons, Joyce knew there were also times when the American's concentration wandered, and she was prone to fritter away routine shots.

Her assessment was accurate. At Troon's sixth tee, Glenna was 1-up but topped her drive. At the ninth she dribbled another tee shot, a blunder that came at exactly the wrong time—Joyce had just missed an easy putt at the eighth, the famed Postage Stamp hole, to even the match.

Miss Wethered made few mistakes. She was a strategist, a great putter, and a woman confident of her own consistency.

"Because I was hitting the ball so surely I was able to avoid what might easily have occurred under the stress of the moment—the slipping of one or two important shots and perhaps the loss of the match as well," she said.

Joyce had six birdies, four of them in a row. She was level fours for the match and closed out Glenna, 4 and 3. Later she remarked that she had never before strung together so many good shots.

Miss Wethered coasted through the next few rounds, then won a hard-fought 37-hole final against Cecil Leitch to capture her third straight national championship.

But the matches at Troon left Joyce tired and dispirited. She was a shy girl, and part of golf's joy was that it offered peaceful solitude.

In contrast, her matches against Glenna and Cecil had been noisy, grueling ordeals. Surrounding towns closed up shop for the championship, and a huge gallery flowed over the course, engulfing the players between shots.

"How it jostled and squashed us and at what a pace it ran!" Joyce remembered.

Dock workers were given a holiday and dragged their wives and children to the golf course, where they ran merrily out of control. Miss Wethered recalled a moment when two men were asked to move aside to let the competitors through.

"Oh, blow the players! We've come to see the match!" the men shouted.

Joyce had tired of the tournament pace. Staying on top was a great strain, and her most diligent efforts were taken for granted. Well-meaning friends and fans didn't help; they accepted her victories stoically, wishing her luck with a casual, "Of course you'll do well."

Likewise, they were shocked when she did poorly.

"That really wasn't like you," they'd say.

And so, after winning at Troon, Joyce astonished her fans by retiring to a quiet, private life.

She felt greatly relieved to be away from the tournament grind and spent long hours fishing, pulling out her clubs only for weekend house parties or to play with her brother Roger in the Worplesdon Mixed-Foursomes. She had played in her last national championship, or so she thought.

After losing to Joyce at Troon, Glenna won the French Open, but it was small consolation. She sailed home determined to return and one day win the British.

In October Glenna salvaged her year by winning a second U.S. Women's Amateur, defeating her old heroine, Alexa Stirling Fraser, 9 and 8, in the final at St. Louis Country Club.

Victory in England became an obsession. She went over in 1926 but never hit a shot. A general strike in England had canceled trains and all manner of other services. Miss Collett's father, alarmed, had cabled her to come home immediately, and she returned to the United States. Eventually, the championship was played, although only fifty-five of the original 124 contestants showed up.

In 1927 Glenna was disappointed again when she lost to the unheralded Mable Wragg at Hunstanton in the third round.

But an exciting rumor raged through the championship at Hunstanton; it was whispered that Joyce Wethered might emerge from retirement for the 1929 British championship at St. Andrews.

Some instinct drives a champion to battle. Not that they are itching for a fight, for many of the finest players have been gentle people at heart. But they search out and put themselves on the line against better players, to prove themselves and to give validity to their own talent. And so, Glenna knew she must accept this silent challenge and once again meet Joyce in Scotland.

In retirement Miss Wethered had become a near-mythic figure, but she had entered the championship for two reasons: First, she loved to play in Scotland. The air, the enthusiasm, and the play itself seemed sharper, keener somehow, and the lure of the Old Course was impossible to resist. As a girl her first trip to St. Andrews was marked by unsteady knees on the first tee and bewilderment at the course's seemingly haphazard arrangement of fairways, bunkers, and greens. But the character of the irrascible old links wooed and charmed her, as it has charmed so many throughout the centuries, and she held these links in deep affection.

More important, in her three years away from the game, Joyce's spirit had healed.

"Much less was expected of me than usual," she said. "I was prepared for anything or everything to happen, however disastrous or extraordinary. It created an enchanting sense of freedom. The moment had merely arrived when I could take part in an event to which I had looked forward for years."

When the championship began, Joyce was pleased to find her consistency intact. In the early rounds she played some of her best golf ever. Her friend Bernard Darwin reported that her progress to the final was "a triumphal procession."

Glenna drew lesser opponents in her opening rounds, fortunately. The American wasn't playing well. Her putter was balky and St. Andrews' huge, rolling greens took a toll.

The British fans went out to watch Glenna, expecting to see a player of even greater skill than she had shown at Troon. At the moment, Miss Collett's game was unimpressive, and the galleries came in, wrote Eleanor Helme, "lulled into a false security."

Joyce knew that Glenna was clearly worried.

"I remember that she dined with us at Russak's on the Thursday night," Joyce recalled, "and I watched her as she walked over from the Grand Hotel, a charming and striking picture in blue and gold against the gray buildings. She was not particularly happy that evening, a little dispirited with the course, and rather depressed and dissatisfied with her golf."

young Glenna Collett hits out of a bunker at St. Andrews in the final round of the 1929 British Women's Open. She was beaten Joyce Wethered.

On Friday Glenna beat two tough opponents, Mrs. J.B. Watson and Doris Park. She had made the final. Shortly after dawn on Saturday, she would once again square off against Joyce in a rematch of huge significance.

It was now Wethered's turn to worry and she spent a restless night.

"[Glenna] showed such convincing form in both these matches that I ruefully, and truthfully, prophesied that evening that there was trouble brewing for me on the morrow," Joyce said.

Early the next morning, the two women shook hands and teed off in front of what Eleanor Helme called "a gloriously impartial gallery." However, Glenna said later that she could plainly feel that the gallery, just slightly smaller than the crowd at Troon, very obviously favored Miss Wethered.

Joyce's uncanny concentration was challenged from the beginning of the match. Because the gallery was so huge, an attendant was assigned to each player. Her aide walked very close to Joyce and carried a stiff, noisy raincoat over her arm. The lady and her coat got on Joyce's nerves until finally she said to herself, "Do I say 'Please move away a little,' or do I make up my mind to put up with it?"

Any remark to the woman might ruin her concentration, so Joyce said nothing and forced herself to think only of her game.

Glenna, one of the earliest women golfers to attack a course, got off to a fast start, made the turn in 34, and was 5-up.

Joyce Wethered during a 1935 match.

"She holed some cruel putts," Bernard Darwin said, "she did everything well and nothing ill."

Eleanor Helme, a golf writer, said Wethered fans quaked in their shoes.

"We tried to encourage each other, as persons on a sinking ship might do," she wrote. "There was only one thing that kept us steady. It was Miss Wethered who was all that amount down. Miss Wethered, on her pedestal, might still achieve the seemingly impossible."

To Glenna, Joyce appeared to be nerveless, but the strain was taking its toll, and the Englishwoman missed several easy putts.

"I have always had the tendency to be nervous and rather jumpy round the hole in the early stages of a match," Joyce once noted.

She tried to avoid looking at Darwin as the morning round ended.

"His dark, angular face was as black as thunder," she said.

Glenna too seemed detached. But of course she wasn't. On the 12th in the morning round, Glenna faced a four-foot putt to go 6-up. Joyce had just three-putted, but Glenna missed the putt and let her off the hook.

The crowd was too polite to heave an audible sigh of relief, but smiles bloomed. Joyce was greatly heartened. The tide of the match had turned. She holed a 12-footer on the 13th and from that moment began to make the important putts. Glenna became uncertain. Her relentless attack disappeared, and Joyce won back three of the five holes by the lunch break. Their best ball score during the morning had been 71, a noteworthy feat, since the Old Course was set at a heroic 6,600 yards for the championship final.

Joyce was superb in the afternoon and stood 4-up at the ninth, a difference of nine holes since the 13th tee of the morning round.

Glenna counterattacked brilliantly, throwing two quick threes at her, and Joyce knew the complexion of the game had changed again.

The final holes were nerve-racking; there were long waits while dogs were corralled and people were cajoled into leaving a few yards of green for the players to pitch to.

At the 15th, Miss Wethered sliced her tee shot and was unable to reach the green in two. She chipped badly, leaving the ball 18 feet from the hole. Glenna was very close in three shots. If Joyce lost a hole here, she would go to the final three holes just 1-up.

Calling it the most opportune putt she had ever made, Joyce holed the long one and kept her lead of two holes.

The match came down to the 35th, the famous Road Hole, an exacting test under any circumstances and playing at 441 yards for the championship. Glenna took four to reach the plateau of the green, while Joyce nervously managed to stay in play.

"It is the most trying of all experiences to keep cool just on the brink of winning," she said, "so easy to lose control and spoil it all."

Joyce couldn't ignore the crowd's pent-up excitement; the people leaned forward, ready to break as soon as she struck the last putt.

"It was a truly wonderful moment, I had wanted this win at St. Andrews so badly and, with Glenna being such a grand opponent, that match was everything a good match ought to be."

When she stroked the putt into the cup for victory, the gallery became a truly frightening force.

"It threatened very nearly to destroy us," Joyce said. "Glenna and I were torn apart and became the center of a squeezing, swaying, and almost hysterical mob."

But she had won. Cheers rang out through the little village of St. Andrews, and the mob shouted until hoarse. Joyce found two large policemen at her side, steering her, yard by yard, through the mass of people. Glenna escaped by another route.

Glenna had again come up empty. In October she would win the United States Women's Amateur for the fourth time and would go on to win six United States Women's Amateur championships, a record that could very well stand for all time.

Joyce Wethered and Glenna Collett were destined never to become great friends. Each respected the other, but they were two strong-minded individuals knocking heads, however gracefully, and they never had the easy affection and shared confidences of true friends. No matter how evenly they were matched, and they were very, very close in ability, Joyce won both of their encounters and later defeated Glenna in singles competition in the 1932 Curtis Cup. And yet, paired by history and by the golden age in which they played, Joyce and Glenna are bonded in one of golf's more remarkable rivalries.

St. Andrews was Joyce Wethered's last championship. In the early 1930s she went to work in the golf department at Fortnam and Mason, the famous London store, and the Ladies Golf Union declared her a professional.

In 1935 Miss Wethered toured the United States, playing exhibitions with such players as Gene Sarazen and Babe Didrickson, at that time a golf novice. Miss Wethered received a reported $35,000 for the tour. While she said it was an opportunity to travel, the tour seemed completely out of character for Joyce. The adventure did nothing to tarnish her image; in fact, the American tour only enhanced her reputation as a player.

Knightshayes Court overlooks the river Exe and the rolling Devon Hills, and from her doorway Joyce Wethered, now Lady Heathcoat-Amory, could watch tourists strolling over the grounds.

They came to see her gardens, among the finest in all of England. Great mounds of color tumbled out of the woodland, borders of white alpine blossoms tripped along a row of stone steps, low carpeting plants spread delicate hues among the flagstones, and a weeping pear tree trailed over a pool.

In her later years, Joyce seldom left her small apartment in Devonshire. She had come to the towering old Victorian house as a bride in 1937 and had lived there with her husband, Sir John Heathcoat-Amory, whom she had called "Jack."

When he died in 1972, the house became part of England's National Trust and Joyce moved to smaller quarters, returning to the quiet, sheltered sort of life she had known as a girl.

With her husband she had turned the gardens into a masterpiece. Each turn of a corner brought a new delight—a pale rose, a shady glade, a carpet of yellow, pink, or white.

In 1980 she wrote a short chapter for a book on English gardens. "I know at heart I am a plantswoman and in company with all those who are devoted to horticulture."

Her private life was quiet. John and Joyce Amory enjoyed occasional rounds of golf until his arthritis worsened, then they dove into landscaping their home. They removed boundary fences around the lawn and each year incorporated a new slice of woodland into their garden, adding footpaths and flowers. When modern machinery became available they carved out larger and larger pieces until finally, with twenty-five acres to care for, they stopped. "But temptation always dwelt just beyond the fence which was pushed back many times," Joyce said.

Gardening suited her. The outdoor life was appealing and the tasks were solitary. Like golf, gardening was trial and error—the woman who had agonized over a lack of backspin with her mashie now devoted long hours to the grounds at Knightshayes Court. As she had torn apart her swing and rebuilt it, so she reworked her gardens, ripping out old plants by hand.

"A certain ruthlessness is necessary," she said.

A modest framed collection of her national medals hung in the old house: four medals as British Women's Open Amateur Champion, five medals for her consecutive victories in the English Ladies' Championship. She gave away her clubs and became so removed from golf after her retirement that Lewine Mair, a writer for *Golf Monthly*, recalled her visit to Knightshayes Court with amusement.

A guide, seeing Mair's notebook, asked if she were writing a story about the gardens. Learning that she was there to interview Lady Amory, he said softly, "So she really is *the* Joyce Wethered."

And yet, Joyce told the reporter, sometimes when she could not sleep at night, she would retrace the holes at St. Andrews, the holes of the Old Course where she had played against Glenna in the match that would become her most poignant golf memory.

5

The British Rebel

No one bridges the years between golf's roots and the modern-day game better than Enid Wilson, who won the British Open Amateur Championship three straight times in the 1930s.

In a game with its share of flamboyant figures, Wilson wore trousers and smoked cigarettes long before such manners were popular. As a child she got herself kicked out of school. As an adult she was booted from amateur golf.

Well into old age, her will remained indomitable, and each day she could be seen tramping among the hilly fairways of her beloved Crowborough Beacon, her white head bowed low, her wiry frame bent under the weight of her old leather golf bag.

Wilson's greatest influence came as a writer. Her journalistic career began in 1927, and in that role she pounded on the holier issues of women's golf for more than sixty years. In print and in private, Enid Wilson chastised British women amateurs for playing from the short tees, railed against officials who let politics influence their selection of international players, and egged on juniors to practice more and socialize less.

Others may have sought to advance women's golf through diplomacy and conciliatory tones—Wilson ruffled golf's feathers.

In 1985, when she was seventy-five, we shared tea and anecdotes at her kitchen table in the tidy cottage in Crowborough, south of London.

"My family here, they're not the least bit golf-minded," she said, nodding out the window. "Why the hell should they be? My cousin, she's just as cuckoo on drama as I am on golf."

Through the window the late-afternoon sun cast a golden glow on pink mounds of rhododendrons and stalks of yellow lillies. Several toddlers, Enid's great-nephews and -nieces, shrieked with joy as they romped on the garden lawn.

My friend George and I sipped tea at Enid's table, happily basking in her brilliant profanity. Our trip had an edge of lunacy to it. I had flown to London that morning, assured by British friends that Miss Wilson expected my visit. George Eberl, an American pal and fellow journalist, picked me up at Heathrow and we drove haphazardly toward England's southern coast, careening through the roundabouts as George muttered vague curses at the car's exotic clutch.

I called Enid Wilson from a telephone booth in the center of Crowborough.

"An American writer? No. Didn't receive your letter," her voice crackled over the line. "Well. Come on then. If you get lost, ring me back."

And she abruptly hung up.

The family estate, Redbridge Farm, stands at the end of a narrow lane. Enid's grandfather bought the property in the 1870s. A cousin lives in the old house and Enid lives in "The Oast," a red-roofed white cottage at the top of a hill. The kitchen, perfectly round, was once an oven where hops were roasted and cured for whiskey and beer.

Enid greeted us at the door. She was slightly stooped, and her white hair was cut in a no-nonsense bob, suitable for her daily battle with Crowborough Golf Club. Her eyes were as bright and curious as those of a small bird.

"Well then, come in, come in," she chirped.

The spotless cottage was sparsely furnished. A 1925 Tom Webster golf cartoon hung near a framed golf print. A sizable book collection, first editions mostly, occupied much of the wall space: *The Oxford Companion of Music, The Companion of Ships and the Sea,* Kipling, Joseph Conrad, and Glenna Collett Vare's small book, *Golf for Young Players,* a memento from the 1984 American Curtis Cup contingent.

Upstairs, Enid's narrow bed jutted from the wall, precisely under the peak of the ceiling. Shakespeare and *Lord Jim* shared her bedside table, and the phonograph needle was poised over Beethoven's "Violin Concerto in D."

A worn brown leather golf bag, survivor of a hundred tournaments and four trips to the United States, stood in the corner. The

From left, Enid Wilson, Dorothy Pearson, Pamela Barton, and her sister Mervyn Barton compete in a rainy British tournament.

clubs were hickory-shafted, polished to the high gleam of Chippendale. Her irons were unnumbered, and their ancient Scottish names were etched on the flanges. Enid's own name was stamped faintly on the niblick and wedge. By holding a club and putting your hands around its worn grip, you could feel the wear from Enid's fingers and, by moving your own fingers slightly, you could pick out the worn spots and feel the club in your hands as she must have felt it. Old golf clubs—every notch as familiar as an old friend, every scratch a memory.

She put a crock of gingersnaps on the table and puttered about her round little kitchen preparing tea. George, who is accustomed to round rooms (he lives in a reconstructed silo in the New Jersey horse country), nestled into Enid's kitchen as if settling into a familiar nest.

"The royal and ancient game of golf became popular when women didn't have to crank the car," Enid said suddenly. "The real emancipation of women was *not* Pankhurst chaining herself to the rails. Women were let loose during the war. They threw off their shackles!

"My father had the Arabic attitude that, to enter heaven, he had got to have a son to close his eyes. When I arrived, he was displeased. And it was made known to me from word naught that, as a woman, I was an inferior in every way. Fair enough. You know right where you are, right from the word go."

Until she was twelve, Enid was taught by a governess, then dispatched to boarding school from which she was shortly expelled for swearing.

"I was the biggest girl in school," she said. "I stuck it out for a year, then I got myself sacked, quite deliberately. My house mistress said, 'Be off, you're a damn nuisance.' Then I started to play serious golf."

For a while we discussed politics. Enid longed for Britain's return to the glory years. She had been a part of it, and she feared that today's British youth was going soft, getting "too bloody idle." Of course, she had special concern for young British golfers.

"We played all our competitions off men's tees," Wilson said. "We played our county matches off men's tees, we played our county championships off men's tees, we played our championships off men's tees.

"What do they do now? They play from the up [front] women's tees," she sneered. "Today they say, 'Oh, we can't make it too tough, otherwise people won't want to play.' It's easy enough to drop standards and its hellish hard to get them up.

"When I was working at the game, I used to play five or six days a week at the Notinghamshire Golf Club. It's an inland course in the valley, with great sands, and on a windy day sand would be blowing about the course. We had great big carries over sand bunkers. Most of our fairways were lined with silver birches. I used to play off the pro tees, played the course at absolutely full stretch, and I played with the men. I could roll it around in the 70s. I had great contempt for these ladies who'd putter around off the ladies' tees. Women have got to be stretched. They'll stretch themselves, if they're made to, but none of us are made to."

Enid Wilson's era fits neatly between the years of Joyce Wethered and those of Pam Barton, England's two best-known players. At fifteen Enid attracted early notice when she won the 1925 Girl's Championship. Three years later, golf writer Eleanor Helme deemed the girl a force in adult competition.

"Miss Enid Wilson was getting steadily better all the time . . . and doing everything else that an earnest young golfer should. By the hour she practiced, by the gross she hit away balls one after the other. At Walton Heath in the autumn, she reaped her reward. . . . In four consecutive championships she had annexed two bronze medals, one silver, and one gold: is further comment greatly needed?"

Miss Wilson's victories came in groups of three: from 1928 through 1930 she captured the English Ladies' Championship; from 1931 through 1933 she won the British Women's Open Amateur Championship; and she played in the very first Curtis Cup matches, in 1932, as a member of the Great Britain and Ireland team.

With a cigarette dangling from her lips even as she swung a club, Enid was a fiercely intense figure on the course. Her soft spot was a streak of strong sentiment for the United States. She made several trips

*1921 U.S. Women's Amateur winner
Marion Hollins at the Hollywood (New
Jersey) Golf Club.*

here, playing well in the U.S. Women's Amateur, where she twice
reached the semifinals.

Her first visit, in 1931, left a lifelong impression.

As a guest, Miss Wilson toured America for more than two
months, playing some of the best courses and meeting wonderful
players such as the stocky Californian, 1921 U.S. Amateur Champion
Marion Hollins, with whom she became fast friends. Marion took Enid
to New York, where they played the great metropolitan-area courses,
and Enid spent one entire night discussing the golf swing with New
York teacher extraordinaire Ernest Jones before returning to the Mon-
terrey Peninsula.

"I fell violently in love with Cypress Point," she recalled, "but I
was so furious because I was so besotted with the beauty of it that I just
couldn't hit a golf ball."

American hospitality prompted her to later donate her collection
of rare handbooks of England's Ladies Golf Union to Golf House, the
museum of the United States Golf Association.

"In 1931 I had played two championships, I had spent two and a
half months in America, and I had spent exactly twenty pounds," Miss
Wilson said. "The Queen herself couldn't have been better looked
after and had more hospitality. There is *no way* I could ever repay. No
way! I'm only too happy, anything they want to have in the museum,
they can have it."

In 1934 Miss Wilson was deemed a "nonamateur" by the Ladies
Golf Union. She didn't challenge the ruling and retired, at twenty-

*Marlene Stewart Streit, a top golfer for
twenty years, and Wanda Sanchez.*

*Frances (Bunty) Stephens, twice winner of
the British Ladies Open Amateur.*

four, from competition. A journalist, she was successful in selling her crisp, pointed prose to most of the golf magazines. She also covered golf for the *Daily Telegraph*, and her commentary gave her great influence in women's golf. Her frequent critiques alienated some of golf's higher-ups, but Enid knew what she was talking about.

In the entry of The Oast, her two-hundred-year-old clock chimed away the afternoon and we talked on.

"Now, one of the greatest of the great had a very frail physique but, by God, the temperament of a tigress! Frances 'Bunty' Stephens. God, nobody had more guts than she had. She was irritating to watch because she had a complete pause at the top, and she took a full practice swing on every shot. I argued with Fred Stephens, her father. I said, 'Look, Frances is absolutely crucifying herself because she doesn't play every shot once, she plays it twice. Now cut out this awful practice swing nonsense.'" And Enid laughed.

Through vociferous longevity and her own good sense, Enid Wilson prevailed and was eventually recognized as a noble influence on British women's golf. In 1982 she was an honored guest in Colorado Springs following the fiftieth anniversary reunion of the Curtis Cup teams, the only member of Britain's 1932 team to attend.

At the U.S. Women's Amateur the following week in Colorado Springs, in the hot August weather, Enid seemed a throwback to another era. Wearing an ancient tweed jacket, she perched upon a shooting stick and keenly assessed the players, just as she had during the six decades of golf to which she is a genuine link.

There exists a very glamourous picture of the young Enid Wilson, taken in the 1930s at the annual Golf Ball in London. In the old photo she wears a sophisticated black sheath with a large white orchid appliquéd on the skirt. Her black hair is pulled back in a sleek chignon, and her eyes are haunting and dark. A man in white tie and tails stands, somewhat forlornly, in the background while Enid grips a golf club, addressing the Oriental carpet as intently as if it were a patch of Sunningdale turf.

"I am," she once declared dramatically, "a slave to golf!"

Nearly five years after that delightful afternoon in Enid's kitchen, I was delighted to receive a letter from The Oast. Enid's black scrawl tracked across the onionskin pages.

For most of the three pages, she recalled Marlene Stewart Streit's 1954 match against Bunty Stephens.

"They had a wonderful match and I recollect that Frances got down in one putt on nine of the last eleven holes of that encounter. When Marlene returned to Ganton in 1955 no one reporting knew that saga of 1954, and Streit can't have mentioned it!

". . . I've always maintained that Marlene was the best woman golfer in the world during the 1950s," Enid wrote.

She followed with a careful listing of matches and, to my great pleasure, added a page of her memories of that match. She even tossed in a headline: "Miss Stephens levels at 18th. Wins at 22nd."

Keen observer, friend of golf for more than sixty years, in the end Enid Wilson remained devoted to making sure that the record was correct.

The flamboyant Marion Hollins.

Marion Hollins

During the 1920s and early 1930s, the forceful personality of Marion Hollins galvanized the early tremors of feminism in women's golf. A strong performer on the amateur circuit who won the 1921 U.S. Women's Amateur Championship, Miss Hollins, more than many champions, stands out. She was flambouyant: she made millions in oil, entertained the pillars of society, and built Pasatiempo, one of California's finest golf courses and resorts, which featured fine estates, stables, tennis courts, a steeplechase course, and a polo field and became known as the playground of the West.

In 1923, just three years after women won the right to vote, Marion Hollins ramrodded the organizing of the Women's National Golf and Country Club on Long Island, hiring architect Devereux Emmet and Albert Tull to design the golf course. The club, today

Glen Head Country Club, was financed totally by women for an all-woman membership.

A large, wide-shouldered woman, Marion Hollins was far ahead of her time. She was independent, cared little for the niceties of fashion, and most often could be seen striding about in rumpled tweeds. She wore her hair in a severe bob and often donned a cloche hat at a rakish angle for golf. She wore skirts but preferred them to have pockets into which she could thrust her large hands, and she set off a look that can, at best, be called casual.

Marion's many interests set her apart from other women of her day. She was an accomplished horsewoman and the first woman to enter an automobile in the Vanderbilt Cup road race on Long Island. She promoted golf, tennis, and horsemanship for juniors, in addition to making her own fortune and playing a primary role in the development of California golf resorts.

Marion Hollins was born in 1893 in Gatsby country—East Islip, Long Island. Her wealthy family was independent enough to accept risk-taking as part of a well-rounded life. Her father, Harry P. Hollins, was a one-time partner of billionaire J.P. Morgan and lost his fortune during attempts to start his own brokerage firm.

Marion, meanwhile, "was always marching up and down New York streets for some cause," said her niece.

In the 1921 U.S. Women's Amateur, Miss Hollins shattered the qualifying record by four strokes and defeated the graceful Alexa Stirling in the final to win the national title. She was a powerful player, and her emergence as champion inspired other American women to try to hit longer tee shots. Glenna Collett, for one, modeled part of her game after Miss Hollins's example and wrote that Marion was one of the five longest drivers in women's golf. Marion was also an adept iron player.

A few years after she won the Women's Amateur, Marion accompanied her family on a visit to California, where she met S.F.B. Morse, developer of the scenic Monterey Peninsula. Morse had brought golf to the area, but he needed help in promoting his golf courses and exclusive real estate. Struck by Marion's zest and obvious intelligence, he hired her as athletic director.

In that role Marion, with Roger Lapham, hired Alister Mackenzie, a Scot, to design the course that would become famous as Cypress Point Golf Club.

In 1928 she began a venture of her own. With partners, Marion bought nearly six hundred acres in the foothills near San Francisco. This was where she could build Pasatiempo Country Club and Estates, commissioning Mackenzie to design another classic in the ruggedly wooded terrain.

Pasatiempo's grand opening, in 1929, featured an exhibition match between her friend Glenna Collett, Bobby Jones, British champion Cyril Tolley, and, naturally, Marion.

U.S. Open Champion Johnny Farrell makes a sand shot at Pebble Beach in a match with Walter Hagen against Glenna Collett and Marion Hollins. The women got six strokes and won, 2 and 1.

She was not yet more than the daughter of a recently wealthy family and had worked hard to attract investors to finance the new resort. But in 1930 she made a propitious oil deal. Convinced by a friend that there was oil in the Kettleman Hills, adjacent to the San Joaquin Valley, she used her eastern connections—including Walter P. Chrysler and Payne Whitney—to raise money for exploration. The Kettleman Oil Corporation was formed with a relatively small grub-stake of a hundred thousand dollars. Its first well struck oil.

Within a few months the company was sold to the Honolulu Consolidated Oil Company and Standard Oil Company of California for $10 million.

The Atlanta Journal announced the deal, noting "a resulting profit of $2,500,000 to Marion Hollins, Pebble Beach, Cal., former women's national golf champion. . . . Persevering financing efforts of Miss Hollins were said Wednesday night to have been responsible for development of the property in Kettleman Hills, arid range in the San Joaquin Valley."

Remember, America was wallowing in the slough of the Great Depression. Marion's $2.5 million might as well have been billions.

Now she began to invest in the indulgences that would lead to her downfall. She sought to make Pasatiempo the capital of west coast entertainment, building incomparable steeplechase and polo facilities (she was a two-goal polo player). She constructed the finest stables and bought a string of racehorses.

Marion Hollins, millionaire.

Actress Jean Harlow in 1932 at Agua Caliente Golf Club, Mexico.

Jean Harlow attended opening day of Pasatiempo's steeple-chase season in 1931, as did other famous actors, authors, and society darlings. The champagne began to flow at Pasatiempo, and celebrities were always on hand to sip from the glass: Alice Marble, Will Rogers, Joan Fontaine, Mary Pickford, Claudette Colbert, the Rothschilds, the Vanderbilts, and Babe Zaharias. This was Marion's circle and she shared close friendships with many. As a reknowned golfer, she was able to break the barriers of the era's class system, which drew distinct lines separating the socially elite, sports figures, and entertainers. Her money made it possible.

She also gave money away in extravagant amounts; a total of fifty thousand dollars went to two friends with whom she had a pact that the first millionaire among the three would "pay off" the other two.

She started a retirement fund for her mother and father but sank most of her bankroll into Pasatiempo, making constant improvements. The money enhanced her own life very little. It was even said that she wore her golf clothes to country club dances.

Ultimately, her passion for her luxurious resort and the financial upheaval of the Great Depression marked Marion's downfall.

The woes of the Depression took a huge toll on the resort and, despite a few bailouts from her well-to-do friends, Pasatiempo was in real trouble in the 1930s.

In 1937 Marion Hollins suffered a severe concussion in an automobile accident and refused medical attention. She was confined to her bed for months and, in 1938, was forced to sell her golf course. She was able to temporarily hold on to the surrounding real estate and her own home but lost both within a few months. Marion struggled to recover from her accident and competed in the 1940 U.S. Women's Amateur.

On August 27, 1944, this remarkable woman, having made and lost a fortune, died of cancer at the age of fifty-one.

Over the years, Pasatiempo suffered severe water shortages and fell into a state of disrepair. The great layout was eventually restored, and in 1987 Pasatiempo hosted the U.S. Women's Amateur Championship. It was a fitting tribute to the 1921 Women's Amateur champion who had made Pasatiempo her last great work.

Four from the Thirties

There was no professional tour, as such, in the 1930s. The decade still belonged to the amateurs and, by far, the most acclaimed were Joyce Wethered and Glenna Collett Vare. While these two dominated the headlines, they also headed a very fine class.

Maureen Orcutt was on the first Curtis Cup team in 1932 and was runner-up in the 1936 Women's Amateur. Helen Hicks won the 1931 U.S. Women's Amateur before becoming one of the first women professionals. Aniela Goldthwaite of Fort Worth, Texas, won the Southern and became a Curtis Cup player. Opal Hill and Charlotte Glutting were Curtis Cup players, as was the seven-time North and South Champion, Estelle Lawson Page.

Mrs. Gregg Lifur, Kathryn Hemphill, Dorothy Traung, and Leona Pressler, who won three Western Amateur titles, also played well.

But four accomplished women of that era, one who died tragically, are worthy of special mention.

As a child, Virginia Van Wie of Chicago was frail and often ill. Her parents kept her out of school, and she seemed doomed to a life of bad health. A wise doctor urged the family to see that their daughter got more exercise and fresh air and suggested that she take up golf.

Virginia soon developed into an exceptional player, a long hitter whose tee shots measured over 200 yards.

"Trying to picture her as a frail young girl strains the imagination," Glenna said.

Miss Van Wie first played in the U.S. Women's Amateur in 1925 but didn't do very well, qualifying with a 91 and losing in the first round.

*Aniela Goldthwaite, two-time
Southern Amateur Champion of the
1930s.*

Leona Pressler, who won three Western Amateur titles.

*Virginia Van Wie, winner of three consecutive U.S.
Women's Amateur Championships.*

The twelfth green at Marion Hollins's classic Pasatiempo Country Club.

In 1926 she wintered in Florida and won the Palm Beach Championship. In 1928 she repeated in the Palm Beach and won the first of four South Atlantic titles.

Now confident, she made steady progress in national events and fought her way to the final of the 1928 Women's Amateur, only to suffer a huge defeat, the victim of Glenna Collett, 13 and 12.

Glenna, however, kept her respect for Virginia's game and rated her among the five longest hitters of the time, with Joyce Wethered, Marion Hollins, Cecil Leitch, and Maureen Orcutt.

"She was composed on the course, a slender girl with strong wrists and hands," Glenna said.

In 1932 Miss Van Wie rebounded beautifully and won the U.S. Women's Amateur at Salem Country Club in Peabody, Massachusetts. It must have given her some satisfaction since, in the final, she beat Glenna, 10 and 8.

With the American Curtis Cup team, Virginia sailed for England. Her play at Wentworth so impressed British golf writer Bernard Darwin that she was the only player he could later recall from that historic encounter. Darwin wrote that Virginia was one of the best lady golfers he had seen, calling her swing "perfection."

The shy, stately young woman won her second Women's Amateur the following year. Her third and, literally, final championship was in 1934 at Whitemarsh Valley Country Club near Philadelphia.

Virginia Van Wie in 1931 with her golf clubs.

With the British Curtis Cup team on hand the field was huge, and for the first time sixty-four qualified for match play. Virginia again defeated her chief rival, Mrs. Vare, in the semifinals, 3 and 2. When she eased past Dorothy Traung in the final, 2 and 1, she had become only the fourth player in history to capture three U.S. Women's Amateur championships in a row.

Following her victory, Virginia Van Wie retired from competitive golf and later taught school near Chicago.

Another of the era's fine players was a Canadian, Ada Mackenzie of Toronto. Americans first saw her in the 1925 U.S. Women's Amateur, where she narrowly lost to Glenna Collett in the second round.

Ada regularly played in the U.S. championship and twice made the semifinals, in 1927 and 1932.

Glenna credited her with having "a good short game and much grit." Miss Collett would know, having had to beat Miss Mackenzie in the final to win the 1924 Canadian Amateur.

Miss Mackenzie won five Canadian Women's Open Amateur titles from 1919 through 1935, and her remarkable reign made her Canada's finest player until Marlene Stewart Streit emerged nearly twenty years later.

In 1932 thirteen-year-old Betty Jameson won the Texas Public Links title. She won the prestigious Southern Women's Amateur Championship in 1934, at fifteen. So began a wonderful career.

Betty Jameson, 1939–40 U.S. Women's Amateur Champion.

Miss Jameson was born in 1919 in Norman, Oklahoma, but grew up in San Antonio and was the first of a long line of great Texas players.

A tall blond with a vibrant smile, Betty had a strong, classic swing. She possessed superb timing, solid fundamentals, and a fine intellect that allowed her to understand the intricacies of the game. Her great hands were another key to her success, hands that gripped the club softly and allowed her to play a variety of shots.

At heart Betty Jameson was an artist and throughout her life devoted much of her time to painting, but she won her fame playing golf.

At sixteen, Miss Jameson won the first of four consecutive Texas

Betty Jameson was the first woman to break 300 for 72 holes, shooting 295 to win the 1947 U.S Women's Open Championship.

state championships and went on to become one of the finest players on the national scene.

Betty seemed to win tournaments in pairs: two Trans-Mississippi titles, two Western Amateur championships, and the U.S. Women's Amateur in 1939 and 1940.

In 1938 she captured the Women's Texas Open as an amateur and won it again in 1949 as a professional. In 1942 Miss Jameson won the Western Open as an amateur and twelve years later won the championship as a professional. When she won the Western Amateur and the Western Open in 1942, she became the first to take both titles in the same year.

The talented young woman became the first woman to break

300 for 72 holes in any tournament, firing a record score of 295 at Starmount Forrest Country Club in Greensboro, North Carolina, to win the 1947 U.S. Women's Open.

Betty Jameson's professional career was a great one, and in 1951 she was inducted into the LPGA Hall of Fame. The following year she conceived the idea of honoring the professional who had the season's lowest scoring average. To that end she donated the Vare Trophy, named in honor of her friend, Glenna Collett Vare.

One of golf's tragic stories is that of Marion Miley of Lexington, Kentucky. Like Pam Barton, who died at the height of her career, Marion Miley's life was a promise unfulfilled.

A tall, exuberant brunette with a wide smile, Marion grew up playing the posh Lexington Country Club where her father was head professional. In 1931, at seventeen, she won the first of six Kentucky Women's Amateur titles.

Marion had many interests. She played bridge and was an accomplished violinist. A good student in college who made nearly all A's, she had hoped to become a doctor, but her diverse talents included an increasing enthusiasm for golf.

Marion Miley was a very strong young woman. She once eagled a 603-yard par 5. In an exhibition match with Babe Didrickson, Miss Miley outscored and outhit the famous athlete.

The year 1935 was a great one. Marion won the Trans-Mississippi, the South Atlantic, and the Women's Western Amateur. In 1936 she again won the Trans and made it to the semifinals of the Women's Amateur. In a great irony, she lost her semifinal match to Pam Barton, the English player who went on to win. Neither young woman would reach thirty years of age.

In 1937 Marion again won the Western Amateur. She won the first of two consecutive Southern Amateur titles in 1938 and reached the semifinals of the U.S. Women's Amateur, winning a spot on the 1938 Curtis Cup team. It would be her last international appearance.

In 1941 Marion was twenty-seven. She worked for an advertising agency and shared an apartment on the second floor of the Lexington Country Club clubhouse with her mother. Her father had accepted a well-paying job at Maketewah Country Club, some eighty miles away in Cincinnati, and, for now, the two women lived alone.

On the night of September 27, Marion played bridge with friends in Lexington, then returned home and went to bed. Shortly after midnight two masked men with handguns crawled into the clubhouse through an open window. They climbed the stairs, broke a glass pane on a door, and entered the Miley apartment.

The men woke Mrs. Miley, demanding the cash receipts from a country club dance. Disappointed at the small amount of money, one of the men knocked Mrs. Miley unconscious.

Hearing her mother's screams, Marion awoke and ran to her aid. A furious fight followed. Marion put up a great battle until one of the men shot her through the neck, then through the head. She died instantly.

The murder made headlines across the nation and today remains one of Kentucky's most sensational crimes.

Three men, including one of the club's caretakers, were later convicted and executed for Marion Miley's murder.

6

Golf's Great Loss

In an old photograph Pam Barton is a sturdy girl, neatly dressed in tweeds and a single strand of pearls. The sun has freckled her nose and tipped with blond the ends of her bouncy auburn curls. She is a wholesome young woman laughing at the camera, merry in her glory, as if the trophies she clutches are the spoils of a great and private joke.

Miss Barton's career was short, brilliant, and finally tragic. She died in a plane crash, killed on her way home from a dance. It was 1943 and she was twenty-six. On the long sad list of British casualties during World War II, maybe the loss of Pam Barton seems of little consequence. She was not, after all, a historical figure in a serious vein, such as in statesmanship or the arts. Nor was her loss as sad, perhaps, as a family's war loss of a father or an only child. Pam Barton was unmarried, childless, a player of games. Yet her death dealt a devastating blow to British women's golf, squelched its most popular voice, and stilled its greatest inspiration.

One of Miss Barton's friends in those years was Maureen Ruttle Garrett. Affectionately known as "Pooh," Maureen is one of those rare women who become, as T.S. Eliot once said of Lady Diana Cooper, "a

*Great Britain and Ireland's 1960 Curtis Cup Team. (**Back row**) Frances Smith, Ruth Porter, Angela Bonallack, Belle McCorkindale, Philomena Garvey, Marley Spearman; (**Front row**) Elizabeth Price, Maureen Garrett, Janette Robertson.*

religion to her many friends." Mrs. Garrett is someone to whom we can turn for an honest appraisal of the period of British golf from 1940 to the present, not only because she was a skilled player but because of her vast knowledge of the game and the players of the last fifty years.

In her flat in Poole, Mrs. Garrett stared pensively through the window as small boats cut through the fog on the bay below. As a girl she had been befriended by Miss Barton, and she remembered being devastated by her death.

"Pam would say, 'Super! Great shot!' to you. She was so enthusiastic. She would like honestly to beat you with her good golf, not because you'd played some awful golf. She would just love to have a great match. I know, because as a competitor you have this sort of feeling about it.

"There are some who'll win by any method and means—if you drop dead, that counts," Mrs. Garrett chuckled. "But if I hit one alongside Pam she would say 'Good shot,' which was lovely.

"The old school was that you must sit on the young and not encourage them, because their day would come. I'd grown up in that era when you stayed out of the way of the older women. There's no way you would seek any help from them, or encouragement, at all. Pam said, 'No, if I can help somebody, I will.' It was lovely to have that.

"I read about her death in the paper," Maureen said. "I was miserable, just the thought that you'd never see her again. Although I was

Pam Barton winning the 1936 U.S. Women's Amateur.

young then, I realized that there was going to be a great hole in British golf. She had been there to be shot at, which was great. Now you weren't going to have her to try and beat. So, after the war we all started with much less. There wasn't anybody really."

Maureen was sixteen when she first played against Pam, who was twenty-one. Maureen had beaten another opponent in the morning, and in the afternoon she went twenty holes against Barton before losing the match.

"At tea time afterwards she gave me lots of encouragement," Mrs. Garrett recalled. "She said that she had only won because I must have been tired having had a game in the morning, whereas she had come in fresh. It was just her nice way of trying to soften the blow and my disappointment at losing such a close match. Her sportsmanship has influenced me throughout my life."

Pam Barton took up the game in the early 1930s, when the swing standard had been set by Joyce Wethered, whose grace and gentle arc were classic.

Pam, however, was a stocky girl with powerful legs and strong hands. While Joyce Wethered stayed so elegantly on her toes through the impact area, Pam Barton planted her left foot firmly on the turf on her downswing. Shifting her weight down and through the ball, her swing had great width and power.

If Miss Wethered typified the graceful swing of the twenties and thirties, Miss Barton, with her solid footwork and strength, was the

Nan Baird, 1934 Scottish Champion.

A teenage Patty Berg, already an excellent amateur in the 1930s.

first woman golfer of the modern era with a power swing.

"Oh, Pam gave the king a scalp, just no two hoops about it, she attacked that ball," said Enid Wilson, the fine British journalist. "One year in the Sunningdale Foursomes, her partner, Alfred Padgham, put her in a clump of heather. Two old gentlemen, probably retired Air Force, whispered, 'Oh, she can't do it.'

"Pam sort of stamped up to the thing and gave it an imperial bash, blasting the ball and the bush over the slope and onto the green. The bush was in shreds," laughed Wilson, "and so were the two old men.

"Pam was a charming personality, but very, very aggressive. She was taught by Archie Compston, a great big rawboned man who gave everything hell. He was her mentor."

In the early 1930s Compston wrote, "Golf is considered the most artistic game in the world. You would imagine that women would have an artistic sense, especially on the putting green. But on the golf course they seem to be absolutely devoid of it. . . . The great failing with women golfers is lack of length from the tee and with the long irons. Lack of length is the principal reason why women golfers will never be able to play on level terms with men."

Compston's estimation of women golfers improved when Pam and her sister Mervyn took lessons from him while in their midteens.

"He told us we were the most lousy golfers he'd ever seen in his life," said Mervyn, "and he worked us to death."

The sisters, daughters of a Surrey tea merchant, had their first great tournament success in 1933, winning the Bystander Foursomes with a combined handicap of 7 and an aggregate age of thirty-four years.

In May 1934 Pam, now seventeen, reached the finals of the British Championship. A few weeks later she was chosen to play for Britain against France, the youngest player ever selected for a British team. Later that year Barton won the French Open at Le Touquet. In the fall she played in the Curtis Cup Match at Chevy Chase, Maryland.

In 1935 she toured Australia and New Zealand with the LGU team and, for the second year in a row, was runner-up at the British Women's Amateur Championship, beating her sister in the semifinals.

It was a remarkable year, and she set herself apart from her peers when, at nineteen, she won the British Women's Amateur Championship at Southport with the American Curtis Cup team in the field.

Compston was prompted to praise his young pupil's character.

"This girl's greatest asset is her attitude of mind," he said. "She has a wonderful power of concentration and wonderful fighting qualities coming up the home stretch where it matters most. Pamela Barton [goes] out there to win."

In September 1936 the U.S. Women's Amateur Championship was played at Canoe Brook Country Club in Summit, New Jersey. The field was formidable. For the first time the USGA had reduced the handicap limit to 6 strokes. Glenna Collett Vare, the defending champion, did not play, but the field included Patty Berg, the Kentucky star Marion Miley, Maureen Orcutt, Betty Jameson, Estelle Lawson Page, and Canada's Ada Mackenzie.

Only Dorothy Campbell, a Scot, had ever won the American and British championships in the same year, and that had happened twenty-seven years earlier. Another Englishwoman, the cheerful Gladys Ravenscroft, won the British in 1912 and the U.S. Women's Amateur in 1913.

Miss Barton was determined to win the double. She made the long ocean voyage to the United States and upon her arrival set up a grueling practice schedule. Each day she played seven holes with twenty balls, an exercise that took two hours, then spent an additional three hours working on her putting, driving, and iron play.

Wisely, she spent most of the week trying to master her nerves, striving to make her mind blank of all thoughts except golf.

"It is a kind of process of self-isolation, of going into a shell, of putting away outside things," she wrote later. "Crack American women golfers are adept at it. They have brought it to the point of perfection. They never talk . . . they seem to press a button and all at once, in their own minds, nobody else exists."

"Pam adored the States," said her sister, "She was put up for the American championship by a very kind couple who she absolutely adored, Mr. and Mrs. Bill Waite. They kept in correspondence for years afterwards."

Bill Waite was most anxious for his young British guest to feel at home.

"Is there anything we do wrong, Pam?" Waite asked one morning, puffing on a foul-smelling cigar.

"Just one thing Bill," Pam said, "I can't take a cigar for breakfast!"

Miss Barton progressed steadily through the tournament and faced Marion Miley in the semifinals. All square at the 13th, Miss Miley hit the green in two. Miss Barton knocked her second shot to the left of the green in a narrow avenue of trees. A low canopy of branches obscured her ball.

"I played a low, straight approach shot out—dead," Pam later wrote. "Shaken, Miss Miley took three putts and I won the hole in four to five."

Pam closed out Marion on the 17th.

The run-up shot was a fine example of Miss Barton's diversity.

"When I was a schoolgirl my idea of good golf was a good drive," she said. "What happened afterwards did not matter. I was perfectly content to suffer the most grievous trouble if I had smacked the ball 200 yards off the tee. Fortunately, I revised my ideas fairly quickly and settled down to practising the various kinds of approach play, determined to master all of them."

In the final, Pam faced Maureen Orcutt. Miss Orcutt played out of the Miami-Biltmore but had competed extensively in metropolitan

Maureen Orcutt during the 1936 Curtis Cup.

New York and was a popular player there. A huge gallery of four thousand tramped around Canoe Brook for the Orcutt-Barton match.

"Pam was thrilled, she was over the moon," her sister recalled. "Maureen was a wonderful sport and the crowds absolutely staggered Pam. People in Britain just politely clap; she'd never encountered a noisy crowd, but they were fantastic.

"Pam was an outgoing person and liked everyone, until she knew better."

Miss Barton was superb. Playing the last 24 holes in one under women's par, she bashed out one long drive after another, rising tee shots that carried 200 yards. Pam simply overpowered the steady Orcutt, winning the match, 4 and 3, to win the U.S. Women's Amateur.

"As I walked round the Canoe Brook course I was not conscious of a single individual," she said.

Pam returned to England a national heroine. She competed extensively in international play and in 1937 wrote *A Stroke a Hole*, a charming instruction book that contains unique photo sequences of her golf swing. If you flip through the pages quickly, the small photographs move like movie frames and Miss Barton's swing can be seen in motion—a visual reminder of her power. (Incidentally, the LGU did not allow her to accept payment for the book because was an amateur.)

Miss Barton repeated as British Women's Amateur Champion in 1939, but war loomed over all of western Europe and games soon came to an end; golf courses were turned into airstrips, clubhouses became hospitals, and tournament golf halted while England fought a more dangerous foe.

England's golfers had a sort of cavalier disregard for their own welfare during wartime rounds. They formed special war rules: They were allowed to take cover, without penalty, to avoid falling bombs or gunblasts. Balls moved by enemy action were replaced, without penalty. There was no penalty for lifting and dropping a ball that lay in a bomb crater, nor for removing shells or bomb pieces from the putting green. If your stroke was affected by a sudden explosion, such as detonation of bombs or mortar shells, or by machine-gun fire, you could play another ball, with a one-stroke penalty.

England's young golfing elite discovered serious new responsibilities. Pam Barton, Maureen Garrett, and Wanda Morgan played in exhibitions to benefit the Red Cross, auctioning off clubs and sweaters for the cause.

Maureen Garrett worked as a doctor's secretary on London's Harley Street, sometimes dodging bombs to get to her office. The doctor innoculated members of England's war cabinet, including Winston Churchill, to keep them fit.

"I could have gone through the war doing that," she recalled, "but on the radio there was a call for a land army. They didn't have enough volunteers and wanted people who could handle horses. I'd always had my own ponies, so I said to Mummy, 'This is ridiculous, I'm sitting in this luxurious office and I don't think I'm doing my war effort.'"

Mrs. Garrett quit her secretarial job, signed up for the land army, and spent the rest of the war milking cows and handling farm horses. But golf was never far from her mind.

"I enjoyed playing golf almost the most during the war because it was so hard," she said. "I would milk the cows on a Sunday morning, then bicycle two and a half miles to whip out of my clothes and into my golf clothes, get my clubs, walk down a lane, catch a bus, go to Moor Park, then walk up a great hill to the clubhouse."

Maureen competed on a men's team made up of "old boys," men too old for the military, against a team of young men from Cambridge and Oxford.

"I was thrilled to be the only woman on a men's team," she said. "They appreciated women because we were bombed as much as they were and had to work as hard. After we played, I had to walk all the way back, get a bus and get home. Before the war, I'd been chauffeur-driven, because everybody was chauffeur-driven, and I'd had a caddie."

Another fine junior English golfer, Jeanne Bisgood, who became a Curtis Cup player, also found life greatly changed. Miss Bisgood's father, a prominent and prosperous stockbroker, was a devoted sportsman who installed a tennis court and a putting green in his garden. An enthusiastic golfer, he encouraged his daughter to compete.

Early in the war, Miss Bisgood attended a convent school in Mayfield at Sussex, and her parents would drive her down to Crow-

Pam Barton (left center) joined the Women's Auxiliary Air Force and died in an air crash in 1943.

borough to play golf. Later she joined the Women's Royal Naval Service and was given a duty vital to England's war effort.

With a group of other schoolgirls, she ran the machines that were used to break the infamous "Enigma" code, the backbone of the Nazi codes. The girls worked in northwest London, in the suburb of Stanmoor. As the Germans invented new codes, the young women helped develop the tools to break the codes. Their work was of the greatest secrecy, and they could not reveal the nature of their war work until 1975.

"We came from schools where we were taught absolutely nothing useful, but we had been taught certain standards of honor. We did not talk, and we did not talk for thirty years," said Miss Bisgood, who later became a barrister.

Pam Barton had enlisted in the Women's Auxiliary Air Force and was given a commission.

By November 1943 her sister Mervyn lived in Calcutta with her husband. One night Mervyn had a strange nightmare.

"I dreamt that Pam had died," Mervyn said. "I dreamt that I got the news in a telegram and in the dream I had thrown it on a chest and said, 'This is of no interest.'"

Shortly after, while Mervyn's husband was in Bombay, a news program was broadcast over the radio.

"A friend rang me up and said, 'Have you got anyone with you?

Get someone round,'" said Mervyn, "I turned on the radio, and I heard of Pam's death. I got the telegram two days later."

Pam had been escorted to a dance in Manston, Kent, by a young pilot. After the dance they boarded a plane. The pilot took off downwind but failed to turn on the plane's gasoline taps. The plane crashed, the young man survived, but Pam was killed. She was buried at Biggin Hill Cemetery in Kent.

"Pam was a brilliant golfer," recalled Molly Gourlay, the veteran Curtis Cup player. "She was never beaten until the last putt was holed. She was amusing and gracious. It was a terrible tragedy."

There had been a brilliance about Miss Barton, something clean and fine that early on gave a glimmer of what women's golf could aspire to—power tempered by finesse, aggression softened by kindness and goodwill—qualities that left a lasting impression on her friends.

"It is terribly difficult for a young golfer always to do and say the right thing," wrote Enid Wilson. "If she remains silent in deference to her elders, she is accounted dumb; if she makes bright conversation and tries to entertain her companions, she is precocious. Miss Barton had the happy knack of being able to say and do the right things in whatever company she found herself . . . she was most popular with the old people and a favorite with the young . . . a splendid sportswoman, modest, unassuming and thoughtful of others."

After the War

World War II ended and British women's golf resumed without Pamela Barton.

"Had it not been for the war, Miss Barton would have gone on winning more championships," wrote Enid Wilson. "Her death made a difference to British women's golf, for had she been able to give the post-war girls an incentive in vigorous hitting, they would not have been so vulnerable as they were to the players from overseas."

The war had temporarily stopped overseas competition. Now the war was over but money was scarce, and England's future matches were threatened. Foreign travel was expensive, and Curtis Cup competition between the British Isles and the United States was particularly endangered.

Finally, after a ten-year lapse, the matches were resumed in 1948 at the Royal Birkdale Golf Club. Some American players, having heard of British postwar austerity and fearing shortages, brought their own food.

When the war had ended, American women golfers organized quickly and began daily practice, but British women were forced to go to work. They coped with haphazard public transportation during the work week and managed only occasional weekend matches at local clubs.

However, the war had unified the British, and it had changed social mores. Before the war only the wealthy played golf—except in Scotland where everyone played—now golf became more democratized.

"After the war we had the greenkeeper's daughter playing on our side," said Maureen Garrett. "We also went into uniform. The idea was to unify us all because the greenkeeper's daughter couldn't afford cashmeres. We were sort of leveling out and I think the wartime did it—it didn't matter who you were, we had all pitched in. The same bombs had dropped on us."

When the British and Irish team lost the 1948 Curtis Cup by a 6½ to 2½ margin, the showing was considered respectable. But British golf was admittedly impoverished, and the LGU could not afford to send a team to the United States for the 1950 Curtis Cup matches. In 1949 the LGU appealed for help in building its International Match Fund to bring British golf back to its formerly high standards. *Fairway & Hazard* magazine suggested that each lady golfer donate a shilling a year. Within a year the fund grew to three thousand pounds, but the pound had been devalued, and the value of the LGU bank account was reduced by about a third.

The Australian opera singer Joan Hammond, a three-time New South Wales Champion, donated proceeds from two of her concerts to the Australian Ladies' Golf Union to finance team travel to England. This gave the British some foreign competition. Still, prospects of sending a team to the United States for the 1950 Curtis Cup matches seemed dim.

The Americans intervened. Margaret Curtis began a campaign that she named "The Pam Barton Fund." At Miss Curtis's urging, American women golfers held a series of "Pam Barton Days," one-day tournaments to raise money for the British. The Cleveland District Women's Golf Association alone forwarded nearly five hundred dollars to England in Barton's name.

"Few people on our side of the Atlantic were aware of this act of kindness in memory of our former champion," wrote Enid Wilson.

Finally enough money was raised, and the British and Irish team sailed for the United States. On September 4, 1950, Jeanne Bisgood and her Curtis Cup teammates—Frances "Bunty" Stephens, Jessie Valentine, Jean Donald, Philomena Garvey, Elizabeth Price, and playing captain Diana Critchley, assembled for the opening ceremonies on the lawn of the Country Club of Buffalo in Williamsville, New York.

The American team had Dorothy Germain Porter, Beverly Hanson, Polly Riley, Dorothy Kielty, Peggy Kirk, Dorothy Kirby, Helen Sigel, and Grace Lenczyk and was captained by Glenna Collett Vare.

Once again the Americans won by a big margin, 7½ to 1½, but,

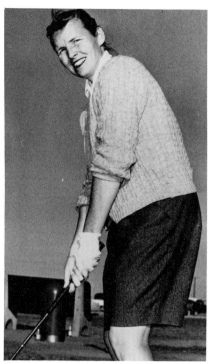

Dot Porter and her daughter in 1949, the year she won the U.S. Women's Amateur.

Peggy Kirk, winner of the 1949 Titleholders Championship.

remarkably, the match had been played.

Two years later a fine little Curtis Cup drama unfolded in Scotland at old Muirfield, ironically, a club that not only prohibited women from joining but had no women's locker room.

Cold winds blustered in from the Firth of Forth over the dramatic 6,460-yard course. The British and Irish team played tenaciously, winning two of the three foursomes matches. Two British players won their singles matches; Bunty Stephens narrowly defeated Marge Lindsay, and Jeanne Bisgood romped over Mae Murray, 6 and 5.

The score was tied, Britain and Ireland, 4 and the USA, 4, with but one match still on the course.

Elizabeth Price, twenty-three, a sturdy, determined young woman, was making her second Curtis Cup appearance for Britain. In 1950 Price had been soundly beaten by Grace Lenczyk, 5 and 4, in a singles match.

This time her opponent, Grace DeMoss of Corvallis, Oregon, was a first-time Curtis Cup player. Miss DeMoss had reached the semifinals in the two previous U.S. Women's Amateur championships, but that had been individual competition, and team play brought entirely different pressures.

During the week, Miss DeMoss had told friends about a dream in which she was playing her final match when her white-coated

Elizabeth Price, British Curtis Cup player of the '50s.

Grace DeMoss, American Curtis Cup player of the '50s.

teammates suddenly appeared over the crest of a hill to tell her that American honor now rested entirely on her shoulders. It was a horrifying premonition.

On the final day, Grace DeMoss was left to battle Elizabeth Price in the match that would decide the Cup's destiny. Miss Price moved into a 2-up advantage, but her opponent was threatening. At the 15th it appeared Miss Price's lead would shrink to a one-hole margin.

Muirfield's 15th, a par 4 of nearly 400 yards, tacked back into the gusty wind off the Firth of Forth. After two mighty wood shots, Miss DeMoss was just short of the green. Miss Price's ball, after three shots, lay in a greenside bunker. If Grace made her simple pitch and got down in one or two putts, the American would no doubt take the hole and would be only one down with three holes to play.

Instead, her nightmare began. Grace addressed her shot to the green, somewhat tentatively. She had chosen a pitching wedge, not her best club, and she was uncomfortable as she stood over the shot. When she struck the ball, it skittered off crazily to the right.

"She shanked it!" the Americans muttered in dismay.

"A socket!" whispered the British.

Miss DeMoss gathered herself and again addressed the ball. She could still pitch to the green and possibly one-putt for a five to halve the hole. She swung the club, and again the ball shot off to the right.

Polly Riley, six-time American Curtis Cup player.

The 1952 British Curtis Cup Team.
(Standing) *Frances Stephens, Moira Paterson, Katherine Cairns, Philomena Garvey, Elizabeth Price, Kitty McCann.*
(Front) *Jessie Valentine, Jean Donald, Jeanne Bisgood.*

Abject humiliation. There was no escape, no hole to crawl into, and no way out but to somehow finish. Again Miss DeMoss stood over the ball. Her American teammates watched helplessly as the little tragedy unfolded. More than one wished that Grace would simply take a putter and bash the ball onto the green, but by now she was in a state of near shock.

Three more times she tried the shot. Each time she shanked it, until she had nearly circled the green, winding up not 15 feet away from the site of her original pitch shot. Miss Price won the hole with a bogey, was 3-up with three to play, and Miss DeMoss was in ruins, incapable now of recovering. Miss Price won the match, 3 and 2, and the British team had won the Curtis Cup, 5 points to 4, for the first time in the twenty-year history of the matches.

Cheers broke out from the five thousand Scots encircling the 16th green.

American player Polly Riley wasn't as distressed as some of her teammates. "The British had never won the Curtis Cup, and they won it fairly and squarely," Miss Riley recalled.

But there was a bizarre conclusion to the United Kingdom's stirring victory against staggering odds. The British victory dinner was in the Marine Hotel. In keeping with tradition, the Curtis Cup was filled with champagne and passed among the assembled players. One of the Americans, a friend of Grace DeMoss, was still smarting over the shanking incident and refused to drink from the cup. To distract attention from the unpleasant scene, Miss Riley grabbed a rose from a vase on the table, clenched it between her teeth, jumped upon the table, and began to dance.

Seldom has the Curtis Cup match been more dramatic than in 1952, but a number of smaller dramas are woven throughout its long history.

Selection to the Curtis Cup team is a rite of passage for the good woman amateur, one of the highest honors in golf, and multiple selection is a symbol of an extraordinary career.

On the American side, several players have been selected a number of times: Anne Quast Sander (8), Polly Riley (6), Barbara McIntire (6), Lancy Smith (5), and Phyllis Preuss (5). Among the Great Britain and Ireland players, Mary McKinna (9), Jessie Anderson Valentine (7), Belle Robertson (7), and Frances Smith, Angela Ward Bonallack, Elizabeth Price Fisher, and Philomena Garvey (all 6 times) are multiple selections.

While the match sparks high interest in Great Britain and Ireland and draws tremendous crowd support for the GB&I team, it draws little notice in the American press.

"The Curtis Cup match is the best-kept secret in golf," said Judy Bell, a two-time player who captained the American side in 1986 and 1988.

Throughout early days the American side dominated, but the contest began to even up in the 1980s, with Great Britain and Ireland winning in 1986 and 1988.

While the Curtis Cup match is a team event, it provides a setting for courageous individual performances. JoAnne Gunderson Carner and Barbara McIntire never lost a singles match for the Americans. Frances Stephens Smith, the wonderful English player, was also undefeated in singles and, in fact, never lost an international match of any kind.

7

The Freckled Fireplug

Patty Berg had deep convictions that she often expressed in a speech she called "What it Takes to Become a Champion."

After a glowing introduction, she would march up to the podium in a navy blue suit, defiantly adjust the microphone, and crack a few jokes. You sat there at your banquet table, thinking about tomorrow's match and not particularly keen on another after-dinner speech. Then she hit you with it, shouting at you about the will to win, inspiration, never giving up, desire, self-control, determination, heart, courage, striving for perfection, faith, aiming for the top, and using your mind.

She was Winston Churchill and FDR rolled into one and, at the end, she told you to take God with you. "God love you!" she shouted, "God be with you! And *God Bless America*!" Then she sat down.

You could hear her speak a dozen times and still get goose bumps. I first heard that speech in May 1966. I last heard it on August 8, 1988, when Patty was honored at the eighty-eighth U.S. Women's Amateur Championship at Minikahda Country Club in Minneapolis. It was the fiftieth anniversary of her U.S. Women's Amateur win.

Friends, Wilson Sporting Goods Company, and members of Interlachen Country Club had commissioned a portrait of Miss Berg, which would hang in Golf House, the USGA Museum in Far Hills, New Jersey.

The portrait was unveiled that night. Judy Bell, a member of the USGA Executive Committee, introduced Miss Berg as "the feisty fireplug from Minneapolis, the former quarterback of the 50th Street Tigers."

Miss Berg's old teaching professional, Les Bolstad, now in his eighties, was there, and the room was crowded with friends and fans. It was the only time I ever saw Patty break down.

Throughout the week, however, she stalked the fairways of Minikahda. A USGA official followed her in an electric golf cart, in case she tired. Patty was, after all, seventy years old, but she followed the matches, frequently stopping to sign autographs and thoroughly enjoying this visit to her old home town.

One afternoon Miss Bell, Barbara McIntire, and I drove Patty to Interlachen, the wonderful old golf course where she had learned to play so many years ago. It had been a long week, and at first Patty seemed tired. The sight of her old club revived her, and she walked briskly to the pro shop, her eyes darting around the old clubhouse.

Miss McIntire had been in a severe slump and was discouraged about her game. She had thought of quitting competition.

"She can't quit!" Patty had said to me, with furrowed brow. "She's too good. Anyone who won the U.S. Amateur twice and the British Amateur and was runner-up in the 1956 U.S. Women's Open has to keep playing!"

And so Patty was going to give Miss McIntire the golf lesson of her life. The August afternoon was steamy hot, and I was concerned about Patty's stamina. I shouldn't have worried. She dumped three large buckets of practice balls on the grass—Miss Bell and I would not be allowed to just observe.

Patty roamed up and down the tee. She teed up each ball and squinted at us through her spectacles, picking out flaws in our grips, shouting instructions like a drill sergeant.

"Drive with those legs! Hold tight with that right hand! Clubhead square at address! Take it straight back! Drive with those legs!"

Even the serious Miss McIntire had to laugh. This only spurred Patty on. After more than two hours, we were slurping each other's iced tea, ignoring whose cup belonged to whom. Storm clubs roiled over the practice tee, the wind nearly knocked us down, but we weren't allowed to stop. "Drive with those legs!" she yelled.

For more than fifty years, Patty Berg appeared in thousands of golf clinics. She strutted across the world's practice tees in her crazy collection of hats, a natural comedian, the rollicking extrovert who loved crowds. She seemed indomitable. As a youngster she barn-

Patty and Babe.

stormed the north country in countless charity exhibitions. As an adult she laid the foundation of the women's professional tour, using good business sense and boundless enthusiasm to promote women's golf when few wanted to listen.

Patty Berg transcended generations: She was a friend to Babe Zaharias and a mother hen to Kathy Whitworth. One of her fans was Nancy Lopez. More than that, she was a wholesome, fresh-faced woman of great kindness and, without doubt, a great player with one of the most sound and powerful swings in the history of the game.

Mickey Wright believed that Patty Berg was the finest woman golfer she ever saw.

"Absolutely," said Miss Wright. "Number one, she had a good grip. She had a simple golf swing that never changed. She had the club square. She hit the ball solidly, she hit the ball high. She knew more golf shots than any other women before, or after."

Miss Berg's contributions to golf and to humanity earned many awards that, in the end, overshadowed her greatness as a player. Several believed that her skill was overlooked because she played in the era of Babe Zaharias.

"Patty got kicked under the rug because of Babe," said Wright. "As a player, as someone who knew golf, all aspects of it, I really don't think she got her due as the fine golfer she was."

Among Miss Berg's qualities, perhaps the most admirable is her cheerful acceptance of her longtime role as Babe's second banana. It

Patty Berg, Jean Bauer, Helen Hicks, and Babe Didrikson at a 1937 Coral Gables exhibition.

was no small personal concession for the redhead: the game is geared to individual achievement. Played in glorious isolation, golf seems to demand total self-absorption from its champions. A splendid exception comes along now and then, however, and Miss Berg chose the high road. While she lived in the shadow of the myth throughout Babe's playing career and even long after Zaharias had died, Miss Berg's grace in accepting that role transcends many sporting acts.

Years after Babe had died, Patty's speeches and commentaries were still full of stories about her old friend.

"She was really one of my idols," Miss Berg said. "I just thought she was terrific. She was a great, great friend of mine too. I had lots of fun with her. I thought she had a great sense of humor and she got a charge out of everything."

Patty Berg was born in Minneapolis, the daughter of Herman Berg, a well-to-do grain merchant who was a member of the Chicago Board of Trade, the Minneapolis Board of Trade, and the Winnipeg Board of Trade. H.L. Berg had a 10 handicap at the famed Interlachen Golf Club, the winding, tree-lined course where his daughter would learn to play. Before golf, however, there was football.

As a moppet in Shirley Temple curls, she quarterbacked the 50th Street Tigers, a neighborhood football team organized by Bud Wilkinson, who would grow up to become head coach of the University of Oklahoma football team. On this team of boys, Patty was the quarterback.

"We had only one signal—22—and everyone ran every which

Patty Berg with touring pro Johnny Revolta at a 1954 Veterans Day benefit.

way," Patty said. "We didn't have any tricky offense, we just had the single wing and I was the only one back there. We didn't have any wide ends, or tight ends, we just had a lot of loose ends. We never lost a game, just teeth! I have a picture of the team and everybody in the line was missing teeth."

Patricia Jane Berg's mother intervened before her daughter could be counted among the toothless.

"Well, Bud told me I was a little slow and that there wasn't any future in football for me," Miss Berg laughed. "Also, I was hurting my legs and tearing my clothes before my dad had even paid for them. Mother said, 'We gotta get this girl into something else!'"

For a while she was a speed skater. Her strong, stocky little legs pumping down the ice, Patty won national medals for the Minneapolis Powderhorn Club. Her interest in golf was inevitable. Her adored father was an avid businessman-golfer, and her brother Herman, Jr., was a fine player. Her father signed her up for lessons from Willie Kidd, Sr., Interlachen's head professional. Later she took from Kidd's assistant, Jim Pringle.

Les Bolstad, one of the nation's foremost instructors, fine-tuned her natural golf swing and taught her to be a great bunker player. She was loyal to his teaching and took lessons from him for forty years.

At the age of fifteen, she entered the Minneapolis City Championship.

"Geez, I'll never forget coming down the night before I was going to play," Miss Berg remembered. "I put my golf bag down and I had a towel draped here, and a towel here, and a towel there, and I said to my dad, 'How do I look?' And he said, 'Well, are you gonna play golf or go swimming?'"

The next day she qualified with an 18-hole score of 122.

"You should have seen that qualifying round," she recalled. "In that 122, I was lucky! I had a lot of lucky things happen to me, it should have been about 140!"

Isolated in the last flight with a woman who qualified with 121, Patty was badly beaten in match play the following day.

"After that, all I could think about was next year's championship. I decided right then and there I was going to dedicate the next 365 days of the year to improving my golf game. So, I practiced and trained, practiced and trained. My dad took me to golf professionals to teach me the right fundamentals of the golf swing—then, I'd practice and play, practice and play, from morning to night. I thought if I worked 365 days maybe I could do better.

"That was the turning point in my whole career, because if I hadn't improved in 365 days, I don't think I would be in golf today."

She won the Minneapolis Ladies City Championship the next year. In 1935 she was invited to play in an exhibition in St. Paul with Walter Hagen, Johnny Revolta, Horton Smith, and Mrs. Austin Pardue, another good amateur of that time.

"They had advertised me as an up-and-comer in the papers, and more people were gathered in that one place than I had ever seen in my life.

"I was very tense and couldn't hit anything straight. I was in the rough all day, and I hit five people in the crowd on the first nine holes. My father was so busy passing out his business card—for insurance purposes with all those people I'd hit—that he was on his knees more than on his feet.

"The first-aid tent was busier than the pop stand. My family and friends didn't want to admit that they knew me. I remember looking at my arms, and my freckles were just popping out at me, I was so scared."

In the next day's paper, Hagen was quoted as saying, "I don't know about that girl. She's dangerous!"

Patty recovered, of course, and that same year got to the final of the U.S. Women's Amateur, losing the last match to Glenna Collett Vare, 3 and 2. At lunchtime, between the double rounds of the match, she received a telegram from Hagen.

"Congratulations," the Haig wired, "All is forgiven. Best wishes and good luck."

Miss Berg made the Curtis Cup team that year. But she had missed so much of her senior year of high school that her father hired a tutor. Later she attended the University of Minnesota for two years, taking general courses in the morning, practicing golf in the afternoon, and studying at night.

As an amateur, she won twenty-nine championships, including three Titleholders (1937–1939). In 1938 she swept virtually every important title, winning ten of the thirteen tournaments she entered, including the Western Amateur, the Trans-Mississippi, the Western Derby, the Doherty, and the U.S. Women's Amateur. She was an easy pick for the 1938 Curtis Cup team, and the Associated Press named her "Woman Athlete of the Year."

In 1939 she won six tournaments, including the Titleholders. An appendectomy prevented her from defending her U.S. Women's Amateur title.

Patty's father, while financing her participation in amateur tournaments, ordered his daughter to contribute something to society.

"I played eight years of amateur golf and every Saturday and Sunday, when I was home, my father had me play some exhibition for charity," she said.

"He said, 'If you're going to play the game, you're going to do some charity work for people. So get started, you're not just sitting at home.'"

Miss Berg's father booked the golf exhibitions. The group of young players, all amateurs, played without remuneration, but admission was charged to raise money for charity. It was Patty's introduction to a lifetime of fun on the road.

"We had a regular schedule, it was really something! We went through the state of Minnesota, a little bit of Iowa, and a little bit of Wisconsin. We'd leave Friday night or early Saturday morning, and sometimes we rode the train, especially if we went up through Duluth to Superior," Miss Berg remembered. "Every time we went on these trips we took the poem, 'Casey at the Bat.' Everyone would do a dramatic reading, then we'd all cheer! We'd sometimes take different poems too, but 'Casey at the Bat' was the main one. I'd get a big buzz out of the way they'd read it."

Patty's exhibition team included Babe Lavore, a Minnesota football player; Kenny Young, a very fine amateur; and Virgil Robby, Bill Maleckar, and Bud Waring. Patty's brother Herman, Jr., also a fine golfer, played occasionally. When the youngsters gave exhibitions, Miss Berg's father would ask the host pro to give a short golf clinic. While the young men hit long shots, Patty demonstrated techniques with the short irons.

On a stint to raise money for the University of Minnesota Student Union Building, she covered nine states with her mother and father, family friends Mr. and Mrs. Obie Pierce, and their son Harmon.

She never forgot her father's concern for mankind and helped charities throughout her life. The Western Women's Golf Association gave her the Director's Pin for her years of work for junior girls' golf. The University of Minnesota Women's Intercollegiate Fund was renamed the Patty Berg Development Fund. She received the Humanitarian Sportsman Award of United Cerebral Palsy of Westchester chapter. In her years on the LPGA Tour, she was considered a soft touch and could seldom say no to a caddie in need. She was a stalwart of the Catholic Church and headed a number of fund-raising projects, including work for the American Cancer Society.

Berg began to refine her performing abilities early. In 1933 Wilson Sporting Goods hired Gene Sarazen to give exhibitions and promote Wilson golf equipment. Wilson hired Helen Hicks for similar work in 1935.

"I used to watch Helen Hicks because she had a marvelous personality and did an outstanding job," Patty remembered. "Any time Sarazen or Helen Hicks was around my area, I'd be there watching."

In 1940, having won every amateur tournament, Miss Berg turned professional and began a lifelong association with Wilson. Her lucrative contract called for a series of exhibitions and clinics promoting the company's equipment, a role she shared with Opal Hill and Helen Dettweiler.

There was an old line on the tour that the two things Patty Berg loved most were God and the Wilson Sporting Goods Company.

Wilson was her main source of income. There was no women's professional tour, as such. Only the Titleholders, the Western Open, and the Women's Texas Open were open to women pros.

In 1941 she won the Western Open, beating Mrs. Burt Weil of Cincinnati in the finals of match play for the first prize, a $100 war bond.

Two tournaments were added to the schedule that year, the Asheville (North Carolina) Invitational Championship and the Lake Champlain Invitational. Patty won three of the four pro tournaments, losing only the Titleholders. Total prize money that year was $500.

Only a handful of women professionals played tournament golf—Miss Berg, Betty Hicks, Helen Dettweiler, Opal Hill, and Hope Seignious—but the pros were indebted to good amateurs like Polly Riley, Maureen Orcutt, Bea Barrett, Helen Sigel, Dot Germain, and Helen Raynor, who rounded out the tournament fields while their friends and families beefed up the galleries.

A near-tragedy struck Miss Berg in her first year as a professional. On December 8, the day after the Japanese attacked Pearl Harbor, she was driving with Helen Dettweiler from Texas to Tennessee when they were struck by another car. Patty's left knee was broken in three places, and she was laid up for eighteen months. Because of adhesions, she couldn't bend the leg and would only regain 75 percent of its use.

After a year of recuperation, she went to Mobile, Alabama, and worked out at a gym owned by ex-boxer Tommy Littleton. Each day she rode a bicycle, took two hours of gym training, hit practice balls, picked them up, and went for long walks. Finally she was able to play golf. On her way back to Minneapolis, she stopped to play an exhibition at Tam O'Shanter Golf Club in Chicago at the invitation of

Helen Hicks, 1931 U.S Women's Amateur Championship.

Patty Berg early in her pro career.

Patty Berg with amateur Marge Lindsay in the early 1950s.

George S. May. After a luncheon in her honor, Patty shot a 78 from the men's tees on rain-soaked fairways.

"You're back!" May said.

Her comeback inspired Mr. May to include women golfers in his All-American that year and later invite them to his World Championship at Tam O'Shanter.

Patty returned to the tour and in 1943 won the Women's Western Open and the All-American Women's Open. When war was declared, she joined the Marines and attended Officers Training School. She served for two years, working in Philadelphia in public relations and recruiting until she was honorably discharged in 1945 as a first lieu-tenant.

In 1944 Hope Seignious formed the Women's Professional Golf Association and launched a women's pro tour, using her own money and that of her father, who was a cotton broker. Miss Seignious was president and Patty Berg was later drafted as vice-president.

Miss Seignious started the U.S. Women's Open in 1946 with the help of Spokane civic groups at the Spokane Country Club.

It was a grueling format: 36 holes of qualifying rounds, then 18-hole matches with a 36-hole semifinal and a 36-hole final. Patty got off to a great start, firing 72-73 to capture medalist honors, then won the tournament to become the winner of the first U.S. Women's Open Championship.

There were many great Patty Berg victories, a number against her friendly rival, Babe Zaharias.

The Weathervane Tournament series was the richest in women's golf in 1951 and 1952. The women pros played 36 holes in each of four sections of the United States. The winner would receive the phenome-nal sum of $5,000. After 144 holes, played in 1951 and 1952, Babe and Patty were tied. There would be a playoff. Both shot 71 in the first round at Scarsdale (New York) Country Club. The following day the two teed it up at Deepdale on Long Island. Patty shot 75, Babe 76, and Patty had won the richest tournament in women's golf.

In 1951 she headed a team of American women pros, Babe, Betsy Rawls, Betty Bush, Betty Jameson, and Peggy Kirk, on a tour of Great Britain. They easily defeated the Irish, Scottish, English, and French girls' teams at the Ladies Course at Sunningdale.

Then they collided with the British Walker Cup Team, made up of the empire's best male amateurs, at Wentworth, outside of London.

In the morning team matches, Babe and Patty lost to Mr. Daven-port and Mr. Beck, Miss Rawls and Mrs. Bush lost, the team of Miss Kirk and Miss Jameson tied their match, and the American women trailed by the score of 2½ to one-half points.

"At lunch, our table had little American flags on it," Miss Berg said. "I said, 'All of those who expect to win their singles, follow me!'

"Babe says, 'Come on, follow Napoleon!' We went out and won all our singles matches and beat the British men, 6½ to 2½."

These were the great tournament memories, spanning more than forty years of competition. But there is another side to Patty Berg: A Berg golf clinic would draw laughs on vaudeville or "Saturday Night Live." Shouting her lines like a Marine sergeant, Patty imitates the world's worst golf swings, cracking jokes with the timing of Bob Hope. They may be the same jokes you heard at the last Patty Berg clinic, but you cannot help laughing.

"I love clinic and exhibition work. I get so much satisfaction out of it because somebody will write me a note, or see me a few months later and they say, 'You know, that little tip you gave on the iron play?

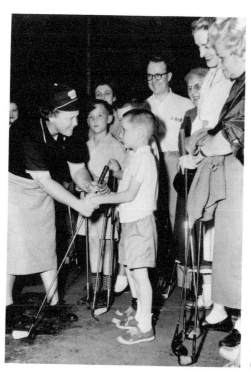

Patty Berg at one of her many clinics.

Well, my irons have improved.' Or they say, 'I came out here and I was down in the dumps but you've given me a few chuckles.' That's very nice to know. When you can do anything to help somebody else through your sport, well, I think that's what I like about it."

"She's a frustrated actress," said Kathy Whitworth, one of Patty's great friends. "But she was a great role model for me, the way she conducted herself, her beliefs. She was thoughtful and always professional in everything that she did."

Her peers in women's professional golf know full well what Patty Berg did for them. While teaching Miss Whitworth how to give golf clinics, Patty also taught her how to play golf.

"I really didn't appreciate everything she did for me until much later," Miss Whitworth said. "But when you look back on your career, you think, boy, I learned a lot during those clinics. Playing in front of people, we had to learn how to hit those shots. And Patty taught me."

Betsy Rawls gives Miss Berg much of the credit for making the LPGA a success.

"She carried the name of Wilson and the LPGA into every corner of the golfing world," Miss Rawls said. "People came to see her time after time, always laughing at the jokes, always admiring the crisp shots, and always loving Patty Berg.

"She has done more to promote golf than any person in the history of the game."

The classic Babe.

A Diamond in the Rough

When Babe Zaharias helped start the Ladies Professional Golf Association, she gave it a kick in the pants and a poke in the funnybone and helped send it on its way. Almost alone, she guaranteed the organization's survival.

Four years later in 1954, in one of the most inspiring victories in sport, she won the U.S. Women's Open a year after a section of her colon had been removed because of cancer. The world cheered her remarkable recovery, and the hopeful fantasized that even cancer could not strike down this remarkable athlete. Babe, however, had begun one of the few battles she would lose. The disease progressed without mercy. In July 1955 she reentered John Sealy Hospital in Galveston, Texas. The end was near.

Allowed to leave the hospital for what would be her last Christmas, Babe and her husband George spent the holiday with R.L. and Bertha Bowen in Fort Worth. The Bowens had befriended the rough, raw young golfer in 1935. Through the years they had given not only loyal support but love.

On December 26, Babe asked Bertha to drive her to a golf course. Their car trundled through the stately old trees lining the fairways at Fort Worth's Colonial Country Club and pulled to a stop near the second green.

"Babe got out of the car, in her bathrobe and pajamas," said Bertha Bowen. "She could barely walk. She just went over and knelt down and put her palm flat on the green. Then she got in the car, and we went home."

"I just wanted to see a golf course one more time," Babe said.

Nine months later, she was dead.

And yet, nearly forty years later we still talk of her and think of her and write of her—this larger-than-life woman, so curiously complex. Depending upon the source, Babe Zaharias was remarkably generous, or petulant and spoiled; she was boastful, or painfully shy. It's entirely likely that the greatest female athlete of all time, controversial in the way that brilliant people sometimes are, was all of these things. But Babe, for all her flaws, was America's first female hero.

The story of Mildred Ella Didrickson Zaharias is uniquely American.

She was the child of an immigrant family, born June 26, 1914, the sixth of seven children of a Norweigan ships carpenter, Ole Didricksen (Babe changed it to "son"), who had immigrated to Port Arthur, Texas. The family later moved to a difficult existence in Beaumont, where Mildred grew up in the rough-and-tumble of neighborhood sports. She was a tomboy, a tough, abrupt girl who correctly thought she could beat every boy on the block. She picked up the name "Babe" for her ability to hit home runs in sandlot baseball games.

Babe at the beginning of her career in the mid-'30s.

By any standard, her athletic skills were memorable. Her high school physical education teacher, Beatrice Lytle, said Babe's ability was the most remarkable of any student in her fifty-year teaching career.

"I saw possibly twelve thousand young women over those years. I observed them closely and I trained a lot of them to be fine athletes but there was never anyone in all those thousands who was anything like Babe. I never again saw the likes of her."

In 1950 an Associated Press poll named Babe Zaharias as the woman athlete of the first half of the century. In the year 2000, other pollsters may well name her as the athletic phenomenon of the century. Her staggering performances in track, field, and golf assure her place in history. It was her human side, however, that guarantees Babe's place in memory. Everything about her was of mythic proportions—her triumphs, struggles, and humiliations.

Babe Didrickson could run, jump, throw the javelin and the discus, play tennis, polo, basketball, marbles, soccer, lacrosse, billiards; she could dive, ride, shoot, pitch, bat home runs, kick, fence, pass, bowl, and skate. She was an exquisite ballroom and adagio dancer, played the harmonica well enough to be a professional at it, excelled at gin rummy, was a good cook and a great seamstress, and could type 100 words a minute.

She was even a one-girl track team. On July 16, 1932, in the combined National Women's A.A.U. Track Meet and Olympic tryouts

Babe's swing was far from classic—she had a "fire-and-fall-back" follow-through.

in Evanston, Illinois, she represented the Employer's Casualty Company of Dallas, Texas, where she worked as a secretary. There were no other representatives from the company. By herself, Babe won the team title. The Illinois Women's Athletic Club, with a full complement of entrants in the various events, finished second.

The lone girl from Texas entered eight of the ten scheduled events. She won the 80-meter hurdles, baseball throw, shot put, broad jump, and javelin toss, was nosed out of a tie in the high jump, and was fourth in the discus throw. That afternoon she set three world records.

She could have been a one-woman track team in the 1932 Olympics, but women were limited to entering three events. In those Los Angeles Olympics, Babe won the 80-meter hurdles and the javelin throw. She was hornswoggled out of the high jump when an official, who had been silent throughout the preliminaries, proclaimed that Babe had illegally dived over the bar after she tied Jean Shiley at world-record height. Her style had been unquestioned throughout the event. Today it is legal.

At the Olympics, sportswriter Paul Gallico asked Babe if there was anything that she didn't play.

"Yeah, dolls," she said.

Babe played her first round of golf at the age of sixteen, impressing her playing companions Gallico, Grantland Rice, and Braven Dyer with drives of up to 260 yards. At first she played only casual golf, three or four rounds a year. But competition was her way of proving herself, and in 1933 she became serious about the game. She began to save money to allow her to compete for three years. Babe practiced "eighteen hours a day" and took lessons from teaching professional Stan Kertes.

In April 1935 she signed up to play in the state championship of the Women's Texas Golf Association at posh River Oaks Country Club in Houston.

Babe's story is no fairy tale; she suffered plenty of embarrassments.

Before she married "she was a pathetic and solitary figure," said Gallico, "neither one thing nor another in the average, normal world of ordinary men and women or even, for that matter, of athletes."

Babe was, after all, that rarity, a remarkable *female* athlete, and her extraordinary ability brought her under the closest scrutiny. She suffered for it. She had a lean, rawboned face, a crooked smile, and a severe haircut. She was a bit *too* athletic, went the whispers, a bit too muscular and strong in the face. This was a different time and, while the world loved the graceful skater Sonja Henie and the fine-looking amateur golfer Glenna Collett Vare, people didn't take kindly to the plain-looking Mildred Didrickson.

Had she been a golfer of ordinary skill, her lack of refinement might have been ignored, but Babe's talents were obvious and stunning. At River Oaks many of her fellow competitors began to gossip.

"It wasn't ladylike to be muscular," said Bertha Bowen. "Of course, there's where her courage came in. I never understood how she had the strength to overlook the snubs and slights and the downright venom of a lot of women. She never talked ugly about anybody and she had every reason to. In many cases people would try to keep her out, really keep her out. But she never held a grudge. She was really too busy to be bothered."

Babe worked her way into the championship finals to play against Peggy Chandler, a fine golfer and a member of golf's social set.

Babe's Olympic victories had made her famous, and a large gallery of fans from her hometown of Beaumont trailed after the match. Dan Chandler, Peggy's husband, who described Babe as a crude, brash woman, believed that her galleries tilted the match in Babe's favor.

In the 36-hole final, Miss Didrickson and Mrs. Chandler were even after 33 holes. On the 34th hole Babe holed a bunker shot for an eagle three to go 1-up. She won the match and the state championship on the next hole, 2-up.

"Babe just didn't fit in, she just didn't, and eyebrows were lifted down there when she won," said Bertha Bowen.

One example of the cruelty that Babe often faced was a story that soon ran in a national magazine. In it an author and close friend of the Chandlers' had written a thinly veiled fictional account of the

Didrickson-Chandler match, in which one character is portrayed as a lady of great character and beauty while her opponent is a swashbuckling, crude golfer who, in the end, is revealed to be a cheat.

After Babe won the tournament, Bertha Bowen invited her and Helen Detweiller, another top amateur, to stay at her Fort Worth home to await the Southern Amateur Championship. Babe was totally unnerved by the wealthy neighborhood.

"They sat out in the car for a long, long time before Babe thought she should come in and stay," said Bertha. "When she did, they stayed three weeks! That's how our friendship started."

Soon, however, Babe would face other trials. She had never played professional golf, yet the Chandlers questioned her amateur status and reported her to the United States Golf Association as having violated the rules.

"There was no question that she was a professional," said Dan Chandler. "No question."

Babe found out about the action when she mailed her entry to the Women's Southern Amateur Championship and it was returned, marked "unacceptable" on the advice of the USGA. On May 14 Archie M. Reid, speaking on behalf of the USGA, declared her a nonamateur for a series of infractions, including having been a professional athlete and for having played other games as a professional. (The Rules of Amateur Status have since been revised.)

Jack Burke, Sr., a Texas professional who had been helping Babe with her game, called the USGA ruling, "the dirtiest deal I've heard of in a long time."

Babe had planned to devote herself to competitive golf. Now she had no events in which to play except the Western Open. Bertha Bowen and her influential Fort Worth friends failed to convince the USGA to rescind its ruling, so they literally invented a tournament for Babe.

"I had started a little three-day stroke-play invitational in Fort Worth," Bowen said. "Bea Thompson suggested that we change that to the Women's Texas Open, so that Babe could play in it. So we did. We didn't know what would come of it, but that's how the Women's Texas Open began."

Babe found few open events for women, but teed it up in those that did exist, like the celebrity division of the PGA's Los Angeles Open in January 1938. Babe was paired with wrestler George Zaharias, a huge man and a fair amateur golfer. Zaharias was nervous about the encounter, but friends assured him that Babe was a great girl.

"You'll never forget her," they told George.

On the first tee, a photographer asked Zaharias to put his arms around Babe. When Babe said, "Sure, put your arms around me," George relented.

In Joan Flynn Dreyspool's excellent story on the pair, written for

Babe and George Zaharias in 1940.

Sports Illustrated shortly before Babe's death, George recalled their romance, saying that he knew immediately that his world had changed. The two had instant chemistry; Zaharias felt "electricity" with Babe and found himself wanting to be close to her. After a few holes, they began tossing compliments to each other.

"Honey, you're my kind of girl," George said.

Babe smiled and said, "You're my kind of guy."

That weekend the two went dancing at the Cotton Club, the Famous Door, and several other clubs. George took her to places where his pals hung out, seeking to show her off. After their evening on the town, they immediately made a date for the following day.

Babe and George were married on December 23, 1938, in St. Louis. Leo Durocher was best man. The newlyweds went to Australia on their honeymoon, where Babe played in golf exhibitions and George wrestled.

After her marriage, Babe began the process of regaining her amateur status. Five years later, in 1943, she was finally reinstated, but women's amateur golf had been suspended during World War II, and Babe was forced out of competition for another three years.

In 1946, after eight years away from competitive golf, she won

Babe with the 1946 U.S. Women's Amateur trophy and the 1947 British Women's Amateur trophy.

the U.S. Women's Amateur, beginning a great run of titles: She won the Doherty with a 12 and 11 victory in the final, won the Broadmoor Invitational by a 10 and 9 margin, and at the Titleholders Championship at Augusta came from 10 strokes behind to shoot a four-day total of 304, winning by five strokes. She won the Women's Texas Open, the All-American at Tam O'Shanter, the Tampa Open, the Palm Beach Championship, the South Atlantic, the Florida East Coast, the North and South, the Hollywood Four-Ball, the Florida Mixed Two-Ball, and the Celebrities Championship.

In 1947 she sailed for England, where she made a much ballyhooed appearance in the venerable British Women's Amateur Championship. Babe's raucous ways dismayed some of the staid British fans.

On the third day of the championship, three elderly British ladies approached Mrs. A.M. Holm, one of England's finest golfers, telling Mrs. Holm they felt Babe to be crass and altogether lacking in refinement.

Holm retorted coldly, "You are speaking of the finest woman golfer that has ever been seen here."

Crashing around the course with her prodigious length, Babe

Peggy Kirk, George, and Babe. Peggy and Babe won the 1947 Hollywood Four-Ball before turning pro.

won the championship, becoming the first American to win the British title. "She is a crushing and heart-breaking opponent," said the *Manchester Guardian*.

On her return, three hours out of New York Harbor, a tugboat loaded with seventy-one reporters and photographers steamed alongside Babe's ship. On deck Babe danced a Highland fling and showed off the championship trophy for the newsreels and newspapers.

Babe and George claimed that she won seventeen straight tournaments in 1946 and 1947 (most historians believe that), but they were simply myth-building. She did win thirteen straight tournaments, admirable enough, but in the 1946 National Women's Open at Spokane Country Club, Babe lost in the first round to amateur Grace Lenczyk. (The Women's Open was then played at match play.)

In 1947, after her second straight victory in the Broadmoor Invitational, a movie company offered her $300,000 for a series of ten golf films. Babe accepted the offer and, this time voluntarily, became a professional.

"I really hated to give up my amateur status I had worked so hard to regain, but that money looked too good," she said.

Babe signed as a client of sports agent Fred Corcoran, who also represented Sam Snead, Stan Musial, and Ted Williams. According to Corcoran, Babe was paid $600 for golf exhibitions when Ben Hogan and Snead were only getting $500.

"They were great guys, but when it came to getting headlines, Babe had them all beat," Corcoran said. "She had a fantastic feel for publicity."

When a press conference started to drag, she'd announce that she was going to enter the U.S. Open Championship—for men—and members of the press would dash for the phones. Babe would scoop up ground balls in appearances at the nation's baseball parks, or play her harmonica in restaurants. For these exhibitions and her tournament victories, Corcoran claimed Babe was hauling in some $100,000 a year, an incredible sum for the time.

In 1949 Babe, George, Patty Berg, Wilson Sporting Goods, and Fred Corcoran created the LPGA Tour. Now Babe had a theater in which to perform. She had tremendous charisma and loved galleries, and they loved hearing her frequent one-liners. In one instance, when one of her fellow competitors pushed her drive into a soggy area, she turned to Babe.

"This is casual water, isn't it Babe? I get a free drop from here?" the player asked.

"Honey, I don't care if you send it out and get it dry-cleaned," Babe purred.

Privately, she could be somewhat profane. "I couldn't hit an elephant's a-- with a bull fiddle," she complained after a bad round.

Peggy Kirk Bell believed Babe was enamored with being part of a game as prestigious as golf.

"Golf was a more social sport then than now and it lifted Babe up," Mrs. Bell said. "It made her appreciate the good things in life. She was so proud of being a golfer. She never even talked about the Olympics or all her other sports."

In those years Patty Berg was one of Mrs. Zaharias's closest competitors and a staunch friend.

"I had a lot of fun with Babe," Patty said.

The brash, sassy Babe was not universally admired by her fellow playing professionals. Several did not appreciate her antics on or off the course, and Babe could pull some real boners. She'd arrange her own pairings, refusing to play with any pro who played too slowly. If she had a bad round and rain began to fall, even lightly, she could convince tournament officials to call the round "rained out." Babe could get away with it, she was the LPGA's chief drawing card.

She was also able to command appearance fees at tournaments, a practice now outlawed by both the men's and women's pro tours. When other professionals complained, Babe held a meeting.

"Let me tell you girls something, the star gets the money because the people come to see the star, right?" Babe said. "Well, I'm

Babe was an ebullient guest, and often entertained friends by playing the harmonica.

the star and I get the money and if it weren't for me, half of our tournaments wouldn't even be."

"Babe," said Patty Berg, "even the star has to have a chorus line."

But Babe could be endearing too, and she was incredibly fair in assessing golfers. She always appreciated new talent, Miss Berg said, offering frequent tips to new players to help them improve their games.

"Babe would say, 'Did you see so-and-so? Boy, she can play!'" Patty recalled.

In the tour's infancy, Babe won dozens of tournaments. Patty Berg remembers that her game improved enormously after sessions on the practice tee with Tommy Armour. Babe wasn't a large woman by modern standards, five feet six inches and 140 pounds, but she had crushing strength. She also possessed a delicate touch. Patty Berg remembers her as the finest ever at making short, crucial putts.

Babe's game wasn't classic. She hit a low, powerful shot that bored into the wind, but she often failed to transfer her weight through to her left side on her follow-through, in a "fire and fall back" method. Her superior athletic ability and great timing compensated for the flaw.

Bertha Bowen ran several home movies of Babe's swing for me, and Babe's unique talent was apparent. She had a remarkably

Babe after winning the 1954 Women's Open by twelve strokes.

smooth, rhythmic tempo, she had the same upright swing on every shot, and her hands seemed almost a part of the club, gripping it with a firm delicacy that isn't often seen. On the film she was more slender than you might imagine, and more serious.

Despite Babe's canny insistence that LPGA tournament courses be played at 6,400 to 6,500 yards in length, to give her the great advantage of her strength, she didn't truly dominate women's golf: Patty Berg, Louise Suggs, and Betsy Rawls were big winners too. Amateur Polly Riley defeated her in the finals of the 1948 Women's Texas Open by a humiliating 10 and 9 margin, a match in which the Babe "was flogging the ball all over the layout and missing putts as if the cup were a thimble," said one news account.

Still, the galleries and press made Babe the favorite in every tournament. She was softer-looking now, and more refined. Bertha Bowen had taught her how to dress, paint her nails, and perm her hair. George was adoring and kind. The rough kid from Beaumont was on top of her game and flying high. In 1950 she captured five of the LPGA's eleven tournaments, including the U.S. Women's Open. In 1951 she won seven of sixteen events. She captured the prestigious Titleholders, the Fresno Open, and the Women's Texas Open in 1952, beating Polly Riley in the finals, 7 and 6.

The year 1953 began well. Babe won at Sarasota in March, then captured her namesake Babe Zaharias Open in Beaumont on April 5.

But she was enduring mysterious aches and pains when, with George, she visited the Bowens in Fort Worth.

"We bought her all sorts of medicine, but she wouldn't see a doctor," Bertha said. "She was rough in spots, but she was modest, too, and didn't like physical examinations. She waited too long, that was the big trouble."

Finally, Babe agreed to undergo a physical. Mrs. Bowen will remember the day for the rest of her life.

"I walked into the guest room where they stayed," she said. "They had come in from the doctor's and George was white-faced. Babe threw her purse on the chair and flopped down on that bed. 'Well, B.B., I've got it, and it's the worst kind, grade three,' she said."

Babe entered a Beaumont hospital a few days later and a colostomy was performed. Her long recuperation inspired an outpouring of affection; letters and contributions to the newly formed Babe Zaharias Cancer Fund poured in.

Yet Babe's beautifully coordinated body was, in her mind, profaned. She was humiliated, and never again would she be quite so brash and bold. But Babe Zaharias, as they say in Texas, "knew no quit." She was determined to again play competitive golf.

"She had many low moments," Mrs. Bowen said. "When she began to try to play she would just break down and cry on the golf course when her strength failed. It was just pure spirit that got her through."

In 1954 she played in a few tournaments. Almost incredibly, she won the Serbin Open in March, then won again in May. Her great goal was to win the U.S. Women's Open, which she had captured twice before. In the heat of July, the Women's Open was a grueling test; 18 holes on Thursday, 18 holes on Friday, and an endurance contest of 36 holes on Saturday.

At Salem Country Club in Massachusetts, she fired opening rounds of 72 and 71, leaping to a seven-stroke lead over Betsy Rawls.

On Saturday, paired with the 1952 U.S. Girls' Junior champion, Mickey Wright, Babe fired a fine 73 in the morning round. The real test would come in the afternoon. Recent history had seen her tire toward the end and frequently blow to high scores, so she took a nap in the clubhouse before the final round.

"On the last four or five holes, the Babe had begun to feel the first faint distress signals. Her tee shots, which had been wonderfully accurate for three days, began to fade and hook badly, a sure sign of fatigue," Al Laney wrote in the New York *Herald Tribune*.

"At the final hole, with all the people lining the course and waiting to escort her home, she sliced her drive badly into a wicked place among trees. She could have used as many strokes as she pleased to finish [she had a 13-stroke lead] and the sensible thing to do was to sacrifice a stroke and play back to the fairway. But the Babe

A happy Babe in the early '50s at the Zaharias fishing camp in Durango, Colorado.

took the position that this was no way to finish. She found a tiny opening and she took a long iron and went through it toward the distant green. A champion's shot and a great roar greeted it. It gave her a chance for a Par 4. She missed it by an inch but she finished in a champion's way."

Babe had won the U.S. Women's Open, by 12 strokes, with the old Zaharias verve and dash. "It is impossible," Laney proclaimed.

"I feel good for 20 more years," she said. "If I've ever had any doubts that I might be able to go on—and let me tell you I've had plenty, they are gone now. For the first time since the operation, I feel like the same old Babe again. My prayers have been answered. I wanted to show thousands of cancer sufferers that the operation I had, a colostomy, will enable a person to return to normal life. I've received some 15,000 inquiries from those who have undergone the operation. This is my answer to them."

Babe didn't have twenty more years. In January 1955 she won the Tampa Open, shooting 4 under par. In March she played in the Titleholders in Augusta.

"That was the last time I saw her," Barbara Romack recalled. "She was just kind of there, but you could kind of feel her presence. I'd see her around the practice tee or sitting on the patio and I remember that the light had gone out of her eyes. She had this look that said, 'My number is up and I know it.'"

In April Mrs. Zaharias won the Peach Blossom Classic in Spartanburg, South Carolina. It was to be her last victory. In July she reentered John Sealy Hospital in Galveston. Off the record, so that she would not know, doctors said she was near the end. She was in and out of John Sealy, and in March 1956 doctors severed spinal nerves to ease her excruciating pain. Early in the morning of September 27, 1956, Babe Zaharias died. She was forty-two years old. Her ashes were lowered into a grave in Forest Lawn Park in her native Beaumont.

Today Beaumont is the site of the Babe Zaharias Hall of Fame. The Women's Texas Golf Association annually hosts a play-day at the organization's state championship for the Babe Zaharias Cancer Fund. Women golfers in Ohio have raised more than three hundred thousand dollars for the Zaharias Fund.

In 1988 I ran a video of the U.S. Women's Open for women members of the Trophy Club, near Fort Worth. They were a mixed lot, some housewives, a few career women, and they ranged in age from about thirty to sixty. This was a posttournament party, and they watched the heroics of the 1988 Women's Open with only polite interest. Then the finale flickered on the screen; the shadowy figures of each past Women's Open champion hit shots, sunk putts, and shook hands. Babe appeared, a tall, smoothly muscled woman in a flowing skirt, and the room erupted in loud and sudden applause.

These women knew other champions, knew that Patty Berg had done more for women's golf and that Mickey Wright was a better player. Only Babe, however, thirty-two years after her death, aroused an emotional response.

Bertha Bowen, who loaned her own dresses to Babe when she had none, is wistful when she speaks of her friend. "She was a good

146

person who was generous with her time when she didn't have the money. She had a hard life. I mean, her life was really hard and rough, but Babe was always grateful for everything good that happened to her. She faced not being welcome, not being wanted, and she was determined to break that barrier. She was fighting a system and she won."

In the end, it wasn't Babe's victories that squelched the venom, but her courage.

Betsy Rawls, four-time U.S. Women's Open Champion.

8

Barnstorming

It's popular to assume that the pioneers who formed the Ladies Professional Golf Association were ironclad, driven women. But in 1950, the thirteen players who founded the LPGA were little more than girls. Most were in their twenties, with a few warps on either side; Marlene Bauer was fifteen, while Babe Zaharias, Betty Jameson, and Patty Berg were in their thirties.

A few possessed the mystical combination of fire and talent to become champions. The rest were golf instructors or simply young women who yearned for more adventure than they'd find in a job as a shop clerk or marriage to the boy next door.

Looking at their photographs, one is struck by how little they look like stereotypical champions of early fem-lib. Instead, they resemble my mother and her friends as they appeared shortly after World War II: gentle girls of the late 1940s, girls who wore tumbles of curls and softly tailored suits.

These golfers were all fine athletes, tanned young women with the clear-eyed zest that comes from a life outdoors. They came from every corner of the country, from families of varying degrees of social privilege, yet they all loved golf. Each had been molded by the Great Depression and World War II. Such hardships had made them independent, and they shared a sort of reckless courage, which they needed if they were going to knock about the country in pursuit of adventure and golf.

"I don't know if it was courage that we had," said Helen Dettweiler. "I think we were probably more curious. It was different than being a secretary or a saleswoman. We didn't really think of the potential of the tour because there weren't that many lady golfers. Men's golf wasn't even doing very well. But we thought it was a great way for us to earn money doing what we liked."

By 1950, when Miss Dettweiler joined twelve other women to file the charter of the Ladies Professional Golf Association, she had already lived an extraordinary life.

Intelligent and unassuming, Helen Dettweiler considered herself a lazy person, but momentous events always seemed to find her. She was a tall, attractive woman with a wide smile and an easy, refined manner that made famous people feel at home in her presence. They liked Helen. She was often surprised that doors seemed to magically open for her, and her conversation was sprinkled with the names of friends who introduced her to new opportunities. She wasn't aggressive, but she was brave and created her own good breaks. In time she became famous herself.

Miss Dettweiler was born in Washington, D.C., where her father owned a bakery and restaurant. The Dettweilers were a sports-minded family, and Helen grew up playing baseball and football with her brothers. One brother, Bill, qualified for the U.S. Amateur at the age of fourteen.

"Bill got me interested in playing golf," Miss Dettweiler recalled. "I would watch him in his tournaments. I wasn't very interested in playing golf myself until he bet me an ice cream soda that I couldn't hit the ball three times if I aimed at it. I took the bet and lost. I went to the pro at Manor Club and told him I'd sure like to learn how to at least contact the ball. Then the bug hit me."

Helen played junior golf around Washington and later won the District Championship and the Middle Atlantic title. She was a student at Trinity College, studying English and political science. At night she attended Columbus Law School but saw little future as a woman lawyer. When she graduated from college, she faced the dilemma of finding something meaningful to do.

In the mid-1930s women's professional golf got its biggest boost from L.B. Icely, the tough, innovative head of Wilson Sporting Goods Company. Icely believed that star athletes could be top salesmen, and he began signing professional athletes to serve on Wilson's advisory staff. In 1933 he signed Gene Sarazen to a contract, and Sarazen toured the country giving golf clinics and beating the drum for Wilson products.

Helen Hicks.

In 1935 Icely signed former U.S. Women's Amateur champion Helen Hicks to promote Wilson's golf equipment for women. Several women had already turned pro in order to give golf lessons or to work in pro shops, among them May Dunn, Bessie Fenn, and Helen Mac-Donald.

Mrs. MacDonald had turned pro in 1924 to help her husband teach at the Golf Studio on South State Street in Chicago's Loop. When she separated from her husband in 1931, she got custody of the Golf Studio, hired an assistant, and gave some fourteen lessons a day, mostly to men. During World War II she sought to close the Golf Studio, in deference to the war effort, but reopened after sixteen months when her students complained about their skyrocketing handicaps.

Helen MacDonald began promoting the idea of a women's professional golf organization in 1940. In July of that year, the *Chicago Daily Times* ran a cartoon lambasting a meeting of the all-male PGA.

A man in the cartoon said, "I tell you we're cooked—sunk!!! Patty Berg's turning pro!!!"

The PGA chairman answers him, "Well don't worry!!! We won't let 'er in this league!!!"

Jean Bauer, Isabel Ogilvie, Jane Cothran Jamison, Kathryn Hemphill, Patty Berg, Helen Dettweiler, and Marion MacDougall at the 1935 Titleholders Championship at Augusta. Hemphill, Berg, and Dettweiler were among the first American women professionals.

Miss Berg had forged an early reputation as a talented athlete. As a youngster in Minneapolis, she won speed-skating medals, played hockey and baseball, and quarterbacked a neighborhood boys' football team. As a teenager she was a great amateur golf star, winning most of the 1938 amateur titles and twice playing on the Curtis Cup team.

In 1940 Miss Berg, twenty-two, was a student at the University of Minnesota. She had few amateur worlds left to conquer, and when a representative of Wilson Sporting Goods approached Patty, her father gave his approval and she signed a pro contract on July 10.

Throughout the early 1940s, Helen MacDonald continued to push for a women's PGA. While the idea did not immediately catch on, she was successful in her own career. She was among the first women signed to an advisory staff and for many years had a contract with sporting goods manufacturers Hillerich & Bradsby of Louisville, Kentucky. As a teaching professional, Mrs. MacDonald gave more than twenty-five thousand golf lessons.

By the late 1930s, six women in addition to Helen MacDonald had turned professional: Miss Hicks, Opal Hill, Miss Dunn, Miss Fenn, former Olympic track and field star Babe Didrickson, and Joyce Wethered, the great English star.

Miss Wethered had forfeited her amateur status when she went to work for a London department store selling sporting goods. In 1935 she cashed in on a lucrative offer to tour the United States in exhibition matches, often playing with Gene Sarazen and Babe Didrickson.

Miss Didrickson had forfeited her amateur status in 1935. Babe signed with the P. Goldsmith Sons Sporting Goods Company, a forerunner of MacGregor, and endorsed a line of clubs with her name on them.

In exhibitions with Sarazen and other top players, her long drives drew appreciative galleries, but Babe's golf skills were raw. She was nowhere near the level of Miss Wethered or Miss Berg at this stage of her career.

For the record, Didrickson faced Wethered twice in those exhibition matches—once at Oak Park in Chicago, where Babe shot 88 and Joyce fired a 78. When they played again, Miss Wethered shot 77 to Babe's 81.

It was Babe's first fling at pro golf. But she had no women's tour on which to compete and in 1940 asked the USGA to reinstate her as an amateur so she could play in tournaments. She was eventually reinstated and, of course, later blossomed into a great player.

In 1939 L.B. Icely had decided to beef up Wilson's women's golf staff. He wanted to add Helen Dettweiler, who had graduated from Trinity College the previous spring.

"My grandmother had given me five hundred dollars for my graduation, which was a lot of money in those days," Miss Dettweiler said. "I had played the Florida winter circuit. I liked it, but there wasn't too much prospect for women in tournaments."

Miss Dettweiler signed the Wilson contract and began an exhibition tour with Helen Hicks. Among the first amateur stars to jump ship, they played in the few tournaments that were open to professionals in 1939. Prize money was meager. When Miss Dettweiler won the 1939 Western Women's Open in St. Louis, an event played at match play since its inception in 1930, she received only a silver Revere bowl for her victory.

Miss Dettweiler had other deals in the works. She was an avid baseball fan and often played golf with Clark Griffith, a Washington Senators executive, and Joe Cronin, the Senators' shortstop. Griffith arranged for her to broadcast play-by-play of the Senators games over national radio for Wheaties cereal; Helen Dettweiler thus became the first coast-to-coast woman sports broadcaster.

By 1941 four tournaments made up a sort of fledgling women's pro circuit: the Western, the Titleholders, the Asheville Invitational, and, in Fort Worth, the Women's Texas Open.

Total prize money on the 1941 women's pro tour was $500. Soon golf took a back seat to more serious matters. War was on the horizon.

"When the war came along," said Helen Dettweiler, "women's golf went downhill. Everything was for the war effort."

Miss Dettweiler got a job as a receptionist for the Air Transport Command. Within three weeks she was assigned to the cryptographic section in Washington. Eventually she headed the section, commanded an all-woman staff, and was sent around the country setting

Louise Suggs, 1947 U.S. Women's Amateur Champion.

up other code-cracking operations. She applied for admission to the Women's Air Force Service Pilots, WASP, and in 1943 was assigned to Avenger Field in Sweetwater, Texas. Helen was transferred to Columbus, Ohio, where she became one of seventeen women pilots who ferried the B-17 bomber, the famous "Flying Fortress."

Patty Berg resumed playing golf in 1943 and won the All-American at Tam O'Shanter and the Western Open at Glen Oaks Country Club in Illinois. After the Western she enlisted in the Marines, where she served two years and was honorably discharged as a first lieutenant.

During the war Babe Zaharias was still on amateur probation and cooled her heels by bowling, playing tennis, and appearing in a few golf exhibitions for war charities. She considered signing up for the WACS, but she was reinstated as an amateur on January 21, 1943, and once again hit the tournament trail.

Other young women sharpened their games during the war. In Dallas, Bettye Mims Danoff, a petite soft-spoken brunette, saw her marriage crumble.

"I came home to Mama and Daddy with my little girl," Mrs. Danoff said. "I thought, Well, this marriage isn't going to work so I'll just concentrate on golf."

Mrs. Danoff's first amateur tournament in the early 1940s was the Western Open in Chicago. She had never been out of Texas.

154

"I didn't decide to go until the last minute," she said. "Joanne Barr Tracy was going, so I scrambled up some money to go. We traveled by train and, I mean, it was pretty rough! We had to carry our luggage and the trains were packed, so we shared a berth."

In Lithia Springs, Georgia, Louise Suggs, at seventeen, had developed one of the game's loveliest golf swings with the help of her father, Johnny Suggs, a former baseball player. Louise won her first big amateur titles during the war years, capturing the Georgia State Championship twice, the North and South, and the Southern Amateur.

Near Detroit, redheaded Shirley Spork had been playing since 1939. Miss Spork would win the 1947 National Women's Collegiate Championship while attending Eastern Michigan University.

"I was majoring in physical education, but that was an era when educators supported intra-mural sports," Spork said. "They were against any national intercollegiate competition. They were for the mass to be involved in sports activities on a local basis. For me to play in the national collegiate, I had to pay my own way to the tournament, which I won."

Momentum was building for a women's professional tour. While there were no outright cash offers, there was tremendous enthusiasm. In 1944 Hope Seignious was named head golf professional at the North Shore Country Club in Milwaukee. Miss Seignious had bigger dreams—she sought to build a pro tour for women and, to this end, founded the Women's Professional Golf Association in 1944.

Several new professionals immediately hopped on board: Betty Hicks, the 1941 U.S. Women's Amateur Champion; Ellen Griffin, a top teacher; Kathryn Hemphill, who had won the Southern Amateur; and former U.S. Women's Amateur Champion, the classic-swinging Betty Jameson.

Helen Dettweiler also joined the WPGA.

"Hope thought it would be a good idea to get some girls together and try to get golf started on a pro basis," said Miss Dettweiler. "She had a lot of great ideas but they were, unfortunately, much too early."

One of Miss Seignious's achievements was the founding of the U.S. Women's Open. In 1946 she convinced the Spokane Athletic Round Table, which enjoyed a healthy income from slot machines, to put up $19,000 in war bonds for a national women's open championship. Patty Berg won the first U.S. Women's Open at match play. Betty Jameson won the following year when the format changed to 72 holes of stroke play.

Women pros began to pick up a few tournaments. In addition to the Western, the Texas Open, and the Titleholders, which was founded in 1930 in Augusta, Georgia, they now had the Hardscrabble in Ft. Smith, Arkansas, and George S. May's "World" and "American" championships at Tam O'Shanter in Chicago.

In 1948 the women professionals still had no firm grip on their own tour. Three of their tournaments had been won by amateurs. Louise Suggs won the Belleair Open, Peggy Kirk and her partner took the Orlando Mixed Two-Ball, and Polly Riley trounced Babe Zaharias in the Women's Texas Open.

That year Louise Suggs and Sally Sessions of Muskegon, Michigan, turned professional. Babe Zaharias, who had won the U.S. Women's Amateur in 1946 and the British in 1947, again turned pro and signed a lucrative deal with agent Fred Corcoran.

But internal dissension troubled the WPGA, and the future looked bleak for the organization. Hope Seignious had used her own savings to finance the tour. Although some financing came from her father, who was a cotton broker, Miss Seignious was running out of money.

Considering the times, a few of the women pros made incredible headway in marketing their talents. In the five years from 1948 through 1953, women pros scored a number of firsts: making their first instructional films, appearing in their first feature-length movie with top stars, designing their first golf course, getting space in national women's glamour magazines, and picking up their first lines of women's golf clothes.

The year 1949 was fairly typical in its tournaments but exceptional for the strides the women pros made in other directions: Louise Suggs and Babe Zaharias starred in their own motion picture short features. RKO-Pathe made a film called *Muscles and the Lady,* in which Frank Stranahan co-starred with Miss Suggs from the posh setting of Florida's Boca Raton Club. The picture was released in the summer of 1948 and was the number one golf movie of the year. In January 1949 Columbia released another short, starring Mrs. Zaharias, called *Babe Didrikson, Queen of Sport,* a ten-minute film in which Babe gave instruction.

In January a photograph of Miss Suggs appeared in *Mademoiselle* when the magazine featured ten young women with outstanding careers.

The magazine said of Louise, "She plays golf with champion style and keen sportsmanship. Now a touring pro, she infuses amateurs with her own enthusiasm."

That same year Alice Bauer, at twenty-one, was the first woman to try to qualify for the L.A. Open, a men's pro event. She shot 85-79—164 and missed qualifying by nine strokes.

In mid-January the women pros kicked off their 1949 tour at the Tampa Open, and Patty Berg fired a 68 in the second round, enabling her to win the $900 first prize by one stroke over Mrs. Zaharias.

The Tampa Open was to be one of the last blasts of the WPGA. Staged at the Palma Ceia Golf Club, gate receipts that year swelled to five thousand dollars. The tournament had 130 entries, although only 103 started. The event was popular with galleries, but only six professionals were in the field: Berg, Zaharias, Suggs, Hemphill, Mary Mo-

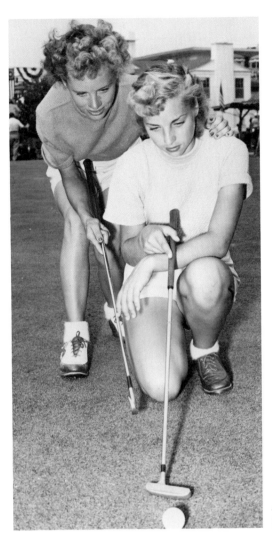

Alice and Marlene Bauer were the tour's first glamour girls.

zel of Portland, Oregon, and Seignious. The remaining ninety-seven players were amateurs of varying degrees of skill, including Polly Riley and Peggy Kirk.

Women amateurs played an important role in early pro tournaments. With so few professionals, they were needed to fill out the field and lure galleries. Playing only for trophies, many top amateurs were early supporters of the women professionals.

"We have to thank all the amateurs of that time because whenever we went into their area, they'd play in our tournaments," said Patty Berg. "They helped us get publicity. A girl is going to bring a lot of people out. You go down to Fort Worth and Polly Riley is going to bring out a lot of friends. We'd go to Minneapolis and Bea Barrett would draw a lot of people. You go over to New York and Maureen

Marilyn Smith, a founding member of the LPGA, was a personable player who twice won the Titleholders.

Orcutt would play and bring out a lot of people. Go to Philadelphia and Helen Sigel and Dot Germain and Helen Raynor would bring out somebody. So we should give them a big, big, big thanks because they did a lot for us."

But the women's pro tour struggled, and the end of the WPGA was near.

"The professional golfing ladies, after a number of starts, have not succeeded in organizing an open tournament circuit, patterned after the PGA's round-the-calendar schedule," wrote Bud Harvey. "The women have a first class show, but they seem to have trouble in master-minding themselves into the lucrative position their skill is worth on today's bullish sports market in the United States."

Shortly after the Tampa Open, Miss Berg, who was president of the WPGA; Fred Corcoran, a former PGA tour official who was Babe's manager; Babe; and George Zaharias met at the Venetian Hotel in Miami to discuss forming a new women's pro circuit.

Corcoran was on the payroll of Wilson Sporting Goods Company and L.B. Icely had asked him to give the women a lift in forming their new organization. Corcoran was to receive a salary from the women of one dollar a year, until the tour was prosperous enough to pay his full fee.

"I think you have to give a lot of credit to Hope Seignious, and her dad, because they helped us a lot," Miss Berg remembered. "She had tremendous vision, but I thought that we just had to get going, that's all. We had to get somebody with Fred's background.

"The first thing he did was change the name from Women's Professional Golf Association to Ladies Professional Golf Association. Fred felt 'Ladies' sounded better than 'Women,' and he thought the name change would give us a little publicity. And that's what happened."

Hope Seignious concurred on the selection of Corcoran, according to *Golf World*, and offered definite suggestions for the new tour. She believed that prize money should be distributed so that all pros would be able to make expenses, even if they didn't win a top prize. She also felt a more even spread of prize money might influence top amateurs to turn pro.

In May 1949, Berg, Jameson, Zaharias, Dettweiler, Danoff, and Hicks met at the Eastern Open in Essex Fells, New Jersey, and officially named Corcoran their tournament manager. Louise Suggs, who didn't play in the Eastern that year, was also invited to join the new organization.

Another meeting was held at the U.S. Women's Open in Wichita. On hand were Berg, Alice and Marlene Bauer, Danoff, Dettweiler, Opal Hill, Jameson, Sally Sessions, Shirley Spork, Suggs, Zaharias, and Marilynn Smith, who had turned pro at the Western Open. This was considered the true charter meeting of the Ladies Professional Golf Association. Miss Berg was elected president, Helen Dettweiler was vice-president, Betty Jameson was treasurer, and Sally Sessions, secretary.

Miss Dettweiler claimed that women's professional golf was floundering until Corcoran came along.

"Nobody wanted to organize it," Helen said. "Our first idea was that we would all put up a certain amount of money and try to get one of the girls to sign up tournaments. Well, none of the girls wanted to do *that*! You know, a girl couldn't go into a men's locker room and sit down and say, 'Now, look.'

"Plus, there was the problem of putting up the money when the girls weren't making enough money on the tour. So the pro tour sort of died in its infancy. Well, not exactly died, but it was awful sick for awhile until Fred Corcoran came along. He really got it underway. He was the one who was really instrumental. He did everything."

In Corcoran's book, *Unplayable Lies,* he recalled his experiences with the budding LPGA with mixed emotions.

"The announcement that we had formed the Ladies PGA touched off a national storm of indifference," Corcoran said. "Potential sponsors were polite when I called them, but you could hear them stifling a yawn at the other end of the line."

In February Hope Seignious and Kathryn Hemphill disbanded the WPGA and joined forces to manage a trucking firm in Greensboro, North Carolina.

The year 1949 was significant in the growth of professional golf for reasons other than the formation of the LPGA.

Four women—Helen Dettweiler, Babe Zaharias, amateur Beverly Hanson, and Betty Hicks—appeared in the movie *Pat and Mike,* a memorable sports story starring Katherine Hepburn and Spencer Tracy.

Golf course maintenance was opening up for women. In Overland Park, Kansas, Chet Mendenhall, head greenkeeper of the Mission Hills Country Club, employed three women as greenkeepers—Mrs. Emma Barker and two sisters, Margaret and Frieda Brown. Mendenhall said the women could handle any job on the course, from driving the gang mowing tractor to hand mowing.

Women were also active as golf writers. England had a number of women who entered golf journalism before World War I, including Mabel Stringer and Eleanor Helme. Enid Wilson later took up the pen for *Golf Illustrated,* the British weekly.

The first American woman golf journalist was Nan O'Reilly, who covered the game for the Hearst newspapers in New York in the 1920s. Maureen Orcutt covered women's golf for *The New York Times* in the 1930s and continued through the early 1960s. Polly Riley covered tournaments for the *Fort Worth Press.* Mrs. Cash Garvey was a golf reporter for her hometown newspaper in Utica, New York.

One of the best of the American golf writers was Ruth Woodward. Miss Woodward, a good amateur, was associate editor of *Golf World* magazine during the 1940s and 1950s. She wrote sparkling copy and insider tidbits about the women's professional and amateur tours.

Two very fine writers emerged in the 1950s; Betty Hicks and Joan Flynn Dreyspool. Miss Hicks, a professional and former U.S. Women's Amateur champion, wrote articles for many national magazines.

Mrs. Dreyspool covered a variety of sports for *Sports Illustrated* magazine. She had the unique ability to inspire confidence among sports figures, and her insightful portrait of Ted Williams, which appeared in several collections of the nation's top sports stories, was "The Splendid Splinter's" own favorite about his career. Mrs. Dreyspool wrote many generous and telling stories about the early LPGA and in the 1960s was chosen by Mickey Wright to edit her book, *Play Golf the Wright Way.*

And so the women's professional golf tour lurched forward through the spring of 1949.

160

Betty McKinnon, Babe Zaharias, Patty Berg, and Betsy Rawls were among the early pros who barnstormed the U.S. playing golf.

In March, Peggy Kirk, an amateur, managed to capture the time-honored Titleholders Championship at Augusta by two strokes over Babe Zaharias and amateur Dot Kirby. It was Miss Kirk's first major title in ten years of competition.

The Titleholders was easily the most beloved pro event. Founded by Mrs. Dorothy Manice, the Titleholders was played at the Augusta Country Club, a Donald Ross course adjacent to Augusta National Golf Club.

The Titleholders was a great social gathering for women golfers. There were tea dances, card parties, and a calcutta. The highlight of the social year was the annual "Titleholders Talent Night."

Betty Dodd and Babe Zaharias would sing a couple of rounds of "Jambalaya" and "The Tennessee Waltz." Alice Bauer, whose dancing had captured two amateur talent contests, annually did the Russian Cossack dance, then joined her sister Marlene and Marilynn Smith to harmonize on "Harbor Lights."

At the Titleholders, Fred Corcoran announced plans for the 1949–50 tournament circuit. He added the Eastern Open and an open event in Dallas. The tour already had the Western, George May's two events at Tam O'Shanter, and the Women's Open.

The infant LPGA boasted a good friend in Helen Lengfeld, a California matron of boundless energy and enthusiasm. Miss Lengfeld sponsored a series of 36-hole women's pro tournaments in California and Nevada through the United Voluntary Services. She was a friend of Alvin Handmacher, who manufactured Weathervane sports clothes for women, and persuaded Handmacher to become involved with the fledgling women's tour.

After a series of indifferent meetings with Corcoran, Handmacher was finally sold on Corcoran's idea for a progressive golf tournament that would skip from one town to another, like a progressive dinner, as a promotion for Weathervane sports clothes.

The Weathervane Transcontinental Tournament, with stops in San Francisco, Chicago, Cleveland, and New York, formed the skeleton of the LPGA tour.

"Let's make no mistake about it. Alvin put the Ladies' PGA in business," Corcoran said. "He set up $15,000 in prize money and a $5,000 bonus for the winner . . . it was Handmacher who cracked the safe."

Several fence-straddlers took the leap from amateur golf to the pros: Betsy Rawls, the Phi Beta Kappa from Spartanburg, South Carolina, Peggy Kirk, and Shirley Spork.

"I went to Chicago, where the women pros were having their tournament," Miss Spork recalled. "Babe asked me to turn pro and I said, 'How do you do it?'

"Babe stood up, hit me on the head, and said, 'You're a pro! Now, go tell 'em on the tee.'"

Bettye Mims Danoff joined the tour in its tournament stop in Dallas.

"I loved that Weathervane tour," Mrs. Danoff recalled. "Mr. Handmacher organized that tour and flew me to New York to model his golf clothes. I stayed in a suite in the Pierre Hotel and went to Broadway shows. That was quite a thrill."

Fred Corcoran's relationship with LPGA members is intriguing. The problem, Corcoran said, was one of locker room meetings. He claimed the players would retreat to the ladies' locker room, stage secret meetings, and emerge with incredible demands. That's when Corcoran ran for his sanctuary, the *men's* locker room.

Still, some women pros prospered. Louise Suggs signed with MacGregor Golf Company and also had a clothing contract. Patty Berg continued to enjoy her Wilson deal, and Babe Zaharias was now picking up five hundred dollars for exhibitions, with six hundred dollars for a Sunday appearance. Babe also signed a deal to be head pro at Skycrest Country Club in Chicago for twenty thousand dollars a year, vowing to play "only in the important tournaments." The club promised to buy an airplane to fly Zaharias to these events.

Patty Berg donated her five hundred dollar check from the 1949 Western Women's Open to help the Western Junior Girls Championship (an event won by Marlene Bauer, fifteen, shortly before she turned pro).

In September, Louise Suggs set a new scoring record at the fourth U.S. Women's Open, outdistancing Mrs. Zaharias by 14 strokes. In November, Miss Suggs appeared in an exhibition at Metarie Country Club in New Orleans and made a prophetic assessment of the state of women's professional golf.

Women golfers were just realizing that there was a great future in the professional field, Miss Suggs said, and were beginning to assert themselves.

"I believe I may have arrived twenty years too soon," she said, "but the day is dawning for women golfers."

Patty, Babe, and the Gang

In 1953, at the Weathervane tournament at Philadelphia's Whitemarsh Country Club, LPGA tournament manager Fred Corcoran said his players staged a locker room sit-down, refusing to play until their demands were met.

After heated discussions, concessions were made and the tournament proceeded. But Alvin Handmacher announced in disgust that, after four years, this was to be the last Weathervane tournament.

Corcoran was sorry to see Handmacher go.

"After a rocky start, we reached a reasonably happy working arrangement," Corcoran wrote. "He understood me and I understood him. Neither of us ever wholly understood the girls."

The sit-down strike was the beginning of the end of the romance between Corcoran and the LPGA. After the tournament, Corcoran resigned.

Now the players would try to run the tour on their own. Babe Zaharias, as LPGA president, took over the tournament director's job in February 1954.

"She didn't last long—just two months, as I recall," said Marilynn Smith. "Then she appointed Betty Hicks as tournament director. Babe never let procedures hamper her when she wanted something done. As I remember it, Betty was the only one on the tour who carried a typewriter with her, so I guess it made sense she should be tournament director."

So began the real barnstorming days of the early LPGA, and what a time it was. Among the small-town tour stops was Carollton, Georgia, "The Pimento Capital of the U.S.A." Louise Suggs's father, Johnny Suggs, a former baseball player and scout, was pro-manager of the host golf course.

"He had taught all the caddies to retrieve our practice balls using a fielding glove," Shirley Spork said. "It was a beautiful sight to watch the Babe send out 150-yard 8-iron shots to her caddy. Shot after shot, he simply reached out for her ball, not moving a bit."

Players often entertained at pro-am parties and sponsor dinners. Betty Dodd, a rookie from San Antonio, played the harmonica while Babe joined her for a duet, singing "Detour." Marilynn Smith played the piano while Shirley Spork sang "Night and Day."

Good times were frequent, but prize money remained meager.

Official Jack Kelly, Betty Dodd, Betty McKinnon, Betty Bush, and Babe Zaharias at the 1952 U.S. Women's Open.

In 1953 the pros played twenty-four tournaments for a total of $120,000, or about $5,000 a tournament.

Babe Zaharias was the star of those early years, and knew it. The galleries came out to see the Babe, and it was a role she loved.

"She thinks she's the whole show," said Helen Dettweiler, "which, of course, she is."

"Babe was an uninhibited, outgoing, colorful athlete; and she shared herself with the public," Betsy Rawls recalled. "She joked, talked, emoted, bragged, and generally made people a part of her golf game. They loved it!"

But Babe had a dark side. She developed rivalries with Louise Suggs and the amateur Polly Riley, among others. In the 1948 Women's Texas Open, Polly had clobbered Babe, 10 and 9, in 36 holes of match play. Babe came back in the 1948 Western Women's Open to nip Polly, 3 and 2.

They met again in the 1949 Western Open at Oklahoma City Golf and Country Club. The tournament got off to a great start when amateur Grace Lenczyk fired a 66 in the qualifying round, breaking the old qualifying mark by five strokes.

Babe disposed of Miss Lenczyk in the second round, due in part to one of her heroic shots. At the 12th hole, a 331-yard, dogleg par 4, Babe elected to take a shortcut and belted her tee shot over the trees, a carry of about 250 yards. The ball finished within nine feet of the cup, and Babe made the putt for an eagle 2, to go 2-up. She won the match, 2 and 1.

A gallery at an early '50s U.S. women's tournament at the Los Angeles Country Club.

Babe faced Polly Riley in a quarter-final match. The two had already had words in a practice round when Babe, standing on an adjacent tee, said, "C'mon Polly, why don't you hit one for the folks?"

Polly retorted, "Whaddaya mean, Babe? These people have been following you for 14 holes, and *you* haven't hit one yet?"

The Riley-Zaharias match was played before a large crowd, and Babe played badly; she got three bad lies against the banks of bunkers, failed to break 80, and lost to her Fort Worth amateur foe, 3 and 1.

Polly went into the press room to chide Oklahoma reporters for their headline that morning, which had read: BABE WINS; RILEY NEXT.

And so, small rivalries and petty jealousies developed on the tour, but they were mostly private little wars. Toward the public, LPGA players were gracious to a fault, tolerating distractions that would unnerve any modern player. Galleries walked elbow-to-elbow with the golfers, often talking with them in the middle of the fairway and even asking for golf advice. The players endured it. Public relations was the tour's lifeblood, and no player was as public-relations oriented as Patty Berg.

"She gave clinics at almost every LPGA tournament for years, just to help bring out spectators and would appear anytime, anywhere, to make a speech," said Betsy Rawls.

"The public identified the organization so much with Patty, that the LPGA took on an aura of being an unselfish, friendly, wholesome, refreshing organization with high standards and All-American

Patty Berg and Betsy Rawls were among the players who drew fans to the fledgling LPGA tour.

values. . . . The love and respect that people had for Patty Berg carried over to the LPGA and helped it survive those early years."

The tour enjoyed mixed benefits in those first days. Sometimes the LPGA played on truly great courses, the classic layouts on which modern-day pros seldom have the opportunity to compete: Colonial Country Club in Fort Worth, Augusta Country Club, Plainfield Country Club in New Jersey, Beverly Country Club in Chicago, Sea Island, Inverness, Pebble Beach, and the Upper Cascades at Hot Springs, Virginia.

Frequently, the early tour stopped at virtual cow pastures. Golf course agronomy was in its infancy, and on these scrubby layouts with bare, hardpan fairways, pioneer women pros learned to play a variety of shots from difficult lies.

Tournament courses were very long. Club members usually set the tees and chose the hole locations, making the layouts as difficult as possible, to prevent low scores and save the integrity of their course.

"It was a matter of pride," Miss Rawls said. "Usually, the tees were moved back each day, so that by Sunday we were playing from the backs of the men's tees. Players hit many more long irons and fairway woods to greens in those days, and some of the good scores that were shot were phenomenal."

Golf courses averaged 6,400 yards in length, Miss Rawls said. The course in Lawton, Oklahoma, was played at 6,900 yards, and carefully manicured Concord, at Kiamesha, New York, was set at a backbreaking 6,950 yards for the 1957 LPGA event. When heavy rains drenched the fairways, Concord played well over 7,000 yards, and Shirley Englehorn's winning score of 77-76-76 was superb, under the conditions.

Betsy Rawls remembered playing with Patty Berg on the tough Richmond Country Club in California and seeing her shoot a round of 64.

"To this day it may be the best round of golf I've ever seen played," Miss Rawls said.

Most players of that early era came from the upper fringes of the middle class, and some had been to college. They came from all regions of the country, and most had parents who played golf, but their families were left behind when they joined the tour. They were part of no organized liberation quest, unless we count the Ladies Professional Golf Association as a movement, but they loved golf and the adventure of the road.

In small towns fan enthusiasm for the LPGA ran high. The tournaments were often the only professional sports event that local residents had seen. The tour hit big towns too—Dallas, Houston, Baltimore, and Milwaukee. Most players drove from one tournament town to another, racking up about forty thousand miles a year.

"We shared wanting to play the game of golf as a group and we had to travel from hell and gone to do that," Shirley Spork recalled.

Miss Spork traveled for a time with Marilynn Smith, which cut expenses. Spalding furnished Miss Smith with a car. Bettye Mims Danoff and Alice Bauer traveled with their children in the summers but soon tired of living out of a suitcase and retired.

There were long distances between tournaments. The Spokane to Waterloo, Iowa, haul was sixteen hundred miles, for example. To help each other avoid trouble on the road, players would caravan.

"A whole string of cars, loaded with golf shoes and clothes and clubs and players, drove from one event to the next," said Marilynn Smith. "[It was] sort of a wagon train to help in case anyone broke down, as we too frequently did."

Peggy Kirk Bell bought her own airplane in Wichita, Kansas. Gloria Armstrong, who was an experienced pilot, flew Mrs. Bell to the West Coast events and eventually taught her to fly. After that, Peggy used a road map for navigation, following the highways from the air.

The players ran their own tournaments. They made pairings, kept statistics, signed the checks, and did their own publicity. Policy decisions were made by the membership. Tournaments were staffed

Patty Berg, Mickey Wright, Mrs. Charles Dennehy, and Betsy Rawls with the U.S Women's Open trophy.

by local club members, and gate receipts usually went to a charity.

If there was a low point in the early years, it was when the LPGA signed to play a tournament in Oklahoma for a percentage of the gate receipts. The golfers trudged away from the first tee in the middle of a dust storm. No gallery showed up. There were no gate receipts, and no paychecks.

Marilynn Smith remembered the other obligations of life on the tour: old friends to see, mandatory tournament cocktail parties, practice rounds, the Wednesday pro-am, four rounds of tournament golf, then another long drive to the next town, not to mention loads of dirty laundry that needed attention.

The stress of the 72-hole tournaments took a toll on even the best players, and soon the LPGA began to abandon that format, favoring a number of 54-hole tournaments to spare the players' health.

In spite of such hardships, many early players wouldn't have traded the adventures of the early years for the riches of the modern tour. They enjoyed a close camaraderie and the excitement of life on the road. Just by keeping women's professional golf alive, they were building the tour. Against overwhelming odds, a handful of golfers had founded and preserved what was to become the oldest women's professional sports organization in the world.

Credibility came to the LPGA early in its history. In 1954 the United States Golf Association assumed sponsorship of the U.S.

Women's Open. In only four years from the tournament's inception, the women pros had earned the USGA's stamp of approval.

Gradually the founders drifted off the tour. Patty Berg made frequent charity appearances, and her hilarious clinics for Wilson Sporting Goods Company drew large crowds wherever she appeared.

Shirley Spork left the tour to live in Palm Springs, California, where she taught golf at Tamarisk Country Club.

Bettye Mims Danoff retired to Desoto, Texas, a small town near Dallas, and spent most of her remaining years enjoying her grandchildren.

Louise Suggs moved to Delray Beach, Florida, made a few rare tournament appearances, and became a popular seasonal instructor at the exclusive Sea Island Golf Club in Georgia.

Alice Bauer retired to Arizona, where she enjoyed her children and her grandchildren and taught golf.

Betty Jameson retired to Delray Beach and retained a keen interest in the game, donating the Glenna Collett Vare Trophy to the LPGA, to be presented yearly to the member with the lowest scoring average.

Opal Hill, Sally Sessions, Babe Zaharias, and Fred Corcoran died before 1975.

Marilynn Smith retired to Richardson, Texas, where, in 1987, she organized the first women's senior professional tournament, the Marilynn Smith Founders' Classic.

Marlene Bauer Hagge, who was fifteen when she became one of the founding members of the LPGA, won twenty-five professional tournaments over the course of her career. In 1990 she was still playing the LPGA Tour and frequently beat players less than half her age.

Helen Dettweiler played a few more years on the tour, then went to Indio, California, where she helped air ace Jacqueline Cochran write the history of the Women's Air Force Service Pilots (WASP). At the urging of Miss Cochran and her husband, financier Floyd Odlum, Helen designed a nine-hole golf course on the couple's thousand-acre ranch in the 1950s, thus becoming the first female golf-course designer. Cochran Ranch, which was later named "Indian Palms," was only the second golf course in the desert, and Hollywood stars flocked to Miss Dettweiler for golf lessons. Helen befriended Jack Benny, Mary Livingston, Desi Arnaz, Lucille Ball, Greer Garson, Ray Milland, and Rosalind Russell. She also taught at Thunderbird Country Cub and El Dorado Country Club in Palm Springs and had a standing golf lesson with former President Dwight D. Eisenhower at 8:30 A.M.

Helen also ran a sportswear shop in Palm Desert. After retiring she played social golf, did charity work for the Eisenhower Medical Center and the Boys Clubs, and made frequent trips to Africa, where she photographed animals. She died in 1991.

Louise Suggs at the 1967 Women's Open. She was the first woman to beat men professionals on a head-to-head basis.

Betsy Rawls, in 1975, became the LPGA's first paid tournament director. In the 1980s she accepted a position with the McDonald's Corporation as chairman of the company's annual LPGA tournament, the McDonald's Championship. The event offered an annual purse of more than $500,000, nearly twice the amount of Miss Rawls's lifetime earnings as a pro.

She admitted that women's professional golf had changed drastically but that the game remains the same.

"For most golfers there is a never-ending struggle to improve and to learn the secrets of this complex sport," Miss Rawls said. "There are many more failures than successes and many more disappointments than joys. To all the people who have played professional golf over the years, however, one thing is certain—the struggle has been worth it."

Silent Champions

Louise Suggs and Betsy Rawls were among golf's quiet people. There's little doubt that each possessed the furious intensity that all great players share, but their inner fires burned silently. Neither caused much of a stir, and during her best years each was overshadowed by more colorful players. But headlines fade and cheers subside, and when giddy publicity is forgotten, their records are enduring testimony to the excellence with which they played.

As close as I can place it, I first saw them play in 1958 in a private exhibition at Atlantis Country Club near Lake Worth, Florida. Louise, Ben Hogan, Sam Snead, and Patty Berg made up one pairing. Betsy, Lew Worsham, Bob Toski, and Mickey Wright played in the other. A small gallery of perhaps five hundred provided a rare opportunity to watch the players from close range. Miss Berg, Snead, and Hogan were jovial. Worsham and Toski ribbed Mickey when she blasted a powerful drive from the first tee. As usual, Louise and Betsy went their quiet way, letting their games speak for them.

People who saw them play remember their styles well—the way Louise stalked a golf course and the languid beauty of her swing, Betsy's heady manufacturing of shots and her never-say-die concentration.

In those days the women professionals spent a lot of time in Florida. It was warm enough for winter practice, and the early months of the year featured tournaments in Lake Worth, St. Petersburg, Sanford, and Miami. LPGA tournaments welcomed amateurs who had handicaps of less than 5 strokes, so I played in a few pro events. I began to know Louise a bit when we were paired together in the St. Petersburg Open. Later we were houseguests of a Mountain Lake resident who annually sponsored a golf exhibition, and we were fellow committee members for a new LPGA event in Delray Beach. Perhaps because I successfully suggested that we name it "The Louise Suggs Invitational," I was the only amateur invited to Louise's tournament party.

While in college I hauled a cumbersome old Wallensack double-reeled tape recorder to her home to interview Louise for a radio sports show. By 1965 standards she was a wealthy woman. Her large stucco house stood on a manicured waterfront lot in Delray Beach. Its interior was cheery and open, each room an uncluttered arrangement of gleaming antiques. A dining room wall was taken up by a glass-fronted cabinet that glittered with rows of silver trophies.

And so, over the years, I began to know Miss Suggs a bit. No one got to know Louise quickly.

Mickey Wright knew her well, of course, and admired her tremendously. Friends said Mickey sometimes inadvertently answered her by saying, "Yes ma'am" or "No ma'am."

Louise seldom let down her reserve, so when we were both guests at a 1988 dinner in New York I was startled to hear her confess that, following a Broadway musical the previous night, she had been so mesmerized by the music that she had taken a friend's arm and they had skipped down Broadway, singing.

Louise grew up learning the game on a Lithia Springs, Georgia, golf course designed and built by her father. John Suggs, a former professional baseball player, had turned to golf and found his daughter to be an apt student.

"I was ten years old then," Miss Suggs said. "In those days Lithia Springs was out in the country; there were no neighbors or anything. Since our house almost had the golf course for a backyard, I just started hitting golf balls."

A slender woman of average height, Louise developed a beautifully fluid golf swing, like Bob Jones, cocking her head slightly to the left as she swept the club back in a lovely, rhythmical motion. She had perfect balance, great feel, and enough power that comedian Bob Hope tagged her "Miss Slugs."

Had Louise come along at any other time, she would have dominated golf, but her game matured just as Babe Zaharias flashed across the scene. Babe won the U.S. Women's Amateur in 1946; Louise won it in 1947. Babe became the first American to capture the British Women's Open Amateur in 1947; Louise won the British in 1948. Her stoic approach was in direct contrast to the Babe's flamboyance, and some have said there were hard feelings between Babe and Louise. Typically, Miss Suggs remains silent on the matter.

If Babe captured attention, Louise won an equal number of big titles. Before turning pro, she won the 1946 and 1947 Western Amateur. She won the North and South in 1942, 1946, and 1948; captured three Doherty titles from 1945 through 1948; and made the 1948 U.S. Curtis Cup team. As an amateur she won two Western Opens and one Titleholders Championship.

Turning professional in 1948, she won a total of eleven major championships and fifty tour victories. Her record in the Women's Open is superb. She won twice, setting a 72-hole scoring record for women in 1952 with a total of 284, and finished second five times.

In 1960 Louise became the first woman to beat men professionals on a head-to-head basis. Playing from the same tees, she defeated a field of LPGA players and a dozen outstanding men, including Sam Snead and Gardner Dickinson, in the Royal Poinciana Invitational at Palm Beach Par 3 Golf Club in Palm Beach, Florida.

While Louise had the heart of a lion, she wasn't one to boast of her victories. "Of course, being in the right place at the right time had a lot to do with it," she said. "I've always tried to play the golf course rather than the person. I figured if I could shoot par golf, even in match play, it would be pretty hard for somebody to beat me."

Betsy Rawls won eight major championships.

Miss Suggs was a steely competitor but an ideal playing companion. Her devout concentration inspired other golfers to keep their minds on business, and some recorded their best scores when paired with her. Generous with her knowledge, she would help younger players learn the strategy of playing a hole just a few hours before a tournament began and frequently offered to play practice rounds with budding superstar Mickey Wright. In 1988 Miss Wright listed

Louise as one of her four favorite playing companions.

A founder of the LPGA Tour, Miss Suggs was a stalwart worker and devoted some of her best playing years to fulfilling additional duties as an officer. Veteran players recall hearing her typewriter as she wrote letters on behalf of the LPGA well into the night. Her loyal efforts prompted little recognition, but acclaim was not what spurred Louise Suggs. In all things her motivation was excellence for its own sake.

Like Louise, Betsy Rawls received little publicity, and her most noted victory was publicized for its flukey nature: In 1957 Miss Rawls captured the U.S. Women's Open. Jackie Pung had recorded the lowest score but inadvertently signed an incorrect scorecard, and the title went to Betsy by default.

It's of little significance now, just a footnote in the record books, because Betsy also won the Women's Open in 1951, 1953, and 1960, becoming one of only two women to have captured four Open titles.

Miss Rawls was introduced to the game by her father at the age of seventeen. Raised in the small town of Burnet in the Texas hill country, she graduated from the University of Texas as a Phi Beta Kappa.

Under the tutelage of noted teacher Harvey Penick, she developed a proficient swing. She was runner-up in the Women's Open and twice won the Women's Texas Amateur before turning professional in 1951. On the fledgling tour she proved her great scoring ability, never quit or showed disgust, and was a wizard around the greens. A woman of endearing shyness, she was a great competitor through sheer strength of will.

When Betsy played you could almost see her mind working, and seldom did she fail to find a way out of trouble. Not the longest hitter on the tour, her understanding of the game was nearly unmatched. And so she crisscrossed the country in the LPGA's early, struggling days and won fifty-five tournaments, including eight major championships. In 1959 she rang up ten victories, a record for the time, and won the Vare Trophy. In 1960, at only thirty-two, she became the LPGA Hall of Fame's fifth member.

When she retired in 1975, after nearly a quarter of a century of professional competition, her role in golf was only beginning. Betsy was hired as the LPGA's tournament director, and no one questioned the choice. Her fine mind was attuned to tournament operation, and she was a virtual genius on administration of the Rules of Golf.

The tour grew, purses increased, and Betsy deserves much of the credit. Disputes were kept to a minimum. Her role as a liaison with sponsors brought new respect from the folks who put up the money, and the LPGA began to take off.

More achievements followed. She was the first woman to serve on the rules committee of the U.S. Open (the *men's* Open), she was elected to the World Golf Hall of Fame, and in 1981 she took her expe-

174

rience to the rich new McDonald's Championship. As executive director for more than a decade, Betsy put her stamp on the tournament to make it one of the LPGA's most successful.

Betsy Rawls, like Louise Suggs, made contributions to golf that received little acclaim. But she made a mark on the game, and that will endure.

9

Catherine the Great

JoAnne Gunderson Carner tagged Catherine Lacoste, the French amateur, "Catherine the Great." Whether or not there was good feeling behind the nickname, Mrs. Carner had hit the mark. Catherine Lacoste *was* great. For a period of three years she was the best amateur in the world, winning the U.S. Women's Amateur, the British Amateur, the Western Amateur, and, incredibly, the U.S. Women's Open.

Other amateurs have won professional tournaments. Polly Riley, Peggy Kirk Bell, Claire Doran, and JoAnne Carner all won weekly tour events. Mlle Lacoste, however, staggered the world of golf when she captured the 1967 U.S. Women's Open. Moreover, she won the Women's Open on alien soil as the first foreign champion, the first amateur winner and, at twenty-two, the youngest champion in history.

Other French golfers had played amateur golf in the United States, most notably Brigitte Varangot and Claudine Cros Rubin. Mlle Varangot, who won three British Amateurs, also played against Mickey Wright on the televised golf show "Shell's Wonderful World of Golf."

Mlle Lacoste blazed across women's golf in the late 1960s, fiery as

JoAnne Gunderson Carner, an amateur rival of Catherine Lacoste, defeated her in the U.S. Women's Amateur in 1968.

a meteor. She was an enigma, of sorts. While she played with great emotion, suffering or celebrating on nearly every shot, the more she won, the less we seemed to know her.

Catherine spoke English well enough, but she was an excitable girl, and when she spoke she bubbled over in a rapid mishmash of language. She had great confidence but, unlike Mlle Varangot and Mlle Cross, made little attempt to make friends.

At the 1967 Women's Open, she kept to herself and made unfortunate remarks to the press. According to the daily newspapers, other contestants in the Women's Open were mean to Catherine, and she was very, very distraught. Prevailing hostility, she said, upset her so that she spent a great deal of time in tears.

Her remarks didn't ring true. The night before the final round, she seemed cheerful enough, whirling so feverishly on the Homestead Hotel's dance floor that her feet slipped out from under her and she fell, laughing, to the floor.

Catherine raised the ire of some contestants when she beat them on that muggy July day, but they weren't hostile, they were embarrassed.

Women's professional golf was struggling. The players ran their own weekly tour events, purses remained low, and endorsement contracts were few. The LPGA didn't have a bad image, it had very little image at all. Television exposure was rare. The ABC telecast of this U.S. Women's Open gave the professionals their only exposure to a national audience. And so, by July 2, 1967, the stage was set for one of golf's more bizzarre encounters.

Nestled in the high hollows of the Shenandoah Mountains, Hot Springs, Virginia, offered splendid isolation, a superb golf course, and two distinctly different resort styles—the luxurious old Homestead Hotel and a cluster of cabins at the foot of a hill.

Network crews, USGA officials, and some players stayed at the Homestead, a romantic old place that society decorator Dorothy Draper had swathed in chintz. An orchestra played show tunes during tea and dinner, and guests dined in evening clothes. On the night before the final round, nimble black-tied waiters stacked a glittering pyramid of champagne glasses, pouring bottle after bottle into a single glass at the top until a waterfall of champagne cascaded into the glasses below. Except for the distinct mountain accents of some of the busboys, it might have been Paris.

Most players stayed in more Spartan cabins at the foot of the hill, but there was fine camaradarie among the golfers. Amateurs were considered serious players and were accepted by the touring professionals, joining them for home-style meals at long tables in the dining cabin. One group that often dined together included Barbara Romack, Kathy Cornelius, JoAnn Prentice, Shirley Englehorn, and four players who would have key roles that week, Murle Breer, Susie Maxwell, Beth Stone, and the stately veteran, Louise Suggs.

There was little conversation about Catherine Lacoste, although she led or was close to the lead all week. Rather, there was a general feeling among the professionals that, in the end, one of their own would win, as they had always won. So they gossiped cheerfully or made an occasional stab at political discussion. None waded into such matters too deeply. Golf prevailed, influencing all that they did. The contestants ate well and early, and rested a lot. Privately, they mulled over stubbed pitch shots and faulty swings, and their minds spiraled around the intrigue of mountain greens. In this way they were alike, yet consideration for the other players kept their thoughts private.

Each approached the game differently. Some were pragmatists, others more mechanical. Louise Suggs, for example, played almost exclusively by feel. With their varied opinions on what it takes to play great golf, they couldn't share their solitary golf selves, and so, after dinner, they adjourned to the porch; in the dark you heard their soft, sleepy laughter and the creak of the old rocking chairs until they went inside to bed.

Evening rainfall meant that the morning players could smell the damp pines and hear the steady dripping of moisture in the mountain forests. The morning fairways were soft, then the sun would glint through the pines, and the superb Upper Cascades course, meander-

Rene and Simone Lacoste, Catherine's parents, were champions in their own right—Rene in tennis, Simone as British Women's Amateur Champion.

ing through the Shenandoah Mountains, played firm and fast. A course with long rough and small, quirky greens, it demanded distance and control off the tee, precision irons, and intelligent putting.

As the championship began, a support group of mothers, sisters, and friends sat on the hillside overlooking the 15th, crocheting or stitching needlepoint as they waited for a favored player to pass below.

Mickey Wright, four-time Women's Open champion, had withdrawn upon the sudden death of her brother, but other wonderful players rounded out the field: Kathy Whitworth, Sandra Haynie, Carol Mann, Donna Caponi, and Judy Kimball, along with good amateurs like Anne Quast and Nancy Roth Syms.

In the first round, Catherine Lacoste fired a 71, one stroke off the lead. A stunning second round of 70 vaulted her into a five-stroke lead, a margin she kept in spite of a 74 in the third round.

Miss Lacoste had exemplary bloodlines. Born in 1945 in Chantaco, France, near the Spanish border, she was the daughter of Rene and Simone Lacoste. Catherine's father was a famous tennis player, known as "The Crocodile" because of his nifty crocodile luggage. He also manufactured the popular Lacoste sports shirt with the crocodile insignia.

Catherine's mother, Simone Thion de la Chaume, was famous in European golf circles. In 1924 Mlle de la Chaume had captured the

Catherine Lacoste (at right) with Claudine Cros and Brigitte Varangot, members of the victorious French team at the 1964 Women's World Amateur Team Championship.

hearts of British golf fans when she won the British Girls' Open Championship. In 1927, near the end of the reign of Cecil Leitch and Joyce Wethered, she won the British Women's Amateur. She won the French championship three times and through the 1930s was the dominant figure in French golf.

English golf writer Eleanor Helme recalled the 1924 Girls' Championship at Stoke Poges, which Mlle de la Chaume went on to win.

"The pitiful sights of suffering parents almost imperiled the gaiety of Stoke Poges," Miss Helme wrote. "The poor dears endured agonies of suspense, and the management wrung shaking hands in the seclusion of the shrubberies or the darkest corner of the clubhouse while a trembling mamma or papa begged to know how the darling was getting on now. . . . Perhaps Pa and Ma banished themselves feeling they could not bear the spectacle of their little one missing an even littler putt."

If the sight of suffering parents in her own junior days prompted Simone Lacoste to become an ideal golf parent, it was Catherine's good fortune. Catherine learned to play at Chantaco, a golf course at the foot of the Pyrenees that belonged to her family, and took her early lessons from Jean Garaialde. As a child she won almost everything she entered and in 1966 startled a strong British field by winning the Astor Trophy medal at Prince's, Sandwich, with a record round of 66.

She was co-medalist in the 1964 World Amateur Team Championships in Paris, where her inspired play vaulted France to the team championship.

But in the final round of the Women's Open, Catherine was approaching one of the sacrosanct barriers in women's golf. The championship had never been won by an amateur, although Barbara McIntire had nearly beaten the odds in 1956 when she tied for first with professional Kathy Cornelius but lost in an 18-hole playoff.

Early in the final round, Miss Lacoste shot to a seven-stroke lead. Susie Maxwell, Sandra Haynie, and Beth Stone, her closest challengers, were unable to rally. Then Catherine began to play poorly, and an attack came from a surprising quarter.

At forty-three Louise Suggs had virtually retired from competition. She had won her first U.S. Women's Open in 1949 and had one of the best records in the history of the Women's Open. She won for a second time in 1952 and had thirteen top-ten finishes in fifteen years, including four as runner-up. A proud woman, she wouldn't have come to Hot Springs had she not been able to play up to her own standards, which were very high.

Catherine Lacoste had made the American trip alone, defying the other French amateurs who were playing in the European Team Championship.

Winning at home is difficult enough, but playing well on foreign soil calls for major tuning. The body's inner clock doesn't seem to work well, and the quality of food, water, and weather become the subject of endless speculation. Accommodations are alien, local dialect unfamiliar, and galleries favor the home player.

In the final round at Hot Springs, Catherine's lead dwindled. The challenge came from Miss Suggs, who had been nine strokes behind when the day began. In a lingering moment of her old greatness, Louise pulled to within one stroke of the lead on the 15th hole. Then, on the 16th, calm and steely-eyed, she hit a crisp iron. The ball reached the top of its arc and descended toward the flagstick. To the moans of the gallery, the ball dropped a foot short of the green, deeply imbedding in the bank of a water hazard. Louise grimly made a double-bogey.

The Americans' last chance rested with Beth Stone, who was also one stroke behind. With determination, Stone parred the last three difficult holes and waited.

Catherine arrived at the 17th knowing that her lead had shrunk to a single stroke. This hole reflects the course's challenge. A creek meanders along the fairway's right side, and the base of a brush-covered mountain juts into the fairway on the left. Under intense pressure, Miss Lacoste rifled her tee shot safely through the trouble.

The second shot on this par 4 is equally challenging; a bunker loomed on the green's left, and the pesky creek guarded the right. Catherine pulled off a remarkable shot, whizzing an iron to within ten

Mlle Lacoste survived the final holes to become the first amateur to win the U.S. Women's Open in 1967.

feet of the hole. With characteristic boldness, she popped the putt firmly. It hit the back of the cup, and fell into the hole. The Americans knew it was over.

Catherine made a fine par on the final hole and became the first amateur to win the Women's Open.

The American professionals were stunned. On national television Catherine Lacoste had ruined their best marketing ploy—their status as the greatest women golfers in the world.

Meanwhile, Catherine's victory at the Women's Open was only the beginning of her short, incredible stretch of great play.

She had been repeatedly frustrated by her failure to win the British Women's Amateur, although she was twice medalist. In 1969 the British was played at Portrush, up the Irish coast from Royal County Down where her mother had clinched the title twenty-three years before. Accompanied by her mother, Catherine arrived at the site a week ahead for intensive practice.

In the final match she fell behind quickly and was four down to Ann Irvin. Again Miss Lacoste rallied and won.

Earlier in the year, she had won the French and the Spanish titles. She now faced the decision whether to go to America to tee it up in the U.S. Women's Amateur, the only important title to elude her. It wasn't an easy decision. The pressure to win was taking a toll on her

Catherine Lacoste with the 1967 U.S. Women's Open trophy.

spirit, and the Women's Amateur was being held in Texas in August, the hottest time of the year.

But, of course, she played. Temperatures hovered above one hundred degrees throughout the week as Miss Lacoste slashed through the field. She came from 3-down to beat Anne Quast in the semifinal. In the final she faced Shelley Hamlin of California.

With several holes left in her match with Miss Hamlin, Miss Lacoste was 3-up when she turned to a USGA official. "When I win," she blurted, "how are you going to ship the trophy to France?"

Brash, indeed, but she beat Shelley Hamlin, 3 and 2.

In 1970 she married, becoming Catherine Lacoste De Prado. She withdrew from top competition and did not defend her U.S. Women's Amateur title.

Six weeks after her marriage, she decided to once again play for France in the Women's World Amateur Team Championship. All week Catherine struggled with her game while her teammates, Brigitte Varangot and Claudine Cros, played well.

In the World Amateur Team Championship, the two best scores of each country's three competitors count as the team's daily total. France bolted to an early lead when Miss Varangot shot 71 and Miss Cros, 70, for a first-day team total of 141. Catherine had shot 74. With one round to play, France had a two-stroke lead.

In the final round, Catherine battled with the Americans as her teammates paced the sidelines. Her lengthy absence from competition took a toll, and she struggled to a 78. France lost by one stroke to the U.S. team.

Although Catherine was co-medalist with Jane Bastanchury Booth of the United States and Marlene Stewart Streit of Canada, had she managed at 76, the French team would have won.

Yet, at the age of twenty-five, Catherine Lacoste de Prado had a remarkable record: In 1967 she won the French Ladies' Open and the U.S. Women's Open. In 1968 she won the French Ladies' Close. She won the French Open, the French Close, the Spanish Open, the British Women's Amateur, and the U.S. Women's Amateur in 1969, and in 1970 she won the French Open.

Catherine showed a final flash of her old talent in 1972 when she again won the French Ladies' Open; then she retired from competition. Today she lives in Spain with her husband and children, having reached her own pedestal in women's golf.

The "Proettes"

The modern, multimillion-dollar LPGA Tour was born in the small towns of America, on putting greens in Visalia, Muskogee, Beaumont, and St. Pete, and on practice tees at Midland, Sutton, and Ocean Shores.

The early players were a diverse collection, some great and some of medium skill, but they had a common goal—to play championship golf and to make the tour, the source of their income, a success.

The tour's difficult first steps, from 1949 to as late as 1964, were made rougher in that the LPGA was conceived during the golden age of amateur golf. Most fine players were making their reputations as amateurs, and the women's professional golf tour was not widely accepted. A requisite of women pros, or "proettes," as they were sometimes called, was thick-skinned immunity to public disapproval. To play the tour, one had to be something of a renegade, in fact. Still, a handful of women turned pro and hit the road. A few wisely invested their winnings and gained lifetime security. Many more did not. And, while they can't take it to the bank, the glory of what the LPGA Tour has become is theirs.

Mickey Wright and Barbara Romack were two great amateurs of the era who chose to turn professional. By the time she was a freshman at Stanford, Miss Wright had won the U.S. Girls' Junior Championship; had been low amateur in the U.S. Women's Open, finishing fourth overall; and had lost to Barbara Romack in the finals of the 1954 U.S. Women's Amateur.

Miss Romack, at twenty-six, had been on three Curtis Cup teams and had won nearly every prestigious title in women's amateur golf, including the U.S. Women's Amateur, the Women's Western Amateur, the North and South, the Canadian Amateur, the Doherty, the Palm Beach Championship, the South Atlantic, and the Florida East Coast.

Barbara Romack, 1954 U.S. Women's Amateur Champion.

Mickey recalled that a lot of her friends played on the amateur circuit.

"Many came from fairly well-to-do families, which allowed them to play ten or fifteen tournaments a year against some of the finest women players of the era," Miss Wright said. "Their main goal was to win the U.S. Women's Amateur and qualify for the Curtis Cup team."

Her own goals differed. "First, I thought Patty Berg, Louise Suggs, and Babe Zaharias were the best. If I was to become the best, I had to compete against them," she said.

An aversion to match play and reluctance to frivolously spend money on amateur golf prompted Miss Wright to join the tour in 1955 with a bank account of twelve hundred dollars, a gift from her father.

"He said when that ran out, there would be no more," she recalled.

Barbara Romack's professional career had a different impetus. Barbara loved amateur golf's great traditions and she loved match play, in which she was such a killer that she was nicknamed "Little Tiger." Her one failure, to win the British Amateur after reaching the final in 1955, was, she said, "an almost devastating blow to my morale."

It was several months before Miss Romack forced herself back to the practice tee. She found it harder and harder to concentrate on her game, and a pro career held little appeal.

"The idea of competing with Patty, Louise, and Betsy Rawls seemed too formidable," Barbara said. "The somewhat negative opinion of the public towards women in sports was another drawback."

Mickey Wright, 1952 Girls Junior Champion, finished fourth in the 1954 U.S. Women's Open, won by Babe Zaharias. After a brief but brilliant amateur career, she turned pro in 1955.

And so, Mickey Wright turned professional while Barbara Romack continued to grind away on the amateur circuit. In 1958, after again reaching the finals of the U.S. Women's Amateur, Barbara heard from Fred Corcoran, the LPGA tournament director. Corcoran urged her to turn pro. Prize money was growing, he said, and Miss Romack, an attractive, vivacious blond, could make money from endorsements and exhibitions.

Intrigued, Barbara made the leap and joined the tour in Florida in the winter of 1959.

"I loved golf, people, travelling, and money," she said, "and I thought that one of these days this tour might really take off and hit the heights."

In Florida she immediately began to learn the hard lessons that Mickey Wright, her old amateur rival, had absorbed for the last four years: Tournament layouts ranged from cow pastures to American classics. Local caddies might or might not show up to tote the golf bags. Good-looking sports clothes for women were expensive and hard to find. A typical drive to the next tournament might be eight hundred miles or more.

The chief of this traveling sideshow of women's golf was Corcoran. After he resigned, Lennie Wirtz, a five-foot-five-inch spitfire and former MacGregor Sporting Goods Company executive from Cincinnati, took the reins. Wirtz, like Corcoran, was a good promoter. He was also father confessor, counsel, diplomat, and a peacemaker who became very close to a number of players. His concern for them became almost an emotional attachment. In the pressure cooker of competition, some were bound to turn on him. Pro-Lennie factions and anti-Lennie factions developed.

Wirtz's finest moment was never publicized: During the racially volatile 1960s, the LPGA tour began to attract new tournaments in housing developments. Developers promoted their real estate by appealing to gallery members as prospective homeowners. Meanwhile, the LPGA now included two black players, Althea Gibson and Renee Powell. Two sponsors, fearing a threat to the all-white home-buying market, decided to bar the black women by calling their tournaments "invitationals" rather than "open" events.

Wirtz broke that barrier, telling the sponsors, "We all play, or we all stay away."

Some developers fell into line, but the LPGA lost several Southern tournaments. Although the tour was desperate for new events, Wirtz's bold position was upheld by the players.

"There is no doubt in my mind that every LPGA player at that time supported and, if necessary, would have backed up that ultimatum," said Mary Lou Crocker.

Through the 1960s Wirtz shepherded his flock. When friction developed with some of the players, he returned to his career as a respected college basketball official.

Before the real estate boom brought the LPGA to housing developments, pro tournaments were sponsored by individual golf clubs, golf associations, and civic groups who used the events to raise money for charity.

The women's tour was welcomed in larger cities like Baltimore, Milwaukee, and Dallas (major markets that, incidentally, no longer host LPGA events), but small towns were the tour's lifeblood.

"Thank God there were thousands of people in Visalia, Las Cruces, Muskogee, and Waterloo willing to devote time, money, and energy to give their small towns a sporting event," declared Mickey Wright.

Barbara Romack also enjoyed these small-town tour stops.

"For the most part, I think our tournaments at these clubs were very well run. The members were always so enthusiastic and proud that we were playing their course in their town," she said. "The townfolk always got in the act by showing interest in our golf and asking for autographs while we were shopping."

Barbara Romack demonstrates her classic swing at a 1965 exhibition with Betsy Rawls.

Rookies had a hard time finding some of the remote settings. Since the tournaments got little publicity, new players who stopped at nearby service stations to ask directions to "the St. Pete Open" were met with blank stares.

Playing conditions could be difficult. At one tournament Kathy Whitworth, Louise Suggs, and Sharon Miller were forced to play the final hole in the dark.

"The members turned on car headlights so we could see to putt, and we signed our scorecards in a telephone booth," Miss Miller remembered.

There were many disasters, and one of the worst was the 1967 Babe Zaharias Open at Bayou Den Country Club in Beaumont, Texas. Bayou Den was surrounded by rice fields, and a week of heavy rains made the course unplayable. For ten days the players tried to finish the 54-hole tournament. The golfers finally managed to complete their first round by playing nine holes, shotgun start, at 2:00 P.M., after wooden planks were laid on the soaked fairways to provide paths to the greens. Water moccasins wriggled everywhere.

"Candy Phillips and I had a lengthy discussion concerning what we would do if we missed one green with our wedge shots," said Mary Lou Crocker. "Candy decided to withdraw if she missed the green because she wasn't going to walk anywhere except on those planks."

Players yelled and gestured to the groups behind, pointing out snakes. Miss Phillips's caddie, cleaning her club in a pond, lifted it

Carol Mann, 1965 U.S. Women's Open Champion.

out of the water to find a baby snake curled around the club shaft. Three more dips, three more snakes.

The golfers went on the offensive, whacking snakes with their iron clubs. One player found a dead snake with a golf tee in its gaping mouth, the tee imprinted with "Aww Shoot," Candy Phillips's favorite curse when she missed a putt.

Despite finding a snake in a ball washer, Marilynn Smith won the tournament on Tuesday of the second week.

Mary Lou Crocker looked back on that week in Beaumont as "degrading and somewhat frightening." Publicly, however, none of the players belittled the tournament. Tournaments were too hard to come by and Beaumont, where country-western music was piped out to the practice tee, had given them many good years.

There were other hazards. Players were sometimes robbed when thieves broke into their cars and motel rooms. Marilynn Smith escaped injury while crossing a creek on a suspended bridge, gallery in tow, when the bridge collapsed. Even worse, Miss Smith had a terrifying experience at a Florida tournament when a sniper opened fire on her group.

"We were playing the second round," Marilynn said. "I was preparing for my second shot on the fourteenth hole when, with a kind of whine and swoosh, this bullet flew past my head! A sniper was hiding in nearby bushes, shooting at us. We delayed play for 45 minutes while tournament officials tried to find the villain. They never could."

The players were fiercely loyal to their tour, teeing off despite injuries and illness. Mary Mills finished a tournament with cracked ribs. Several golfers completed another tournament in the throes of viral pneumonia. Carol Mann won at Midland, Texas, walking the final round on crutches. Sharon Miller, bothered by hip spasms after stepping in a hole at Waco, cut her backswing and follow-through to a three-quarter motion and finished second. The next week at Corpus Christi, Sharon dared not sit down, fearing that her hip joint would lock. She won the tournament. She twice finished tournaments by swinging forward only with her left arm, because her right was injured.

Attendance at sponsors' cocktail parties and pro-am dinners was mandatory.

"We had no means of really promoting ourselves other than local television, radio, and press," said Sharon Miller. "Cocktail parties were a way for us to mingle with the sponsors, pro-am partners, and members of the club. . . . For two years we had one of our players appointed to check off names of those who attended."

At the last tournament of her first season on tour, Miss Miller was told by Lennie Wirtz that she had lost "Rookie of the Year" honors to Jan Ferraris. Although the two were close in the money standings, Wirtz said Jan had won the award because she attended one more cocktail party than Sharon.

The tour rattled on with player morale bolstered by the sincere friendliness in small towns. Shirley Spork remembered Waterloo, Iowa, with fondness.

"I generally placed a check in the collection basket at the Catholic Church," Miss Spork said. "The good monsignor, an ardent golfer, noticed I had not finished well that week. I received my check back with a note saying, 'You need this more than God does. Also, if you are ever in our area again, we have a good cook at the rectory. Stop any time.'"

For many years the LPGA Championship was played at Pleasant Valley Country Club in Sutton, Massachusetts, a favorite stop. The golf course was grand, and Cuzzy Mingola, the principal owner of Pleasant Valley, was a great supporter of the fledgling LPGA.

Mingola wasn't afraid to offer critical advice to the players. He believed that all tour stops could be as good as the Pleasant Valley event "if we sacrificed our egos, improved our games, and did all the little things necessary to improve our image with the public and with sponsors," Mary Lou Crocker said.

"I know for a fact that half the people I met at the tournament that week knew very little or nothing about golf," said Mary Lou,

191

"but they were marshalling, working, and supporting the event because that was the way people in that area did things. No matter how bleak other tournaments may have seemed, there was always the memory of Pleasant Valley."

All players remember a sense of family among the players.

"At dinner, we ate together at big tables," said Patty Berg, "and we'd talk about current events. Everyone joined in these friendly conversations and we learned a lot and stayed current. Since we spent so much time together, we became a very close-knit group. We came to really *know* each other."

In Columbus, Ohio, in the 1960s, a bunch of players included the veteran Miss Berg in a touch football game in a parking lot.

"Miss Patty was no spring chicken, so we passed the word to take it easy on Patty, we didn't want her to get hurt," recalled Sharon Miller. "She creamed us! The next day I asked her if she was sore and she said, 'Not a bit.' The rest of us ached all over."

Parties were frequent. There were fines for players who muttered a swear word or who tossed a club in a fit of anger. The money was used to stage an end-of-the-year party for the offenders. Card games were a favorite diversion, and an occasional snipe hunt was staged. At one such hunt, Mickey Wright and Betsy Rawls purchased a plucked chicken from a local butcher, pulling the "snipe" out of a pillowcase at the end of the hunt.

A favorite stop was Prospect, Kentucky. A country motel there had generous acreage for playing softball, darts, shuffleboard, or hitting golf balls.

Its restaurant was great. Home-cooked food was at a premium on the road. If a player discovered a motel with in-room kitchens, the other players crammed in, making note of the motel phone number for next year's reservations. Some players cooked in crock pots and electric frying pans in their motel rooms. Marlene Hagge could whip up a gourmet dinner or chicken-fried steak on a moment's notice, and peeling carrots in the bathroom sink was one of her regular chores. Marlene, who had been on tour since 1949, was known for her familiarity with every cafeteria and shopping mall in America.

In the 1950s and 1960s some players began traveling in trailers and campers. Bev Hanson, Mickey Wright, Susie and Dale Berning, Don and JoAnne Carner, Sue Roberts, Debbie Austin, Kathy Postlewait, Sharon Miller, and Jerilyn Britz were among the first campers.

"We got to be a close campground family," Miss Miller recalled. "At one of our cookouts in Rochester, New York, we invited a few guests and set up a chipping contest to see who won the leftovers. Jerilyn Britz won the beans."

Most drove automobiles from tournament to tournament. Air travel was too expensive. As one player said, next to her golf clubs, a player's most important equipment was a good car. Mickey Wright, Barbara Romack, Betsy Rawls, Louise Suggs, and others who were

JoAnne Gunderson Carner, two-time U.S. Women's Open Champion.

making money drove Cadillacs. The big cars were comfortable and had trunk space for three suitcases (one for winter clothes, one for summer clothes, one for dress clothes), golf clubs, dozens of pairs of golf shoes, a small ironing board, iron, briefcase, record player, typewriter, a charcoal grill, pots and pans, hair dryers, shag bag, and a gross of golf balls. A few players had guitars, and several traveled with cats or dogs.

For a while the top players enjoyed a courtesy Oldsmobile, a deal promoted by Lennie Wirtz. Each of the top ten money winners was given a big white Olds with her name and the LPGA insignia on the door. Sandra Haynie was stopped by a policeman as she whizzed through a town on her way to a tournament. The officer wanted to know why she had driven through the town ten times, each time exceeding the speed limit. Miss Haynie spent several minutes trying to explain the new LPGA perk.

Marlene Hagge was a notorious speedster, known to outrun the police. Barbara Romack rode with Marlene just once, she claimed.

"Relax," said Miss Hagge, "at least nobody can hit us from the rear!"

Most players traveled in caravans of six to eight cars, signaling each other when to pass and holding up signs that urged the others to stop for "food," "gas," or "potty."

Marlene Bauer (Hagge) and her sister Alice, here with their parents, joined the LPGA while still teenagers.

And so they beat down the highways for eight to fifteen hours at a stretch. Once they hit the road, the players didn't return home until the end of the season. Life on the tour was a commitment.

For most, golf's challenge was the lure. Only on the tour could they measure their games against the world's top players. Some of the greatest, like Kathy Whitworth and Mickey Wright, claim to have learned the game on the tour.

For Barbara Romack, who gained endorsements and did a number of appearances, it was a profitable career. Despite a wonderfully classic swing, the former amateur champion was never able to fully adjust to stroke play, although she finished among the top ten money winners in her early years before back injuries ended her career.

For a few it was a sort of golf holiday. Players who performed well could make a living. Most could get by. A total purse of $7,500 was average and $15,000 was a bonanza, but the strength of the American dollar meant that players could live well on $150 to $200 a week. A steak dinner cost two dollars, a fine motel room was eight dollars to ten dollars a night.

"I was surprised that, during my first year, I made more money than I would have made teaching school," said Betsy Cullen.

Players were sensitive to the financial woes of the lesser lights.

194

Sandra Palmer, 1975 Women's Open Champion, was on the tour in the 1960s.

"It was a team effort in many ways," said Miss Romack. "There were times when we knew one of our group was hard-pressed for money, yet too proud to say anything. There would be a silent collection among the players to help her get to the next stop. Sometimes the club members would chip in. The money would mysteriously appear, sealed in a nondescript envelope, in the player's incoming mail."

To help the tour grow and to encourage lesser players, a motion surfaced at a 1964 players' meeting that more money be distributed at the bottom of the money list.

"The top players, particularly Mickey Wright, who would have the most to lose, voted to take money off the top and put it on the bottom to help the struggling players," said Betsy Cullen. "That was impressive to me as a rookie, to realize that the players took pride in pioneering their organization and would sacrifice their own best interests in its behalf."

Several women played the tour with their husbands and children in tow. One of the first was Bettye Mims Danoff, a Dallas player who was one of the LPGA's founding members. Since 1950 Bettye had traveled with her two daughters. In 1956 Mrs. Danoff teed off in the Dallas Civitan Open just two weeks and two days after her daughter Debbie was born. Walking every hole, she finished the 72-hole event.

In 1960, when her daughter Kaye had a child, Bettye was promoted as the tour's first grandmother. Patty Berg started the moniker in her famous "Swing Parade," a pretournament clinic where she introduced each player to hit a few shots.

One week, when Patty started her spiel, introducing Mrs. Danoff as "our first grandmother," Bettye limped onto the tee, leaning on a cane, a parasol over her head, wearing a long black skirt, high-button shoes, and a floppy hat. Her hair was sprayed with gray dye. Gold-rimmed granny glasses perched on her nose. Her picture, hitting a 3-wood in her absurd get-up, made the front page of the local newspaper the following day.

Tour families got a lot of ink, but their lives were somewhat unusual. Entertaining the children while Mom played golf was one of the more difficult chores. Kathy Cornelius's daughter Karen and Peggy Kirk Bell's daughter Bonnie watched Miss Berg's clinic so often that they knew the routine by heart. The two played make-believe by doing their own version of Patty's clinic.

Karen began traveling with her mother and father in 1957 when she was two years old. The LPGA became the toddler's extended family.

"As the only full-time child on the tour, I had many aunts," Karen said.

Karen's birthday parties were a bonanza, and she still has the Tiny Tears doll that Patty Berg presented at her fourth birthday party in French Lick, Indiana.

Karen and her father followed Kathy every step of every round. It could be a distraction. In Wykagyl, New York, Karen fell into quicksand. Her dad pulled her out and brushed off the mud. At the 1961 Women's Open, Karen and Bonnie dug up the tulip bulbs in the Baltusrol Golf Club's flower beds and were caught red-handed by the dignified Joseph C. Dey, Jr., executive director of the USGA.

"I think he was more amused than angry," Karen said.

When the tour stopped in Phoenix, Karen nearly caused one of her mother's fellow-competitors to be disqualified.

"I had just gotten a pocket knife and talked Mary Mills, a former U.S. Women's Open champion, into playing mumbletypeg," Karen said. "Unnoticed, we played near the first tee, oblivious to the calls for Mary to go to the tee. Her group finally teed off without her and she was given a two-stroke penalty."

Karen's sister Kay was born in 1966. Kay grew up to be a very fine player herself and was 1981 U.S. Girls' Junior champion. As a toddler she could throw a noisy tantrum, her sister said. Avoiding a room next door to the Cornelius's became a tour joke.

Eventually Karen, Kay, and Bonnie Bell were joined by Judy Rankin's son Tuey, Murle Breer's daughters, and Robin Dummett's son. The children brought their books to the tour and were taught by their parents, although most big tournaments were played during the summer school vacations.

Karen's role changed to that of baby sitter, and with Mrs. Rankin's sister Liz she took tour children to carnivals, zoos, and swimming pools.

Karen remembers those days with pleasure.

"How many children have been to forty-nine states, Canada, Japan, and Mexico?" she said. "I met so many nice people at each tournament, and had so many adults who cared for me and watched over me."

10

Golf's Golden Girl

Mickey Wright turned professional in 1955 at the age of nineteen. With the charming frankness of youth, she announced a lofty goal.

"I'm going to win," she predicted. "I'll work harder and harder and I'm going to be the best woman golfer in the world some day."

She became that. During her career Miss Wright rewrote the record book and won more than one-fourth of the tournaments she entered. Most believe she was the greatest woman golfer of all.

It was a happy accident of near-perfect casting. Blond and graceful, an intellectual who expressed herself in a modulated, low timbre, Mickey made an instant impression on galleries and was a great boon to the struggling LPGA. But she was followed by a ghost—her own nearly impossible expectations that finally drove her from the tour.

Kathy Whitworth, with whom she had a pleasant rivalry, believed Miss Wright to be the finest golfer in history. She said the great male players had only one advantage; while Mickey was very strong, she couldn't generate the sheer power of a man. For pure skill and shotmaking ability, however, Miss Whitworth maintained that Miss Wright was the best ever, man or woman.

"We could all see she was just so far superior to anyone else," Kathy said. "People don't remember just how good she *was*."

Unlike Babe Zaharias, Mickey's gallery appeal was based on her performance, rather than on her personality, which was reserved and even shy.

"Mickey gave the LPGA credibility in the area of skill and competence," said Betsy Rawls. "No one would ever doubt, after seeing Mickey, that women could be great golfers.

Miss Rawls, as a rules official and tournament director, remains a close observer of contemporary LPGA players, yet stands her ground when comparing Mickey to modern greats.

"She set a standard of shot-making that will probably never be equalled," Betsy said. "Mickey's swing was as flawless as a golf swing can be—smooth, efficient, powerful, rhythmical, and beautiful. Her shots were something to behold. She was the longest hitter of her era, but it was more the character of her shots that separated her from the rest. Her shots were always high, with tremendous carry. Even with a two-iron Mickey had no trouble hitting over a bunker or a lake guarding the green. She contacted the ball at precisely the right point in the arc of the swing and with such clubhead speed that no shot was impossible for her. She was a spectacular golfer to watch."

Kathy Whitworth remembered a shot she saw Mickey play at a course in French Lick, Indiana. Mickey hit her tee shot near the base of a large tree in the middle of the fairway on a par-4 hole. The ball lay behind and slightly to the right of the tree. She had room to make a full backswing but would not be able to strike the ball without hitting the tree on her follow-through. Additionally, she faced a carry of about 160 yards to an elevated green.

"Mickey pulled out an iron, made a full backswing, hit the ball just as hard as she normally would, and *stopped* the clubhead at impact," Miss Whitworth said. "Just POW! Hit the ball onto the green! And, the funny thing is that I had seen her *practice* that shot!"

Mickey Wright was an enigmatic champion. By almost every measure she was too sensitive and emotional to be a winner, her mind too finely tuned to subtleties to be a stoic war maiden on the golf course. She wasn't very competitive. You could needle Mickey, spurring her on for a hole or two, and she'd hole a difficult putt or make an impossible shot just to show you she could do it, but she seemed without killer instinct. She viewed golf as a form of self-expression rather than a contest between people. Competition was impersonal to her, each hole a separate game. At the end she simply added them up and went on.

Her graceful appearance was deceptive. She was a fine athlete and could generate great power. Some twenty years after retiring from golf, she easily kicked a football nearly sixty yards in a high, spiraling arc from her own back yard to the adjacent golf course. When lured into a game of catch with a softball and gloves, she'd play "burn-out"

Mickey's great extension was a key to her swing.

until her opponent's hand was red and stinging.

She had a delicate touch—with a fly rod she could cast precisely to a small shadow on a pond—and great feel for the golf swing. There was no weakness in her game nor in her swing. Her shots had a long, soaring beauty and a distinctive sound. Even with her irons she produced a loud crack at impact, a sound that only the best men generate.

It's difficult to believe that Mickey Wright has been away from competitive golf for more than twenty years. Her imprint on the game was so strong that, while it's hard to imagine her without golf, it's even more difficult to imagine golf without *her*.

For all practical purposes, she retired to a quiet life in Florida in 1971, although she played in an occasional tournament through 1980. She left without fanfare, a departure that suited the quiet side of her nature, but the years have put her talent in perspective, and those who saw her play believe that she was in the elite class of Harry Vardon, Bob Jones, Ben Hogan, and Jack Nicklaus. (Miss Wright believes such a hypothesis to be impossible, saying that superior strength gives men the edge in every shot in golf, including putting.)

She grew up in San Diego, and her first teaching professional was Johnny Bellante. After only a few sessions, Bellante asked a newspaper photographer to come to La Jolla Country Club. A few days later, Mickey's picture ran in the San Diego Union with the caption, "The next Babe?"

She once did me the great favor of running a home movie taken during this period. Mickey watched it with her chin in her hand and

Mickey Wright and the swing acclaimed by Ben Hogan and Byron Nelson as the greatest ever.

shook her head, watching the child hit golf balls. The swing embarrassed her, she said, how terrible it looked to her now.

There was something sweetly earnest about the girl hitting balls: with long blond hair, in a dainty dress tied with a sash, she was a child with a gift. She hadn't harnessed it yet, her footwork was awkward, but the swing was there—the familiar wide arc and her right shoulder driving through in her trademark downswing. Even power was evident.

In a raw form, it was the same swing that amazed men professionals competing against her in the 1985 Legends of Golf tournament, a men's senior event. In Austin, Texas, at the age of fifty, Mickey came out of retirement and hit the ball with such forceful beauty that men playing ahead of her would turn to watch.

"Did you see those approach shots!" they exclaimed to each other.

It's the swing that Byron Nelson and Ben Hogan called the best in the world. In 1988 I asked Hogan about her. He leaned forward in his chair and placed both hands flat upon his desk.

"She had the finest golf swing I ever saw, man or woman," Hogan said. "What a swing!"

In 1986 Byron Nelson told me during a casual round that, for sheer fundamentals, Mickey Wright had the best swing he had ever seen.

Herbert Warren Wind wrote about Mickey in 1965, lumping her in a triumvirate with Joyce Wethered and Babe Zaharias. He was reluctant at the time to place her above the other two. In 1975, after he'd had time to mull it over, Wind concluded in another article that Miss Wright was the best. He pointed out that Mickey was a much finer shotmaker than Babe and that her competitive record far surpassed that of Miss Wethered.

202

(Today the longevity and great shotmaking ability of Kathy Whitworth would probably elevate her into that elite group.)

Most often we measure a golfer by her victories in major championships: Miss Wright won them in bunches. She's the only woman to have held the four major titles at one time. She accomplished this grand slam in 1961 and 1962. In 1961 Mickey won the U.S. Women's Open, the LPGA Championship, and the Titleholders (the major of its time, in a category with the modern Dinah Shore Championship). She then began the 1962 season with another victory in the Titleholders in April and won that era's fourth major, the Western Open, in May.

Altogether she won four Open titles, in 1958, 1959, 1961, and 1964. She captured the LPGA Championship four times, in 1958, 1960, 1961, and 1963. She won the Titleholders twice, in 1961 and 1962, and she won the Western Women's Open three times, in 1962, 1963, and 1966.

In 1963, a year in which she won one of her four LPGA Championships, she was second in the Titleholders, and won the Western Open. It was a phenomenal year by any standard. She won thirteen tournaments, or 40.6 percent of the events in which she played. By 1986 prize-money standards, her 1963 season would have captured at least $810,000. In 1962 and again in 1963 she won four tournaments in a row, a record she shares with Miss Whitworth.

Venue seemed to make little difference. From 1960 through 1964 she won fifty tournaments, an average of ten victories a year, on every type of layout—from Baltusrol's grueling lower course and tempestuous Sea Island Golf Club, to the sporty little Palma Ceia in Tampa. She won grandly on courses designed by Donald Ross, Albert Tillinghast, and the team of H.S. Colt and Charles Alison. But she also won on obscure municipal courses and on the flat, beat-up confines of public links.

In 1965 Mickey made a stab at retirement and returned to college, but golf's lure was too great. She came back to the tour the following season, winning the Western Open and finishing second in the LPGA Championship.

Her two competitive rounds of 62, which remains the LPGA 18-hole scoring record after more than twenty-five years, were shot under very different circumstances. In 1964 she fired a 62 in the last round of the Tall City Open at Hogan Park Golf Course, a relatively flat, par-71 layout in Midland, Texas.

"I was 10 shots out of the lead going into the last round," she recalled. "Sherry Wheeler was leading. I was playing with Kathy Cornelius and Clifford Ann Creed and I just knew my good round was eating Clifford up, which I'm sure spurred me on. I just putted the eyes out of it that day, the best putting round of my life."

The 62 put Miss Wright into a playoff with Miss Wheeler, and they went two extra holes. Mickey won when she fired birdie, eagle, to Sherry's birdie, birdie.

She refers to her other record round as her "good 62." She actually set the record on the long, hilly Hunting Creek Country Club in Louisville, Kentucky, a few weeks before Midland. That day, before she played, Lennie Wirtz, LPGA tournament director, jabbed Mickey with a quick aside.

"You'd better shoot 65 today," Wirtz needled.

Mickey's reply was a slick 29 on the front nine.

"I hit the ball so well, hit all the greens and made a couple of good putts, mostly short putts," she said. "Going over to the tenth tee I couldn't wait to see Lennie, just couldn't wait to see him. Sixty-five, huh? Well, I had 29!

"'You better keep it going,' he said, '64 is the record.'

"He used to casually do those things to me, which was helpful.

He needled me. He needled me a *lot* about not practicing putting. He made me very angry because I wasn't quite sure it was any of his business but, of course, I spent a lot more time practicing putting because of it.

"I played steady golf on the back nine and on the eighteenth hole I had a birdie putt to shoot 61. I made a good putt at it and missed."

Because Hunting Creek's new fairways were in poor condition, the field had been allowed to improve the lie. Miss Wright improved her lie once. The LPGA, in those days, was a real stickler about records, and Mickey's 62 wasn't included as an "official" record. Today the association includes all rounds, even those played under winter rules, in such categories as scoring average for the Vare Trophy and in season totals of eagles, birdies, and putting. Under those circumstances, the omission of Miss Wright's first record 62 seems, at best, a whim.

Tired of the grind and suffering from wrist and foot injuries, Mickey retired in 1971 to play in just a few events a year. In 1973, after two years of playing little more than the stock market, she decided to enter the Colgate–Dinah Shore Championship, the star-studded tournament at Mission Hills Country Club near Palm Springs, California.

Even par after 54 holes, she was four strokes behind the leader, Joyce Kazmierski. In the final round, Mickey pounded the front nine with a 32 and on the last green holed a curling, 25-foot birdie putt for a 68. It was a flash of the old Wright stuff, and she won the tournament by two strokes.

In 1979, after nearly a decade of inaction, she pulled on her sneakers, which she wore because of a foot ailment, and shot 70-74-72 to tie for first in the LPGA's Coca-Cola Classic at Clifton, New Jersey. She lost in a five-way playoff, but it still seemed almost as if she could win at will.

Mickey Wright with the U.S. Girls' Junior trophy in 1952.

To assess what so many call the greatest golf swing in history, it's useful to follow Miss Wright's evolution as a golfer: Her breakthrough came when she won the Southern California Girls' Junior at the age of thirteen. During this period of her life, she had played a lot of golf at La Jolla Country Club with Margaret Grizzle Allen, a fine woman amateur. To Mrs. Allen, Mickey seemed to have the talent, but not the fortitude, to become a champion.

"We never thought Mickey would win a lot of tournaments," Mrs. Allen recalled. "I really believed she was just too shy and too nice to win. She didn't seem to have a killer instinct."

Mickey, however, had great determination to go along with her golf swing, which, incidentally, she always referred to as "the swing," never "my swing," as if it were a valuable but somewhat separate, mysterious thing, even to its owner.

Mickey believes that much of her success is due to the great teachers to whom she entrusted the swing. One key teacher was Harry Pressler, a respected California instructor. Pressler was pro at San Gabriel Country Club where Mickey won the Southern California Junior. After he saw her play, he offered to help. At thirteen, Mickey considered the offer with great seriousness.

"I talked to Johnny Bellante about it," she remembered. "He thought it was a wonderful idea because Harry had such a wonderful reputation. He had taught two California amateur champions and his wife, Leona, who won the Western Amateur. So, I got on the phone, and I'd like to emphasize that I got on the phone, not my mother or my father. I called him and set up an appointment."

The following Saturday Pressler began working with his new pupil in front of her mother's living room mirror. He took her through the golf swing, helping her to move the club to the top of the backswing and showing her, in the mirror, what a square clubface looked like. They worked for nearly two hours.

"I was so excited," Miss Wright said. "I just felt as if I had taken a giant step toward becoming a great golfer."

Throughout her career she consulted Pressler and referred to her own way of swinging the club as "Harry's swing."

After three lessons from Pressler, Mickey won the 36-hole Indio Invitational with scores of 70-71.

"I had never come close to playing any golf like that, score-wise, before Harry," she said. "It was unbelievable how I took to his method."

Pressler taught her through repetition, putting her in the correct positions repeatedly until she could "feel" her swing. He taught her to feel when the clubhead was square, and when it was not. Another crucial swing principle was Pressler's theory that the weight shift must work *across* the feet.

"Harry thought that a golf swing is a moving of the weight from the left foot to the right, and a returning of the weight to the left foot," Miss Wright said. "At the start of the downswing, the hands do nothing. They stay there, and the weight moves across the right foot.

"All I ever did was just move the weight across the right foot. You coordinate that, it squares the clubhead, and you'll contact the ball squarely with a square clubhead. That's really all there is to it, but it took so much repetition."

Over the years she sought out great teachers and added something from each to her own technique. In 1954 she took lessons from Les Bolstad, the Minnesota instructor famous for helping Patty Berg. Bolstad coached Mickey on what he called a "counter-clockwise" swing theory, which stressed using the inside muscles of the legs and arms. She incorporated that and shortly after made a great showing in the 1954 U.S. Women's Open in Peabody, Massachusetts. Babe Zaharias won, but Miss Wright, then eighteen, was low amateur and finished fourth in the championship.

"None can dim the lustre that is Babe Zaharias's following her climactic triumph, . . ." wrote Harry Molter, in the *Christian Science Monitor*. "But the player who captured the imagination of many was youthful Mickey Wright—an heir apparent from the city of champions.

"One of the most wholesome and refreshing things to happen to women's golf since the Bauer Sisters, Mickey has the long game to be a top-flight player and lacks only tournament experience and improved chipping and putting. Though still an amateur, at the moment, Mickey has soared into national prominence and gives real promise of attaining championship stature in the near future."

Even Mrs. Zaharias got into the act. After Mickey outdrove her on several holes, she quipped, "What are you doing, copying my swing?"

Very often such promise fades in the limelight of top competition. Potential can be a terrible burden, and early acclaim becomes an end unto itself. But Miss Wright was no flash in the pan. That summer she was runner-up in the U.S. Women's Amateur to her fellow-Californian, Barbara Romack.

In 1956 Mickey sought out another top teacher, Stan Kertes of Chicago. Kertes helped her correct two old flaws: a tendency to close the clubface and to drop her left shoulder on her takeaway, which produced some fat shots and sweeping hooks. Kertes taught her to feel as if she fanned open the club slightly on her backswing, although she was simply keeping it square. He also corrected her left shoulder, and soon she was able to blast a driver from a tight fairway lie. Thanks to a swing exercise from Kertes, she added fifteen to twenty yards to her length.

Later in her career, she took lessons from professional Earl Stewart in Dallas. Stewart had won several PGA Tour events, and he taught her to make quick decisions in order to ease the pressure that built up in the later years.

Touring professional Jackie Burke also gave her a lasting gift when she was a youngster. In San Diego, Burke watched her hit a few balls.

"That's very good, young lady, but you have one last thing to do," Burke said. "You can hit the ball fairly high. Learn to hit it higher."

Mickey learned to hit high shots by standing as close as possible to a tree and hitting practice balls over the tree with the longest club she could manage. Her towering shots became a trademark of her game.

On the LPGA Tour, fellow players helped her refine her game. Patty Berg helped her learn to play from the sand. Louise Suggs played practice rounds with her and gave Mickey advice on the practice tee. Betsy Rawls, who possessed a dazzling short game, helped her to become an expert around the greens.

"They were all influential in their own way," Miss Wright said. "Harry taught me what I think is the best way to swing a golf club. When I teach, I teach his principles. Stan Kertes did a little refining and made it a little easier for me to strike the ball well under pressure. Earl taught me how to play golf. . . .

"I was really lucky to hit these people at the right time when I needed them. I learned so well, I think, when I was with them, and worked so hard, and practiced so much, that I didn't have to be taught again. I really learned the *feel* of all those swing principles."

Mary Kathryn Wright had many gifts. Her father, Arthur Wright, was a prominent San Diego lawyer and president of the California Bar Association. She inherited his keen, analytical mind and, as an adult, she could cut cleanly through lesser meanderings and nail an issue with a single word. But she was kind about it, and I felt as if she never really flexed her intellect on anyone, except on matters of principle. She was very stern on principle. Honesty and loyalty mattered a great deal to her, and if you wavered over the line, you had to account for it. She was ramrod straight, but her intensity was appealing because you knew you could count on her, and she almost always let you know where she stood.

She was very open about most things and, as powerfully intense as Mickey sometimes was, she found joy in simple things. After she retired to a villa in south Florida, she seemed mostly happy to be away from the competitive grind. Nature was a comfort to her. She would put food out for the squirrels, rabbits, and birds that flocked to her yard. She was thrilled by a family of sandhill cranes that made daily visits. The cranes returned each winter and she fed them, gave them all names, imitated their calls, and mourned for them when they died.

Her haven was her kitchen, a simple, clean arrangement of stove and countertops with a few chef's knives near the stovetop and a dozen cookbooks on a shelf over the sink. Her recipes were mostly Southern, and she attacked cooking with single-minded energy, serving tasty dishes to her grateful friends.

The way she moved was graceful rather than athletic. It was what you first noticed about her. There was grace in her walk, in the way she moved her hands, and in the way she spoke, which was with a polite reserve and kindliness that made conversation easy and reflected the Southern side of her nature. In this she was like her mother, Kathryn, a Southern belle from Conyers, Georgia.

Intellectual men were attracted to Mickey's fine mind, and she enjoyed friendships with lawyers, doctors, and financiers. The latter taught her the subtleties of investments so that she could handle her own affairs, which she did brilliantly, and in the early morning, with her first cup of coffee, she would bend over her desk and draw intricate graphs of stocks.

She was a voracious reader and had gone through all the classics, but in her retirement she leaned toward adventure tales, animal stories, and mysteries. Her own book, *Play Golf the Wright Way*, edited by Joan Flynn Dreyspool, who wrote the biographical material, was published in 1962. A good writer with a fine, clean style, Miss Wright worried that she expressed herself with too much conviction. But, after agonizing over the text for two years, she created an eloquent little jewel of theory. If you have not read it, then you haven't read about golf.

When she was younger, Mickey's achievements had complicated her life. In later years she seemed to strive for a sort of symmetry. She sought to scale down, bought a smaller home, weeded out her possessions, and narrowed her circle to a few close friends. And she relaxed. She seemed to enjoy more and viewed life with a quick humor that surprised and amused her friends.

"Isn't knowing Mickey fun!" remarked Betsy Rawls.

It wasn't so easy: Miss Wright's consuming dedication to golf wasn't readily erased. She had a high energy level, and that and her retirement were a difficult combination. Years after she retired, she'd suddenly jump up from her chair and bolt through the back door. Soon you'd hear the crack of her favorite old 6-iron as the rippling, powerful swing boomed shots nearly 170 yards out across a nearby fairway.

During her career she had won more tournaments in a shorter time than anyone else. When she had gone higher and farther than anyone, she knew it and all of the other players knew it. She was the best. She wouldn't have quit, otherwise. However, *not* playing was very hard for her and, if she found a simpler life away from golf, I felt that she never really found tranquility.

She seldom watched televised tournaments. She enjoyed the great players and fine courses she could see while watching the Masters and the U.S. Open, and she might tune in if a favorite friend was near the lead, but most of the time she couldn't watch. Golf had meant too much to her.

The duality of Mickey Wright was that she was practical, yet her emotions were strong and ran close to the surface. The fine mind and the great heart at war—it can be a costly battle.

Once, in conversation, she mused over the mental attitude that had made her a great player.

"I hate to lose," she said. "The perfectionist bit in golf doesn't have as much to do with doing it perfectly as the total rejection and horror of doing it badly. And I don't know which comes first, or which is more important. Winning really never crossed my mind that much. It's trite, but I knew if I did it as well as I could, I would win. If I did as well as I could, it would have been better than anybody else did it, and therefore it would win.

". . . I look back on it like it's somebody else. It's like a dream, another life. What amazes me is that I could have done it as long as I did."

During the most strenuous times of her career, she fought the immense pressure she felt by indulging her passion for art. During her triumphant 1963 season, she escaped by sneaking off to galleries. Anonymous, she strolled through the rooms, peering at the blithe colors of the Impressionist paintings she loved.

Her gift was her burden. For some five years Mickey Wright *was* the tour. She attended luncheons, gave speeches, and reigned over all

Mickey Wright ". . . set standards of achievement that have not been surpassed."

of the press conferences that her role demanded. She was the tour's only star. Patty Berg, Louise Suggs, and Betsy Rawls had played their best golf a few years before. Kathy Whitworth was just beginning to emerge. Sandra Haynie and Carol Mann would have their best years later. Sponsors called Mickey and threatened to cancel their tournaments if she didn't play. The pressures were immense.

"The main emotion going into any new season was fear," she said. "Every season, just every season. It was the fear that no matter how good the previous year had been, this year would not be as good, and the pressure to win that first tournament was unbelievable.

"It's really like a monkey on your back. You have to get it off at some point because it really wears you out. If you spend your life trying to impress or please other people, it's a tremendous strain because you can't do it. Nothing is ever enough. I think I spent my whole golf life that way."

The 1964 and 1965 seasons overwhelmed her. An injured wrist just before the 1965 U.S. Women's Open in Northfield, New Jersey, forced her to withdraw the day before the championship began.

"I drove home to Dallas and cried practically the whole way, because it hit me that it was the end of my golf career," she recalled. "That was one miserable drive and I can't go through Erie, Pennsylvania—

because that was part of the route—without thinking about it. I don't know if all the pressure made it necessary for me to find a physical excuse to get out from under it, or if the physical things just plain happened. I really don't know."

And so, at the age of thirty, Mickey retired and returned to college. (She had attended Stanford University before turning professional.) It wasn't the end of her career. Quitting the game she loved was to be a long procedure, a gradual withdrawal that would take several years, and she returned to the tour in the spring of 1966. Her first tournament was the old St. Petersburg Open. We were paired together in the first round. She seemed content to be back, if a little tense, but she recognized that the pairing was an awesome experience for any young amateur, and she chatted amiably on the first tee. Her kindness put me at ease and, to be perfectly candid, the round was the most enjoyable of my life.

Despite a gallery of several hundred, Mickey played quietly, but the precision of her round was startling. She split each fairway from the tee, and I recall that she missed only two greens. The 16th was a narrow little par 4 that doglegged gently to the left. She drove with a 3-wood, then hit some sort of midiron just to the right of the green. She faced an odd little pitch, slightly uphill. In winter Florida's turf is very thin, and her ball seemed to be sitting mostly on grass roots. Using a straight-faced club, she played a delicate little pitch-and-run. When she holed the shot, she broke into a broad smile. She fired a 68 that day and, while it was far from her best score, it was very, very fine and a round I will never forget.

What it is that makes a champion? Mickey's bloodlines were certainly strong: her grandmother was the first woman pharmacist in Illinois, her grandfather was an inventor, and her father once rode horseback from the Midwest, through the Rocky Mountains, to the Pacific coast. Perhaps an accident of genes combines to produce that rare individual with athletic coordination, determination, and strength of character. Whatever its source, Mickey Wright had the gift.

Perhaps Pat Ward-Thomas, the fine British golf scribe, put it best when he wrote, "She had set standards of achievement that have not been surpassed, the most lasting contribution any player can give to their game, especially when, as with Mickey Wright, it is gracefully borne."

Broken Barriers

On September 17, 1956, Ann Gregory teed off in the U.S. Women's Amateur at Meridian Hills Country Club in Indianapolis and became the first black woman to play in a national championship sponsored

Ann Gregory, the first black woman to compete in the U.S. Women's Amateur.

by the United States Golf Association.

There would be other good black women players: Eoline Thornton of Long Beach, California, played in the 1958 Women's Amateur; Renee Powell of Canton, Ohio, turned pro in 1967; Althea Gibson, Wimbledon and U.S. Open tennis champion, took up the game at thirty-two and in 1963 became the first black golfer to play on the LPGA Tour. But Mrs. Gregory was the first black woman to compete on the national scene and, arguably, the best.

"She was a determined and confident golfer," said Renee Powell, "and she was such a warm-hearted, inspirational individual that she helped me by her example, by the kind of person she was. Not enough people know about Ann. She set the stage for every other black female who came into golf after her."

I first met Ann when we were contestants in the 1963 Women's Amateur in Williamstown, Massachusetts. A handsome woman with great warmth, she was by then a veteran who mingled easily with the other contestants, but there had been an embarrassing moment earlier in the week.

Polly Riley was unpacking her suitcase when she caught a glimpse of Ann, dressed all in white, walking in the hall of her inn.

Mistaking Ann for a maid, Riley called out, "Hey, can you bring me some coat hangers?"

Moments later Mrs. Gregory came into Polly's room and handed her a bunch of hangers with a big smile.

"I saw then that she had on golf clothes," said Miss Riley. "I was terribly embarrassed. We've laughed about it many times, although that type of thing must have been very difficult for her."

Ann Gregory endured worse insults: she was barred from the public golf course in her hometown, denied rooms in white-owned hotels, and refused entry to the players' dinner at the Women's Amateur in 1959. Golf's delicate rituals, however, allow the psyche no room for vengeance, and from some deep well of character, Mrs. Gregory was able to forgive the indignities.

"Racism is only in your mind, it's something that you overlook, or you look at it," said Ann, leaning against a locker at the Sea Island (Georgia) Golf Club. The 1988 U.S. Senior Women's Amateur would mark her last appearance in national competition but, at seventy-six, she radiated the vitality of a much younger woman.

"Racism works best when you let it affect your mind," she said. "It was better for me to remember that the flaw was in the racist, not in myself. For all the ugliness, I've gotten nice things three times over. I can't think ugly of anybody."

In 1956 there had been few real social advances in women's golf. At the turn of the century, British suffragettes had used acid to burn militant slogans into golf course greens. In 1950 Babe Zaharias and Patty Berg had opened new careers for crack women golfers when they spearheaded the founding of the LPGA. When Ann stepped onto the tee at Meridian Hills four years later, the burning issue in women's golf was whether to allow players to forsake skirts in favor of Bermuda shorts (to the knee).

Until that moment the women's amateur arena was isolated from emotional racial questions that now tested the nation. In 1954 the U.S. Supreme Court had ruled on the landmark case of *Brown vs. Board of Education of Topeka*, banning racial segregation in public schools. A whole body of legislation was evolving in Congress, and court actions were aimed at stopping segregation in schools, housing, and voting. Earlier in 1956 Rev. Martin Luther King, Jr., had led bus boycotts on the streets of Montgomery, Alabama.

In contrast, the women's amateur circuit of the 1950s was a sort of enclave of golf debutantes. These were fresh-faced, athletic young women who vied for silver cups on a tour of private clubs and resorts, Palm Beach in February, Pinehurst in April, Colorado Springs in July. The era produced great players—Mickey Wright, JoAnne Carner, Marlene Streit, Barbara McIntire, and Anne Sander—but amateur golf was expensive and, while a few had jobs, many were well-to-do. Their backgrounds, so different from Ann Gregory's humble origins, worked in her favor. If they were somewhat sheltered, they were also sporting and polite, and she would never hear hostile comments from another player.

Born in Aberdeen, Mississippi, on July 25, 1912, Ann was the daughter of Henry and Myra Moore. Her parents died when she was

Ann Gregory began competing in the 1940s.

a child, and she was raised by a white family, the Sanders. Fed, clothed, and housed, she also served as the family's maid. In 1938 she married Percy Gregory and moved to Gary, Indiana.

"That family cried like babies," she said. "They said people in the north were so cold and that I didn't deserve being treated like that. I said, 'Mrs. Sanders, you've prepared me very well for mistreatment.'"

The new Mrs. Gregory was a good athlete and won the Gary city tennis championship. In 1943 she joined the all-black Chicago Women's Golf Association and took golf lessons from Calvin Ingram, a good black player who worked at a Chicago club.

In the 1940s Mrs. Gregory won the CWGA title, the Joe Louis Invitational in Detroit, and the championship of the United Golf Association, an organization for black golfers. Black newspapers hailed her as "The Queen of Negro Women's Golf," and in 1947 George S. May invited her to play in the Tam O'Shanter in Chicago.

"Mr. May told me if anyone said anything to me, to let him know," Ann said. "No one did. The galleries were just beautiful to me, but I was lonely. For a whole week I didn't see any black people.

"My neighbors drove up from Gary to see me play the final round and, when I saw them, that's the only time I felt funny. It just did something to me to see my black friends among all those white people, and I cried."

The Gregorys lived in a comfortable house in Gary, where Percy

Ann Gregory, shown here with the champ, won many black tournaments, including the Joe Louis Invitational.

worked for U.S. Steel. Ann catered for the University Club, served on the Community Chest and United Fund committees, and in 1954 became the first black appointed to the Gary Public Library Board.

Ann yearned to play in national tournaments. Her ambition startled members of the Chicago Women's Golf Association. Some feared she wouldn't be allowed to play in white tournaments, others said she might shame them if she played badly. But in 1956 the Chicago group became the first black organization to join the USGA, so that Ann could play in USGA championships.

Mrs. Gregory immediately entered the 1956 U.S. Women's Amateur and drove to Indianapolis with Jolyn Robichaux, a friend from the Chicago Women's Golf Association.

"We were so excited about the idea of her being in the championship that we didn't notice any problems," said Mrs. Robichaux. "Ann was the type we needed to break that barrier. She was outgoing, told jokes, and was very compassionate and encouraging to the other golfers. They immediately liked her. Joe Dey, the USGA's executive director, was very eager to do everything that he could to see that her participation was pleasant."

The Associated Press noted the historic day: "A starting field of 105 players, including the first Negro in its history, was paired Saturday for match play in the 56th USGA Women's Amateur. . . ."

There was no escape from prejudice. Ann's first opponent, Carolyn Cudone, a Curtis Cup player from Caldwell, New Jersey, recalled an ugly run-in. A parking attendant told Mrs. Cudone's father, "Your daughter better win today, or you'd better not come back to this parking lot."

Introduced on the first tee, Mrs. Cudone got a huge ovation and Ann received polite applause.

"Every reporter in Indianapolis was there," said Carolyn. "You couldn't stir them with a stick! She must have been nervous as a wet hen because, as we left the tee, she said if she didn't count her strokes right, it wasn't on purpose."

Mrs. Cudone had her hands full. Making several great escapes from bunkers, Ann gained a 2-up lead, then began to drive wildly. Her lead collapsed and she narrowly lost the landmark match, 2 and 1.

"My husband said I didn't have a snowball's chance in hell," Ann confided as she shook Mrs. Cudone's hand. "I guess I fooled him."

In 1957 Ann returned to the Women's Amateur and advanced to the third round without incident. But she was targeted for conflict at the 1959 championship at Congressional Country Club in Bethesda, Maryland.

A UGA event was underway in Washington, D.C., and members were angry that Ann had abandoned them to play in a white tournament. On top of that, Congressional simply didn't want her. In a flare-up of bitter prejudice, the club barred her from the traditional players' dinner on the eve of the championship. Joseph C. Dey of the USGA broke the news.

"They have decided that you are not to have dinner with them," Dey told Ann, explaining that host clubs ran social events at USGA championships.

"I told Joe Dey it was no big deal," Gregory said. "I said, 'I realize the money I paid to enter the tournament didn't buy stock in the clubhouse. I'll eat me a hamburger and be just as happy as a lark, waiting on tee number one.' I didn't feel bad. I didn't. I just wanted to play golf. They were letting me play golf. So, I got me a hamburger and went to bed."

One of Ann's best performances in national competition followed. She eased through an extra-hole match against Mrs. Thaddeus Owings of York, Pennsylvania, 1-up in the first round. In the second round she faced the Georgia state champion, Mrs. Curtis Jordan.

The Georgia player was heavily favored by the gallery and dashed to a 2-up lead. Ann enjoyed her own fans. When Frank Stranahan, an Ohio professional, cheered her from the sidelines Ann began to rally. She squared the match on the 17th. On the home hole she hit a clutch shot, firing a 3-iron over a pond to the putting surface. When Mrs. Jordan hit her ball into a bunker and bogeyed, Ann had two putts to win the match.

Mrs. Gregory often gave clinics for white golfers.

"I stroked my putt, turned my head away, and heard the ball fall into the cup," she remembered. "All of the people began to applaud for me. When I made that deuce to win, my caddie turned a somersault. The club fired him for that. When I asked for my caddie the next day, the caddie master told me he had been fired."

Ann lost her third-round match, 6 and 4, to Diana Hoke of Chartiers, Pennsylvania.

"After I lost, the club president invited me into his office," Gregory said. "He told me that I had exhibited myself as one of the most beautiful ladies to ever walk that golf course and he wanted me to know that I was welcome to play there anytime I was in that area."

"I thought, 'He's got to be crazy! I would never come back there to play after all of the things they put me through.'"

There would be other incidents: The manager of a white hotel in Tulsa ignored her reservation during the 1960 U.S. Women's Amateur and sent her to a shabby black hotel without air conditioning. Ann and Percy sat on the hotel steps eating ice cream until she was tired and cool enough to sleep.

Gleason Park, a public course in Gary, restricted black golfers to a short nine-hole layout. Whites played the 18-hole course. In the early 1960s, Ann slapped her money on the counter and announced that she had outgrown the short layout.

"My tax dollars are taking care of the big course and there's no way you can bar me from it," she said. "Just send the police out to get me."

Without looking back, she teed off and played without interference. Soon Gary's black golfers began to make tee times on the longer course.

In 1971 Ann nearly won the U.S. Women's Senior Amateur at Sea Island Golf Club. In the final round of stroke play, only one woman stood between her and a national championship, her old rival from so many years ago, Carolyn Cudone.

Mrs. Cudone parred the last hole to beat Ann by a single stroke. Over the years they had become friends and often shared lunch at women's senior events.

"Ann was a lady and she could play," said Mrs. Cudone. "She was a fine competitor; a good winner and a good loser. She played the game as you wanted to see it played."

I last saw Ann in 1988. I asked for photocopies of her tournament records. Instead, she shipped her scrapbooks to me and I leafed through the pages, greatly moved by the nobility of the life that unfolded in yellowed newspaper clippings. On one page she had pasted her invitation to a 1963 tournament in the South. I too had saved that invitation, but I knew that Ann's invitation meant so much more.

In the summer of 1990, during a visit to Golf House, the USGA's museum in Far Hills, New Jersey, I learned of Ann Gregory's death. Museum curator Karen Bednarsky handed a letter to me from Ann's daughter.

Her mother, a fine golfer, had died earlier in the year at the age of seventy-seven, the woman wrote, offering Ann's trophies to the USGA.

"Did you know Ann Gregory?" Karen asked.

Yes, I knew Ann Gregory. She teed it up during a difficult era against odds that few of us can ever know. She endured painful slights with warmth, humor, courage, and good sense. More that most of us, she cherished the game and, in the end, she honored it. I knew Ann Gregory. She was simply a golfer. A very fine one.

The Golden Age of Amateurs

The years from 1950 through 1968 marked an extraordinary era, spawning more fine amateurs, and more great ones, than any other.

It was the last era in which there were more serious amateurs than professionals, a virtually unchanging cast of forty-five amateurs of international stature and a hundred more who were devoted competitors.

Their golf inspired huge galleries—six thousand fans turned out to watch the finals of the 1954 Hollywood Four-Ball—and bigger headlines than at any time before or since.

And never since have there been so many key amateur events: counting the three open events—the U.S. Women's Open, the Women's Western Open, and the Titleholders—the schedule included twenty important amateurs tournaments. It was amateur golf's last great stand.

"It was really one of the most fun times of my life," said Edean

Ihlanfeldt, a Montana player who captured several key tournaments.

Recalling the old Florida winter Orange Blossom Circuit, she remembered playing nine or ten tournaments in a row.

"Wonderful memories," Mrs. Ihlanfeldt said, "because we travelled together and everyone was really closeknit. The big hotels in Palm Beach and St. Augustine were unbelievable. They gave us rates of $7 a day, and that included three meals. Often, we found rooms in homes for $10 for the week."

The stars of that time included Barbara Romack, a glamorous platinum blond from Sacramento, California, and Polly Riley, the little Texan who was one of golf's most feared match-play competitors. Washington produced two great amateurs: Anne Quast, a slender, emotional young player who possessed inner fire and great staying power, and the rollicking JoAnne Gunderson Carner, "The Great Gundy." Barbara McIntire, of Toledo, Ohio, was reserved and won with fierce tenacity, yet had great charm. Another great player was Marlene Stewart Streit, an elfin golfer from the Canadian frontier whose tiny stature belied the size of her heart.

Like the other competitors, they were golf's last debutantes. Fawned over by fans, they adorned magazine covers, while the nation's newspapers boasted of their triumphs in big headlines.

Mary Lena Faulk, the soft-spoken Southerner, compiled a record several notches better than most. Tish Preuss and Nancy Roth Syms began to play their finest golf during the era's latter years, and Mary Ann Downey, Pat Lesser, Pat O'Sullivan, Brigitte Varangot, Jean Ashley, Judy Bell, Judy Eller, Helen Sigel Wilson, Barbara Fay White, and Carol Sorenson also had outstanding records.

A teenager in the early years, Mickey Wright wouldn't reach her peak until she turned professional, but her brief amateur career was brilliant. Catherine Lacoste, the French golfer, broke records and has a section of her own in this book.

Intense competition came from some thirty very fine players: Jane Nelson, Wiffi Smith, Phyllis Semple, Betty Probasco, Marge Burns, Marge Lindsay, Edean Ihlanfeldt, Carolyn Cudone, Cookie Berger, Dot Kirby, Grace Lenczyk, Ann Johnstone, Meriam Bailey, Dot Porter, Joanne Goodwin, Alice Dye, Clifford Ann Creed, Dot Kielty, Claire Doran, Grace DeMoss, Mae Murray, Barbara Fitton, Fee Fee Matthews, Connie Day, Ceil MacLaurin, Doris Phillips, Ann Richardson, Mary Patton Janssen, and Natasha Matson.

The majority of these players were career amateurs. A few had jobs but most were supported by families who sent them to the best teachers and financed their summer championships, then shipped them to fine old resorts like Pinehurst and Palm Beach for competition in winter and spring.

Sending a daughter on the amateur golf trail was somewhat less costly than letting her dabble in show horses or sailing, but not much.

Pat O'Sullivan.

Phyllis "Tish" Preuss.

Helen S. Wilson, a lifelong amateur, at the 1965 U.S. Women's Open.

There was no real future in it, other than golf itself. Amateur golf was a commitment one made to oneself.

Near the end of the era, in the early 1960s, I joined the amateur circuit. I remember that we played because it was fun, because we could play great courses like Pinehurst and the Broadmoor, and be-

Jean Ashley, 1965 U.S. Women's Amateur Champion.

cause it was a chance to put ourselves on the line against fine players. A lot of it had to do with the opportunity to just play the game, to feel our spikes crunching into the early-morning turf, to hit soaring 5-irons and zingy little 4-woods.

There was another reason, more subtle. I remember us during those years at the Palm Beach Championship on the old Donald Ross course connected to the Breakers Hotel. A policeman would hold up his hand on County Road, long lines of Cadillacs and sparkling Rolls-Royces would glide to a halt, and we'd walk across to the fifth tee, our spikes clacking on the pavement, our heads down, brows furrowed in concentration, our little galleries trooping behind us. We were very earnest. We tried very hard.

I think now that there was a great deal more to it than the glory; it was also that those soaring iron shots and pinpoint fairway woods really *mattered*. They meant something. Those were different times and, for women, the doors of opportunity had opened only a hair. *The Feminine Mystique,* the landmark book that ushered in women's liberation, was just a gleam in Betty Friedan's eye. This was a chance to achieve, to do this one thing really well.

Friendships were shy, reducing life's personal issues to holes won and holes lost, and our group floated in a little bubble of naiveté above a world in cataclysmic political upheaval. This strikes home when some contemporary, someone who marched for civil rights or protested the draft, asks what I was doing in the sixties. "I played golf" is my reply.

Marion Turpie, Southern Amateur Champion in 1928 and 1931.

In the 1920s, when women amateurs first played on the Orange Blossom circuit, they dressed like this.

Edith Quier, 1936 Eastern Amateur Champion.

Nonna Barlow, winning the Women's Eastern Championship in 1912.

Mary Fownes, winner of the 1909 Women's North and South.

We were a sheltered little troop, and somewhat innocent. At most clubs we had been allowed to forsake skirts only for Bermuda shorts. No one lugged her own golf bag then, except to get it out of the car. And I seldom heard anyone swear.

We played golf, and we played it nearly year-round, in tournaments over and above the state championships. The U.S. Women's Amateur commanded the best field, but there were dozens of others: the Western Amateur, established by the Women's Western Golf Association in 1901; the North and South Championship, played at lovely old Pinehurst since 1903; the Trans-Mississippi (which later became the Trans-National) began in 1927; the Broadmoor Ladies' Invitational dated to 1928; the Eastern Amateur began in 1906; and the Southern Amateur was first played in 1911.

Young players enjoyed their own championships. The Women's National Collegiate Championship began in 1941, the U.S. Girls' Junior in 1949, and the Western Junior Girls' in 1920. International events included the Women's Canadian Open Amateur, which began in 1901, and the British Ladies' Amateur, played since 1893. And there were good regional events, like the Pacific Northwest Ladies Championship, which began in 1899.

International team competition included the Curtis Cup Match, which began in 1932.

The old Florida Orange Blossom Circuit was unique. At its peak the tour was made up of eleven tournaments and ran from January through March. Eight events were for amateurs only: the Harder Hall Invitational in Sebring, the Palm Beach Championship, the South Atlantic Championship in Ormond Beach, the Doherty Invitational in Miami (originally called the Miami-Biltmore Invitational), the International Four-Ball in Hollywood, the National Mixed-Foursomes at the Everglades Club in Palm Beach, the Florida East Coast Championship in St. Augustine, and the International Two-Ball, a mixed event in Orlando.

Some amateurs were invited to play in three pro tournaments—the venerable Tampa Open, the Titleholders Championship in Augusta, Georgia, and the Sea Island (Georgia) Invitational.

In the 1920s, players of stature, like Glenna Collett, Dorothy Campbell Hurd Howe, Edith Cummings, and Mrs. Caleb Fox, had enjoyed three additional Florida tournaments; the Midwinter Championship and the Belleair Championship, both played at the old Belleair resort, and the Florida Championship at Mountain Lake.

Living frugally, alternating between second-rate motels, huge resort hotels, and the fine homes of club members, we drove from stop to stop. All but four of the eleven events were match play, and it was a grueling schedule if you played well enough to get to the late rounds.

"You had to lose, sometimes on purpose, to get a rest," said Barbara Romack.

Miss Frances Munn at The Breakers in 1932.

Those who traveled the Orange Blossom Circuit, however, enjoyed benefits that set them a little apart from other young women. They were invited to play at posh courses, like the Everglades Club, Gulfstream, and Ponte Vedra. They danced at the little clubs on Worth Avenue in Palm Beach and, if they were especially charming, socialites might trot them out to Seminole to show them off.

The Florida circuit began in the 1920s. Henry Morrison Flagler, a northern oil magnate, had opened the sunshine state to winter tourism shortly before the turn of the century with his Florida East Coast Railroad, which extended the full length of the Atlantic shore to Key West. Along the route, he built towering resort hotels. St. Augustine's massive Spanish revival edifice, the Ponce de Leon, opened in 1888, and Flagler later built the Ormond Beach Hotel near Daytona, the magnificent Royal Poinciana, and the less pretentious Palm Beach Inn, which became the Breakers.

In the 1920s wealthy northern visitors rode Flagler's trains to his great hotels. Women's amateur golf, meanwhile, was riding on the coat tails of a collection of young players—Virginia Van Wie, Maureen Orcutt, the glamorous Edith Cummings, and especially Glenna Collet, whose vivid personality and wonderful game were getting headlines.

Flagler died in 1913, but Florida's tourist industry remained strong, and the Orange Blossom Circuit was devised as a way to entertain winter visitors staying in the huge hotels.

Glenna Collett loved her winter sojourns in Florida. She believed that women who played in the winter events had an advantage in the summer championships, and she became a fixture on the Florida circuit in the 1920s.

"I was able to make the trip to Palm Beach last winter for the first time and took part in the championship there," Collett wrote. "It was my good fortune to win the title which I would dearly love to defend this season.

"Palm Beach is a wonderful place," she continued. "I had never thought it possible that there was a hotel in any land quite as large as the Royal Poinciana. They say it is the biggest hotel in the world, and I believe it. . . . One of the most delightful trips that I had in Florida was when I motored from Palm Beach to Belleair. It took just a day. . . . We were in a Rolls-Royce and made fine time."

The first tournament, the Palm Beach Championship, was founded in 1919 at the Breakers Golf Club, a sporty little resort course set at 6,008 yards in those early years and connected to the Breakers Hotel. Bessie Fenn, a good amateur player on the national scene, was the winner. Miss Fenn won again in 1922. It was her last amateur event. The indomitable Bessie, a rotund woman in wire-rimmed glasses, turned professional to run the Breakers' golf operation.

Miss Fenn had absolute rule and was described as "a beloved marinet, who bosses tycoons and debutantes rigidly and makes them

Tom Draper, Rhonda Glenn, Marlene Streit, and Hobart Manley at the 1966 International Mixed Foursomes.

like it," by golf reporter Tom O'Neill. A favorite story about Bessie Fenn took place in the 1960s. At the time, the Duke of Windsor was enjoying the hospitality of Palm Beach; simply put, it was royal treatment—which meant, to him, gratis. The duke played frequently at the Breakers. One balmy day he teed off and had reached the first green before Bessie charged down the fairway roaring, "Dooook! Doook! You forgot to pay your green fee!" The duke paid.

Glenna Collett won the first Florida East Coast Championship in 1925. The tournament was played at Ponce de Leon Golf Club, originally laid out by Alexander Findlay, a Scot in charge of constructing and operating golf courses along Flagler's railroad. Donald Ross redesigned the course in 1916, and it meandered along the marshland near the great hotel. Buffeted by ocean winds, the course was set at 6,148 yards in the 1950s. By 1965, following the example of the LPGA players, who competed on long courses as a point of pride, the women amateurs were playing Ponce de Leon at 6,600 yards, par 71.

The South Atlantic Championship, familiarly known as "Sally," began in 1926 on the old Ormond Golf Club, another Alex Findlay design. The course, today called Oceanside Country Club, has an intriguing history. The club's publicist, future columnist and television star Ed Sullivan, promoted the Sally tournament in the 1920s, and millionaire John D. Rockefeller played the course during visits to his winter home across the road. In 1950 a former Georgia automobile dealer, Merrill F. Ellinor, bought the course and named it Ellinor Village.

Often blasted by cold winds and rain, the South Atlantic Championship became famous for "Sally weather." This duneside course was played at slightly over 6,100 yards. The first Sally was won by Dorothy Klotz of Minneapolis.

In 1933, Opal Hill won the first Helen Lee Doherty Championship at the Miami-Biltmore. The tournament later moved to Miami Shores Country Club. Late in the 1950s, the Doherty moved to Coral Ridge Country Club in Fort Lauderdale, a Robert Trent Jones course that played at 6,500 yards.

The National Mixed-Foursomes tournament was played at the Everglades Club in Palm Beach in 1936 and remained there for twenty years. The event was a rare pairing of distinguished men and women amateurs. Pairings were made by a tournament director, and the event lured a fine gallery. In 1957 the Mixed-Foursomes moved to the Boca Raton Hotel and Club. In the 1960s it was staged at Lost Tree Country Club, north of Palm Beach.

The Hollywood Four-Ball Championship began in 1946 at Orange Brook Golf Club in Hollywood. The field was restricted to sixteen pairs, who were seeded for best-ball, match-play competition.

For many years amateurs enjoyed February's International Mixed Two-Ball Tournament at Dubsdread Country Club in Orlando, which began in 1937.

The last entry on the Florida circuit, the Harder Hall Invitational, a 72-hole stroke-play event, began in 1956. The field played Harder Hall Golf Club, near Sebring, at 6,600 yards. In its first years the tournament attracted only a few top players, but the inaugural was won by a fine Baltimore golfer, Evelyn Glick.

The Orange Blossom tour lured golfers from Europe, including England's Maureen Ruttle, a Curtis Cup player, and French amateurs Claudine Cros and Brigitte Varangot. Monica Steegman came over from Germany, and Mexico's Cha Cha Martinez often played.

Big crowds came out to watch the matches. Around Miami and Fort Lauderdale, many were tourists with a certain new vagabond interest in golf. These mysterious fellows placed huge bets on our matches.

I never knew of any gambler to actually approach a player, but Miss Romack noticed two with their heads together after she won a semifinal match at the Doherty. When she showed up for the final, her trusty sand-wedge, which she used with great delicacy, mysteriously disappeared from her bag moments before she teed off and miraculously reappeared just after she lost.

Carol Sorenson, Barbara McIntire, a French hostess, and Barbara Fay White Boddie at the first Women's World Amateur Team Championship in 1964.

My own grueling days of golf would end with nightly calls from two or three older Palm Beach friends who wanted to know if I'd won. Years later my mother told me these friends had big wagers on my matches.

The Palm Beach galleries were made up of wealthy, older fans. We'd see them scattered around the Breakers golf course, seated on shooting sticks under the palms with wide-brimmed straw hats shading their eyes and silk scarves tucked into their collars. They discussed the game knowledgeably, chatting about Miss McIntire's ability to feather a shot or the intense concentration of Polly Riley.

"Ahhh, moved her head," they'd tsk, when one of us hit into a bunker.

Served elaborate lunches on silver trays, we enjoyed the company of the Palm Beach social set when playing at the Breakers or in the mixed event at the Everglades. Their company sparked some interesting incidents.

"Golf clubs, purse, wearing apparel and other valuables owned by Miss Maureen Ruttle, famed English golfing star, were stolen from an automobile on Worth Avenue late yesterday afternoon," reported a Palm Beach newspaper.

"Miss Ruttle and Reginald Boardman had participated in the semi-finals of the Invitational Golf tournament at the Everglades Club and following the match decided to visit a Worth Avenue restaurant.

"While they were in the restaurant thieves looted the car of Miss Ruttle's property."

During the Florida East Coast Championship, competitors stayed at the Ponce de Leon, a spooky old hotel of Spanish medieval ambience. Afternoons brought a command appearance for mint juleps with the tournament director. Social highlights included horse-drawn carriage tours of old St. Augustine and, early on, there were tennis tournaments in which golfers played mixed-doubles with famous male tennis professionals.

There was always a lot to do during those winter months in Florida, and the prizes we took home were grand. Most were sterling silver—shimmering samovars, tea sets, glittering trays, pitchers, inscribed cigarette boxes, and graceful Revere bowls. For a time the Hollywood Four-Ball awarded heavy 14-karat gold jewelry, delicate pearl-studded pendants and huge gold bracelets with jeweled charms.

In the spring we headed for the Southern Amateur and the North and South Championship. Summer brought a round of important tournaments: the U.S. Women's Amateur, the U.S. Women's Open, the Western Open, the Western Amateur, the Broadmoor Invitational, the Eastern Amateur, the Trans-Mississippi, the Canadian Open Amateur, and the British.

Barbara Romack picked up a lot of the loot during those years. The bubbly blonde from Sacramento, California, was not only a great player, she was a fashion plate. Petite, at five feet four inches, Barbara sported finely cut silk Bermuda shorts, a collection of golf shoes that ranged from zebra stripes to silver, and colorful cashmere sweaters. She traveled in great style, thanks to a supportive father who owned a plumbing supply business and to her own later career as an insurance salesperson. Barbara's name appeared in the social columns almost as much as in newspaper sports sections. She was befriended by movie stars, once dated Bing Crosby, and was invited to the White House by Ike.

Miss Romack's flamboyant lifestyle was deceiving. She took golf seriously and was a fierce competitor. She possessed a big, classic swing, developed with the help of that era's great teachers, Tom LoPresti and Harry Pressler. In 1952, at the age of nineteen, she won the prestigious North and South, and the South Atlantic, and reached the quarter-finals of the U.S. Women's Amateur.

The following year she repeated in the South Atlantic, became one of the few Americans to win the Canadian Amateur, and again reached the quarters in the Women's Amateur. The year 1954 was notable because she won the U.S. Women's Amateur, defeating her fellow Californian, a very young Mickey Wright, in the final at Allegheny Country Club in Sewickley, Pennsylvania.

She was named to the 1954 Curtis Cup team, the first of three appearances (1956, 1958) in that international match. Her great record continued. She very nearly won the 1955 British Amateur, but lost in the final, and was low amateur in the 1955 Titleholders. She won three tournaments on the 1957 Florida circuit—the Florida East Coast, a third South Atlantic title, and the Palm Beach Championship. In 1958 she repeated in the Florida East Coast and was runner-up in the Women's Amateur to Anne Quast.

One of Barbara's friends was Polly Riley of Fort Worth, Texas. Polly had begun to play well in 1948 and made that year's Curtis Cup team after winning three big tournaments and reaching the fourth round in the Women's Amateur.

Miss Riley began learning the game at thirteen at Fort Worth's River Crest Country Club. Short and somewhat stocky, she mastered a great array of shots around the greens. She wasn't long off the tee, but long enough, and as a great fairway wood player she was a threat on long courses.

Polly was a golf-course strategist. She was bright and funny but could be an unnerving match-play opponent. Taking it upon herself to set the pace of play, she slowed down against fast players and speeded up, often appearing impatient, against slower players. Polly worked at this psychological warfare on and off the course. In the locker room she isolated herself, played solitaire, and sought to intimidate players by ignoring them. It worked often enough, and Patty Berg called her one of the two best competitors she had ever known, the other being Kathy Whitworth.

Holding a number of jobs to support her amateur career, Miss Riley even became a golf reporter for the old *Fort Worth Press*, where she worked next to Dan Jenkins and Blackie Sherrod, two rising stars of reporting who tried to ignore the fact that there was a woman in the sports department.

Over seventeen years Polly piled up an incredible record: She was low amateur in the 1955 Women's Open and won three Palm Beach championships, two Florida East Coast championships, three Trans-Mississippi events, six Southern titles, two Western Amateurs, the Doherty, and the South Atlantic. Her failure to win the U.S. Women's Amateur was a rare disappointment, but her record in the championship was impressive. She went to the fourth round of match play no less than eleven times and was runner-up to Mary Lena Faulk in 1953. As late as 1965 the veteran made it to the semifinals. In 1950 Riley won the budding LPGA's first tournament of the year, the Tampa Open.

*Five-time U.S. Women's Amateur
Champion JoAnne Gunderson Carner.*

Mary Lena Faulk, the 1953 U.S. Women's Amateur Champion, was a soft-spoken Southerner with a graceful, repeating swing. Miss Faulk was not a long player, but she hit a low draw and got great run on her tee shots. She was one of history's finest fairway wood players, had a delicate touch on short shots, and was a fine putter. A student of Harvey Penick, the famed Austin, Texas, professional, Mary Lena had wonderful deportment on the golf course. She was a gracious winner as well as a gracious loser. Miss Faulk beat you quietly and politely.

For a three-year period, from 1951 through 1953, she not only captured the national title but won three Florida East Coast championships, two Doherty events, and, in 1954, advanced to the semifinals of the Women's Amateur.

One of golf's greatest rivalries, however, began to take shape in 1956 when four superb amateurs began to spur each other to new plateaus of achievement.

They would dominate for more than a decade. From 1956 through 1968, the four won fifty-seven major titles. More remarkably, they won eleven of the thirteen U.S. Women's Amateur Championships and, five times, one of the four finished as runner-up.

Well into their senior years, each would go on to win many

Barbara McIntire won the U.S Women's Amateur twice.

more tournaments, but the 1950s and 1960s marked their prime. It was one of golf's most competitive eras. Marlene Stewart Streit, Jo-Anne Gunderson Carner, Anne Quast Sander, and Barbara McIntire had varying styles of play, but they were so near in ability that one cannot be considered better than the other three.

Barbara McIntire

Of the four, Barbara McIntire, a sedate brunette, emerged first on the national scene: in 1952 she finished as runner-up to Mickey Wright in the U.S. Girls' Junior and won the Western Junior.

Born and raised in Ohio, Barbara enrolled in Rollins College in Winter Park, Florida. By 1956 Miss McIntire's career had not yet taken off, and the star at Rollins was Marlene Stewart, Women's National Collegiate Champion.

That same year Barbara, twenty-one, signed up to play in the U.S. Women's Open at the Northland Country Club in Duluth, Minnesota.

The year had been a dark one for women's professional golf. Babe Zaharias was fatally ill with cancer. Deprived of its top drawing card, the Women's Open failed to attract much attention, and the USGA had slashed the purse by $1,500, to $6,000. The field of forty-six included twenty-three amateurs.

Despite Babe's absence, an elite field teed off for the final round. After 54 holes, Kathy Cornelius, a professional from Lake Worth, Florida, led at 223, 2 over par. Marlene Bauer Hagge was just a stroke behind.

Patty Berg, Joyce Ziske, Louise Suggs, Betty Jameson, and Beverly Hanson were all within seven shots of the lead. Miss McIntire was far back, at 10 over par and eight strokes off the lead.

Early in the round, Mrs. Cornelius and Mrs. Hagge faltered. It was a good opportunity for someone in the middle of the field to pull even with a hot round. That round, to the shock of everyone in the championship, came from Barbara McIntire.

Barbara played the game politely, striding down the fairway with her shoulders braced forward, but she had a truly solid game. Her wood play was accurate, and she was one of amateur golf's finest long-iron players. She owned a precise short game, and few women could play a soft wedge shot more beautifully.

A dedicated, serious player, Barbara was also a good loser and a sporting winner. Her's was the old-fashioned deportment that served the game well. She commented quietly on an opponent's good shots and reacted not at all to poor ones. When she sank a long putt or made a good bunker shot—and as a superb bunker player she made many—she might respond with a slight smile, but that was all.

In match play, opponents found that a loss to Miss McIntire was not as unpleasant as losing to less thoughtful players.

Yet Barbara was disciplined: her greatest asset was that she kept her emotions in check in competition. She was no showboat, yet had many fans. They admired her often-flawless play and her great style, part of which was an elegant wardrobe in conservative browns, blues, tans, and grays. And reporters seldom failed to mention her dimples. In the coming years she would get plenty of publicity and in 1960 would be featured on the cover of *Sports Illustrated*.

But her reputation started at the 1956 Women's Open. Over the final 18, she very quietly fired the best round of the championship, finishing birdie, par, eagle, for a 3-under-par 71. Her total of 302 was, incredibly, leading the Women's Open.

The great finish had drained Barbara's emotions and, after the round, the leader of the championship sat on a locker room bench, staring at the floor and waiting.

Mrs. Hagge and Mrs. Cornelius finished immediately behind her. Kathy's best effort that day was a 79, good enough to tie Barbara for the lead. Marlene, however, faced a short, uphill putt on the final green to tie. She thought she had hit it perfectly. Aghast, she watched her ball hit the back of the cup and pop out to rest on the high side of the hole. It was one of the greatest disappointments of Mrs. Hagge's career. While Barbara and Kathy would enter an 18-hole playoff the following day, Marlene would cry all the way to the next tour stop.

Barbara didn't win the playoff, shooting 82 to Kathy's 75, but she had nearly won the Women's Open and had finished higher than any amateur in history. She had proven that a good amateur was still able to match the top professionals, and she had done it in golf's most prestigious championship.

A young Mark McCormack, getting his sports talent agency underway, offered her a contract, but Barbara decided against a pro career and began to compile a great amateur record. From 1957 through 1963 she won two North and South titles, the Western Amateur, and the South Atlantic and twice finished as low amateur in the Open. In 1959 she won the U.S. Women's Amateur and, in 1960, the British Amateur, thus becoming one of only a handful of players who have captured both national titles.

In 1964 Barbara defeated JoAnne Gunderson, at the height of her powers as "The Great Gundy," to win the U.S. Women's Amateur for a second time. Before the end of the decade, Barbara McIntire won another Western, three North and South championships, and two Broadmoor Invitationals and again finished as low amateur in the Women's Open.

In 1971 she would win the North and South for the sixth time. It was her nineteenth major title.

Marlene Stewart Streit

When Marlene Stewart first flashed upon the American women's amateur scene, she was an underdog. For one thing, she wasn't an American at all but a Canadian. For another, there was her size. A five-footer, except in gymnastics or ice-skating, seldom makes much of a dent in major athletic arenas. No yardstick, however, could measure the size of her heart.

In the era of match-play giants, Marlene won a slew of important titles: the U.S. Women's Amateur, the National Women's Collegiate, four Doherty titles, two North and South championships, ten Canadian Open Amateurs, and the British.

She became one of only two women to capture the American, British, and Canadian national titles, a feat matched by Dorothy Campbell Hurd Howe.

Like other golfers of those years, she worked hard at her studies (at Rollins College), yet made time to play in a handful of big tournaments. She was frugal, wearing her old worn glove until it was too stiff to be of any use. She was sporting and polite to opponents, conceding a great number of short putts (too many, some said), which she did by picking up your ball and handing it to you, with a smile.

Somewhat shy, she was tempered by the limelight of competitive golf. It gave her polish, and she could stroll through posh resorts with dignity and finesse.

Her early life, however, was unlike the lives of the other players. Miss Stewart's childhood on the Canadian frontier was light-years

Marlene Stewart Streit was only the second woman to win the U.S., British, and Canadian women's amateur titles.

removed from the rich green fairways and the lilting tinkle of glasses on the clubhouse veranda.

Reporters wrote breathless summaries of her putting grip (reverse-overlap) and her practice routine (putting, chipping, and hitting a hundred full shots), but their analysis never grasped the roots of her strength. When you have been up against locust plagues and have rumbled through the northern wilderness in a horse-drawn wagon, when you have forded the Red Deer River in your mother's arms, even the Great Gundy can't stare you down.

Marlene Stewart was born in 1934 in Cereal, a small town on the Canadian plains in southern Alberta. The following year, small farms along the prairie were attacked by hordes of locusts that rattled through the fields like a hail storm, cutting crops to the ground.

The locusts plugged up car radiators. They were so thick on the inclines that cars would slide off the road.

*JoAnne Carner and Marlene
Streit in the final match of the
1966 U.S. Women's Amateur,
which Mrs. Carner won.*

The Stewarts tried to save their farm. Mary Stewart, Marlene's mother, drove across the fields in a buggy, Marlene at her side, and shoveled poison mixed with sawdust over what was left of the crops. It was a losing battle. After another locust attack the following year, Harold and Mary Stewart and two-year-old Marlene left the farm.

They set out on a six-day journey by horse and wagon to the rich irrigation lands in southern Canada. Crossing the Red Deer River, Mary held Marlene tightly under her arm while the wagon was pulled by winch, to hold it against swirling currents.

Their horses dragged the Stewart's wagon up and down rocky mountain slopes to the irrigation district, which had hazards of its own.

"Sand storms would blow down off the dry lands and shut out the sun," said Mary Stewart. "The sand was so fine that it blew into the house and into our beds. It blew into the tractor mechanism and, when Harold tried to start the tractor, the sand had ruined the motor."

During World War II the Stewarts left the rugged existence of the farm forever, settling in Fonthill, Ontario, about twelve miles from Niagra Falls. Marlene was introduced to golf by a playmate and, at the age of twelve, became a caddie at Lookout Point Golf Club.

Gordon McInnis, the club's professional, became fond of the tiny girl, hired her to carry his small canvas bag, and gave her golf lessons.

"She was really handicapped because she was so small," McInnis said. "But right from the beginning she could pull off all the shots. She had a real long sweeping backswing and a good shoulder turn, so that she got everything out of her little old body that was possible.

"Nobody had any confidence in her except my wife, Bunny, her parents, and me. She was so persistent in her practicing. She got it right from the beginning and stuck to it.

"Her father asked me, 'How far can she go?' I knew what she could do, how she could concentrate and how much stamina she had. I said, 'She can go the limit. She can be the best.'"

After winning some junior tournaments as a teenager, Marlene enrolled at Rollins. In 1956 she won the Women's National Collegiate Championship. That summer she won the U.S. Women's Amateur. Her opponent in the final was JoAnne Gunderson, seventeen, of Seattle, the reigning U.S. Girls' Junior champion.

After Marlene's 2 and 1 victory, a handful of Canadian rooters shed tears of joy, and Miss Stewart was photographed clasping the Canadian flag to her chest.

"It's unfair to Marlene, a great player and totally deserving of the title, to say that her victory was unpopular," wrote golf reporter Jimmy Mann, "but the main body of the gallery of 2,000 favored the youngster from Seattle."

Years later Mrs. Streit pondered her unique role in American golf.

"I never dwelled on it because, within, I know what I did," she said. "And yet, certainly, I felt it when my American friends would win and their pictures were on the cover of a golf magazine, and I would win the British Amateur, or whatever, and there would be a little blurb in that same magazine. I didn't dwell on it because I would never have played as well as I did, if I had. Within myself I knew. I guess the players knew. I got enough recognition."

After college Marlene married J. Douglas Streit and as Marlene Streit continued to compile a great record. In 1966 she again battled JoAnne, now Mrs. Carner, for 41 holes in the longest final in the history of the U.S. Women's Amateur, before losing, 1-up. That gave her a one-hole advantage over Mrs. Carner in their 76 holes of final-match competition, a remarkable feat when you consider that sending Marlene in against JoAnne was a little like sending in a hummingbird to fight a bear. Had there been a weigh-in, Marlene would have been logged at five feet, 115 pounds, JoAnne at five feet, seven inches, 150 pounds.

During her career, Mrs. Streit's perseverance, talent, and courage made her one of the best amateurs in history. She developed a compact swing and owned a great all-around game. She lacked great power, hitting her tee shots 210 yards, at most, but she was a wonderful fairway wood player, a fine iron player, and a good putter. She concentrated better than almost any of her peers.

In 1989 British golf writer Enid Wilson speculated that, in the 1950s, Marlene Stewart Streit was the greatest woman player in the world.

It's an opinion to consider carefully.

JoAnne Gunderson could flatten opponents with the force of her swing.

JoAnne Gunderson Carner

A large, good-natured girl, JoAnne Gunderson could be very casual in competition. In the final of the 1956 U.S. Women's Amateur she met Marlene Stewart. Seemingly bored with the pace of play, Miss Gunderson lay down on the apron of the green while her opponent stood over a crucial putt.

She was only seventeen at the time and perhaps unaware that such antics can be distracting to opponents, but she never lost that relaxed approach, joking with her fans or using extreme body English when one of her putts approached the hole.

She could rock opponents simply with the force of her swing. It was a good, smooth swing, especially in those early years. Her backswing was shortish, and at times the club wouldn't reach horizontal. But Miss Gunderson was so strong and used her legs so well that she could generate tremendous power, hitting tee shots that approached 260 yards.

Born in 1939 in Kirkland, Washington, the strawberry blonde achieved quick success on the amateur circuit. She was runner-up in the 1955 U.S. Girls' Junior, losing to Carole Jo Kabler. When she won the Girls' Junior in 1956, only one opponent managed to take her past the 15th hole. "Gundy," as the other players called her, won a golf scholarship (rare for young women in those days) to Arizona

"The Great Gundy" in 1957 with the U.S. Women's Amateur trophy.

State University and captured the Women's National Collegiate Championship in 1960.

By then she was a seasoned veteran. She had won the 1955 Western Junior. She had romped through the 1957 U.S. Women's Amateur, at the age of eighteen, defeating Ann Casey Johnstone, 8 and 6, in the final. In 1959 she won the Western Amateur. She won it again in 1960, defeating Jean Ashley.

Her five victories in the Women's Amateur are second only to Glenna Collett Vare, who won six titles. Miss Gunderson won the 1962 version with a stunning 9 and 8 victory over Ann Baker in the final, making eight threes in the round, four birdies, and an eagle. In 1966 she beat Marlene Streit in a 41-hole final.

JoAnne won her fifth Women's Amateur Championship in 1968, defeating Anne Quast Welts, 5 and 4. These two had a great rivalry of their own. In eleven of the thirteen previous years, either JoAnne or Anne had reached the final.

JoAnne's casual play was deceptive. She practiced a great deal and played so hard in the U.S. Women's Amateur that, after the championship, she would collapse into bed for a solid week.

She became a ferocious match-play competitor but sometimes fell asleep against easy opponents.

"Basically, I'd always lose to players I could beat very easily," she said. "I'd seldom lose to a good player. I'd be up for that."

Miss Gunderson in the 1963 U.S. Women's Amateur.

Her semifinal against Catherine Lacoste in the 1968 Women's Amateur was a good example. JoAnne had been the reigning queen of amateur golf when Mlle Lacoste, the French amateur, had startled all of golf by winning the 1967 Women's Open.

The cocky French girl's success had somewhat unnerved Jo-Anne, and she referred to Lacoste, somewhat snidely, as "Catherine the Great." At Birmingham (Michigan) Country Club, Mrs. Carner planned to show Catherine who had the best stuff. Their match was a thriller. Lacoste and Carner were even after 11 holes, then JoAnne put on a devastating finish, making a par on the 12th and firing birdie, birdie, birdie to close out Catherine, 4 and 3.

She won the Trans-National in 1961 and was low amateur in the 1962 Women's Open. JoAnne played the Florida Orange Blossom Circuit rarely, but in 1968 she made an appearance and clinched the Harder Hall Championship and the Doherty.

She shone as an immense talent and unique personality, with her chorus-line kicks, wisecracks, and her deep, rumbling, Beatrice Arthur voice. But in the heat of a tight match, when stoicism counted, she sailed down the fairway, head high and elbows out, serene as the Queen Mary.

No one really *wanted* to play against her, so intimidating were her big tee shots and her sheer confidence in her own ability. She cut doglegs that others wouldn't dare attempt, hit blistering long irons, and could hit even medium-length par 5 holes in two shots.

"The Great Gundy," as we began to call her, was afraid of no one. But it was hard not to like her.

Always an amateur at heart.

I remember the 1963 Women's Amateur at the Taconic Golf Club, in Williamstown, Massachusetts. The players' dinner in the old clubhouse was a warm, lovely affair. The committee in navy blazers at the head table. Candlelight. Harp music. Inspiring speeches about sportsmanship and the glories of amateur golf. The revered Joe Dey was the master of ceremonies. Glenna Collett Vare was remembered, and the ghost of the Babe hovered about the room. This was our national championship, a time to be in awe.

As defending champion, Gundy was asked to say a few words. She walked staidly to the head table. She was lovely and slim in the candlelight, and her blonde hair gleamed. Our champion. The committee smiled expectantly. The room was hushed.

Gundy turned up one corner of her mouth in a wry smile, then her voice rumbled up from Bankhead depths. "A lot of people have noticed that I've lost a lot of weight," she said quietly. "Well, it's because I'm in love."

We held our collective breaths. "Yeah, I wanna tell you," she bellowed, "I'm in love—with MYSELF!"

She then regaled us with just how she fell in love with herself after her third national championship, and the very positive aspects of falling in love with oneself.

We almost fell on the floor. Loosening his striped tie, Joe Dey threw back his head and roared. There was a strange and wonderful energy in the air; nothing was sacrosanct.

It was, Gundy had reminded us, only a game.

After fifteen years as an amateur star, the Great Gundy left all of us behind. She won the Burdine's Invitational, an LPGA event, in Miami in 1969 and became a professional. Perhaps in the flush of that startling victory by an amateur in a field of pros, Gundy said she could get together a team of amateurs and whip any team the pros had to offer.

The pros, of course, were insulted, and later JoAnne rather regretted that statement. But more than one of us heard this flagrant display of sheer guttiness and thought, "Yep, that's Gundy. The game is on!"

She had a tough time on the professional tour at first but eventually came into her own, winning two U.S. Women's Open championships (and contending in a dozen other Women's Opens), and she eventually played her way into the LPGA Hall of Fame.

As a professional, JoAnne Gunderson Carner would win the Bob Jones Award for her sporting conduct, and during her long career she would make many friends for the game. She was no longer "The Great Gundy." Her friends on the tour began calling her "Big Mama."

JoAnne didn't mind. Golf was fun for her. She made a great deal of money, but she simply loved to play the game. And, while she became one of the leading lights of the LPGA tour, I will always believe that she remained an amateur at heart.

Anne Quast Sander

Anne Quast was the fourth player in this group of rivals. Born in 1937 in Everett, Washington, Anne had deep roots in the Pacific Northwest. Her grandfather homesteaded land thirty-five miles from Seattle, land on which her parents, Tom and Joan Quast, later built Everett Golf and Country Club.

"My parents didn't play golf, they ran the course strictly as a business," Anne said. "They never envisioned me as a golfer, but I grew up on that course."

At thirteen she was a promising player when Helene Kendall and Helen Ingram, family friends, took her to the Washington Women's Public Links championship in Seattle. Anne advanced to the final and, while she lost by a large margin, loved the competition. It was to be the beginning of one of golf's longest and most successful amateur careers.

In 1952 Anne, now fourteen, became the youngest qualifier in the history of the U.S. Women's Amateur. At the U.S. Girls' Junior, she fired a 76, tying Mickey Wright for medalist honors.

"No one had ever heard of me," she remembered. "I didn't know how hard the game was then, and I really became determined because I realized I could compete. I would always dream about making a 10-foot putt to win the National."

In 1954 she won the Western Girls' Junior and in 1955 entered the University of Washington (she would later transfer to Stanford).

244

Anne Quast Sander was one of the four truly great amateurs of the 1960s.

Mrs. Sander won the U.S. Women's Amateur in 1958, 1961, and 1963.

Her great career was just beginning.

A slender, attractive brunette, Anne, like her rivals—Gunderson, McIntire, and Streit—had a devoted following, "the darling of the galleries, win or lose," wrote one reporter.

Her swing was somewhat mechanical, but it was repetitive and reliable, and she seldom strayed from the fairway. She was tenacious in match play but also recorded wonderful scores in stroke play.

Anne was a year younger than JoAnne Gunderson, who was from Kirkland, Washington. A natural rivalry developed between the two Washingtonians when they were in their early teens, and it was a teasing relationship from the beginning.

"The first time I met JoAnne, she was fourteen and I was thirteen," Anne recalled. "I was putting. I'll never forget it, she came up to me and said, 'Whatcha practicing for? Afraid I'm gonna beat you?'"

JoAnne defeated Anne in the semifinals of the 1955 Girls' Junior. Their next meeting was in the semifinals of the 1958 U.S. Women's Amateur.

"I had to make a downhill, three-foot putt to win," Anne said. "The ball wasn't in the hole yet, and I swear she threw her arms around me and said, 'I knew you were going to make that one.'"

And she remembered Miss Gunderson's unique approach to her own tournament battles.

"In the first round of the 1961 Women's Amateur, JoAnne was going extra holes against her opponent and she just creamed it off the first tee, but far out of bounds. I just remember how much she laughed at herself. That was typical of JoAnne, you never knew—she was either spectacular or she would do something awful. She hit it so far, it would go anywhere. You'd never see Barbara McIntire hit the ball out of bounds on the nineteenth hole, she was so steady. But JoAnne was spectacular, that's why everyone loved watching her."

Anne's career as a schoolteacher kept her from the Florida winter circuit most years, although she won the 1956 South Atlantic and the 1957 Doherty. In the summer championships she was outstanding. In 1956, despite a broken toe, at eighteen she became the youngest winner of the Western Amateur and was medalist with a score of 70.

In 1958 Anne and JoAnne were selected to play on the Curtis Cup team for the first time. The two were paired as partners for a 36-hole foursomes match (played at alternate shot). The match was a long one for both players.

"We were disasterous together," Anne said. "I was a very short, but straight, hitter. But JoAnne would hit the ball into an unbelievable place, then laugh and say, 'Let's see you get out of that one,' knowing darn well I didn't know how to get out of it. We were embarrassed because we lost badly."

Three teachers have influenced Anne Quast Sander's game. Her first instructor was Chuck Congdon. While a student at Stanford, she took lessons from Bud Ward.

"Bud's the one who really made it possible for me to finally win," she said. "In 1955 I hit a few balls for him. He was a tough character. One day he said, 'Why are you wasting your money coming up here? All you care about are boys and school.'

"I got so mad that I was going to prove to him that I could do it. When I won the 1958 Women's Amateur, I could hardly wait to see him again. He said, 'That was pretty good but you know that anyone can win once, not everyone can win twice.'

"My determination wasn't just my own," said Anne, "it was also the determination that he instilled in me. But Bud quit charging me for lessons once he realized that I really did care."

After her victory in the 1958 Amateur, reporter Tom O'Neill wrote, "So ended a quest of six years by one of the game's greatest personality girls." Her picture ran on a 1959 cover of *Sports Illustrated*.

Anne was to fulfill Bud Ward's ambitions when she repeated as Women's Amateur champion in 1961, overwhelming Tish Preuss in the finals. It was a superlative display of golf. That week Anne played 112 holes at 9 under par. She was never over par in any match, and lost only six holes during the championship.

In 1963 she joined Miss Gunderson as a three-time winner of the Women's Amateur, beating Gundy in the semifinals, 3 and 2, and easing past Peggy Conley, a sixteen-year-old from Spokane, 2 and 1, in the final.

Anne was runner-up in the Women's Amateur three times, in 1965, 1968 (losing to JoAnne), and 1973.

Mrs. Sander was an excitable player who at times lost shots when she became overwrought, but her game had few weaknesses. Her longevity is almost unmatched. She won the British Amateur in 1980 at the age of forty-three. Then, in 1986, she began taking lessons from Ed Oldfield and gained new inspiration.

"I had ceased to be competitive," she said. "It wasn't fun anymore."

Oldfield helped her make key changes in her swing, telling her that the changes would be difficult so late in her career. But Mrs. Sander worked hard on her game and proved her new swing by winning the U.S. Senior Women's Amateur in 1987, 1989, and 1990.

In 1990 she advanced to the semifinals of the U.S. Women's Mid-Amateur at the age of fifty-three. After a practice round before the championship, we shared lunch and I was delighted to discover that Anne Quast Sander's great enthusiasm for the game was intact. She maintained a vigorous practice schedule, she said, and her quest for the ideal competitive golf swing continued.

Anne played for the winning American side in the 1990 Curtis Cup match. She had been named to the team in five different decades, beginning in 1958. The 1990 match marked her eighth Curtis Cup appearance—an American record. She remains part of a unique era of great players, women who continued to prove themselves well after their prime.

In 1990 JoAnne Gunderson Carner continued to play on the LPGA Tour and, at fifty-four, sometimes managed to play her way into the thick of the fight.

Barbara McIntire finished fourth in the 1990 U.S. Women's Senior Championship, and Marlene Stewart Streit finished as runner-up. She tied for the championship, then lost the title in an 18-hole playoff against Anne Sander.

It was a wonderful year in which to remember their rivalries of old.

*hy Whitworth winning her
*h official tournament in
tsmouth, Virginia.

11

The Modern Monarch

In the last pearly hour before dawn, the air conditioner rattled at the window and the motel room seemed as damp and cold as the inside of a refrigerator. Mail, bottles of vitamins, and packages of peanut butter crackers were scattered on a table. An old putter leaned in the corner, and three golf balls lay on the carpet.

Kathy Whitworth stole a few extra minutes from the clock radio. Her legs ached and her eyes felt swollen and burned from constant exposure to the glaring sun.

Soon the warm whirr of her hair dryer drowned out the air conditioner. The fried eggs and sports pages arrived, and she ate breakfast, blessed by a Sunday sermon flickering from the television.

In an hour she was strolling across the parking lot, a lithe, tanned woman in golf clothes, her hazel eyes extraordinarily bright. She frowned and clenched her jaw but walked smoothly, timing each stride to some careful inner rhythm.

Nervousness hit her as she drove to the golf course and made her vaguely cross, but she expected it, needed it.

Take dead aim, she thought. She could almost feel the old putter,

". . . a flinty squint of resolute will . . ."

the slight imaginary pressure of her fingers on its tattered leather grip as the invisible pulse took over, a rhythm that timed her stroke to her own heartbeat. The feel, individual as her fingerprint, thundered and flashed through the small sensors of her perception, pulsing in a beat as steady as the pendulum of a clock.

She made her mind go blank. Think of nothing. Eyes on the road. Relax.

In the dining room of the Brookfield West Country Club near Atlanta, she stared into a cup of coffee. It was 1983. A year before at this site she had broken Mickey Wright's record of eighty-two career victories. If she could hang on for one more win, she would break Sam Snead's record of eighty-four official career titles.

Golf was waiting.

The strain made her feel out of sorts. Media hysteria surrounds such feats, but she knew that she was being protected by LPGA officials.

"They form a cocoon around me and keep people from asking me about it," she said. "If I think about it too much, I'll blow it. Even the press is getting real quiet about it, I notice. I think, Well, OK, that's over now. In fact, it feels a little funny because everybody has stopped talking about it."

Her game was in a sort of swale, a natural wind-down from the peaks of the twenty-four years of her great career: three LPGA championships, two Titleholders victories, the Dinah Shore, leading money-

A wonderful putting touch was one of Miss Whitworth's assets.

winner eight times, Player of the Year seven times, Vare Trophy winner seven times.

Who could forget?

The years had been kind to Miss Whitworth. Her natural dignity gave her a certain stateliness. Despite decades of sun her face was unlined, and her ageless eyes, flecked with blue and brown, darkened and lightened with her mood, sparkling when she laughed, narrowing into a flinty squint of resolute will when she stared down one of the ten thousand fairways she had walked.

What she wanted this dewy spring morning was all that she had ever wanted, to just be allowed to play golf and to play it well. She could not, of course, be let alone. The young players, the press, the galleries saw her as an icon of sorts, a terribly uncomfortable role. It was hard for her to think of herself as anything other than a golfer who had heroes of her own—Patty Berg, Mickey Wright, Betsy Rawls.

"I'm playing with one of the rookies today," she muttered.

"So?" said her companion at the table.

"You don't know how it is," she said. "She'll be nervous, so she probably won't play well. Then I'll feel bad about it. I'll worry about how I'm affecting her game, when I should be thinking of my own."

"Why don't you talk to her now, before you tee off? That's what Nicklaus does when he's paired with a young player."

"What in the world can I say?" Miss Whitworth asked.

The friend tried to lighten the mood.

Carol Mann, Kathy Whitworth, and Sandra Haynie during Kathy's World Series of Golf victory.

"You could always tell her about your eighty-three victories. Shot by shot. That ought to loosen her up."

Kathy glared across the table.

At this point in her career, to accept her great record was to acknowledge its longevity.

At the end of the 1988 season, I began to see Kathy differently. There were the inevitable signs of aging: Her silky putting touch had mostly deserted her. Tendinitus wore away at her knees, and she struggled to walk up hills, gritting her teeth in pain. The sun glinted off the silver in her hair. But she managed a full schedule and, just as she had for three decades, she would stride down the fairway, tall and erect, the quintessential professional athlete going about her business.

She was intolerant of bad play. After a round of 71, she was taken to the press tent, muttering over some shots that got away. A reporter asked her why one under par made her seem so unhappy.

"If I'm happy with it, I'll never shoot 70," Whitworth said.

She could still pull off some wonderful shotmaking. These were shots that few modern women knew, but Miss Whitworth had learned them early while watching Miss Berg, Miss Wright, and Miss Rawls. Without her early power, she was still good off the tee; with her driver she could fade the ball toward a small mound beside a bunker, draw it slightly to take advantage of a slight breeze, or cut the shot to hold the line into a crosswind.

Miss Whitworth made this 50-foot putt on the final hole to win the LPGA Championship, one of four wins in that tournament.

Her great gifts were a wonderful innate touch and a keen mind that saw new ways to attack strategic problems. But in 1988 few believed that she would win again.

She recalled sitting near the younger Pat Bradley and Mary Dwyer in a locker room. Miss Bradley was trying to talk the slumping Miss Dwyer out of quitting the tour.

"Pat told Mary, 'Look at Whit, look at how many times they've written *her* off!'"

Kathy laughed. "I didn't know I'd been written off that many times!"

She was still the most interviewed player on the tour, and her appearances in the old tournament towns were nostalgic. The situation reached laughable proportions in 1987. A Rochester, New York, reporter had asked her when she would retire. If she couldn't turn her game around, she said, then it would be time to quit.

She had no intention of quitting in the near future, of course, but on Sunday morning a headline proclaimed, WHITWORTH PLAYING IN LAST ROCHESTER INTERNATIONAL!

Cheering galleries sent her off the first tee that day, and fans around the course shouted, "We'll miss you!" She walked to the final green to an emotional standing ovation. To her mortification, play was stopped when tournament officials gave her red roses while, back in the fairway, Pat Bradley stood with hands on hips and glared at the delay.

It was hard to imagine what the LPGA would be like after Miss Whitworth retired. Almost alone she is a reminder of the barnstorming days when the players rattled around the country in their caravan of cars. Not that she built the tour alone, but she had been there, she had helped. When she left, it would be the end of a slam-bang time in women's golf.

Let us go back to the LPGA's vintage years. Burneyville, Oklahoma, site of the Opie Turner Open. Oklahoma oilman Waco Turner sponsored the tournament and named it for Opie, his wife.

Miss Whitworth was in her early twenties, and everything was ahead of her. Like everyone, she was trying to adjust to this tournament's unique format.

Turner's sunbaked golf course is hard as a rock, and the course setup committee, tour husbands Bill Cornelius and Bob Hagge, can only pound the putting cups into the hard surface and leave them in the same spot all week. It gives them something to do. Waco has ruled that all players must stay in a player's dorm, off-limits to the husbands. At night the bored wives join the other players in furious poker games. By day they play Waco's meandering layout. After holing out on the front nine, the players jump into old wrecked Cadillacs and a truck tows the old cars a couple of miles to the 10th tee.

Each day Waco announces a lunch break at the end of nine. The players are hauled to the bar for a few hours, then they pile into the old cars to be towed back to the course in a cloud of red dust. Waco has imported Miss America for the closing ceremonies. The lovely and talented Mary Ann Mobley presents the trophies, while the players and caddies applaud and Bill Cornelius packs his car.

They were a merry band, these few, playing bridge and poker, cooking meals on a hot plate, running their own tournaments, and dreaming of somehow making it all work. By 1988 not many of them remained on the tour, but Marlene Hagge and Kathy Whitworth were still out there, and they had been known to change a tire or two together in the old days.

Kathy loved that life.

"We would always have a good time," she said. "There wasn't that much money involved. It was just a game back then. After a tournament, everyone kind of celebrated together. Usually, the winner would pay for the drinks because she was the only one who had any money."

In that era she visited the winners circle nine or ten times a year. By 1988 her role had changed. She couldn't play as well, of course, and it grated on her nerves. She often slammed clubs in frustration but, oddly, kept her self-control even in her outburst. When she missed a green with a poor iron shot, she remained calm. She finessed a lovely little pitch, then slammed the club into the ground. Startled observers thought she was very angry because she hadn't holed the pitch shot. It wasn't that.

254

"I was furious when I missed the iron shot to the green," she said, "but you have to stay in control, at least until you've hit a recovery shot, or it will cause you to miss the next shot."

Such was her strength. She had terrific determination and the inability to quit. Atlanta sports columnist Furman Bisher once wrote that Kathy Whitworth was the type of woman you'd want on your side when the Indians attacked, the sort of woman to whom he'd hand a rifle, saying, "Here, you hold 'em off and I'll go for help."

Bisher's scenario wasn't far off. Miss Whitworth's roots were in the American West. Her grandparents migrated from Kansas, Missouri, and Georgia but homesteaded in New Mexico when the federal government offered acreage to anyone who would build a home. Homesteading called for pluck, providence, and boundless energy to settle the parched southeastern corner of the state. According to a minister of the time, "These people had not come as adventurers to see how they would like it. They had come to stay and see the thing done."

Kathrynne Ann Whitworth was born September 27, 1939, in Monahans, Texas, where her father worked for a lumber company. Soon after, the Whitworths returned to Jal, New Mexico, near the Texas border. Jal, named for the ranch brand J-A-L, was dominated by the oil and gas industry. Its outskirts roll out over huge sand dunes, punctuated by cactus and the mosquito-like pump jacks that suck oil from beneath the desert floor. The land looks like a big, brown blotter, but the sky offers wide freedom and glorious sunsets.

Kathy loved that openness. "Not a tree to spoil the view," she laughed.

The Whitworths owned a hardware store. Morris Whitworth, a thoughtful, philosophical man with a keen sense of humor, wrote a weekly column for *The Jal Record*. He ran the hardware store and, eventually, the town. During Jal's most progressive years he served on the city council and was elected mayor three times.

Dama Whitworth, Kathy's mother, was one of those dignified Western women who civilize a community, glue it together, and give it grace. She kept the store's books and attacked church work, charity functions, and social life with determined energy. If something needed to be done in Jal, Dama Whitworth could be counted on to get it done.

On a visit home, Kathy addressed the annual meeting of the Jal Chamber of Commerce.

"A lot of people have asked me how to achieve success," she began, "and I tell them, first you have to get yourself born in a small town."

The backing of the town and her family reinforced Kathy's dream, both simple and complex in its challenge.

"All I ever wanted," she said, "was to be the greatest woman golfer in the world."

The youngest of three girls, she played the bass drum in the Jal Panthers high school marching band. She excelled in sports, and one

Miss Whitworth, a fine bunker player, learned the shot from Patty Berg.

day in 1954 she first tried golf. At fifteen she joined three school friends at Jal Country Club. She remembers the day as the most frustrating of her youth. She played horribly, but golf fascinated and challenged her. She was hooked, and from that day she began to work at the game, often hitting practice balls in a cow pasture on the edge of town.

Hardy Loudermilk, the Jal Country Club professional, took her under his wing. He was, she felt, a key to her eventual success. One day Loudermilk said, "I've taken you as far as I can. I'm going to call Harvey Penick and ask him to help you now."

Penick, the famed Texas teacher who taught Betsy Rawls, Ben Crenshaw, and Tom Kite, remained Miss Whitworth's teacher throughout her career. She returned often to Penick's Austin, Texas, practice tee. One summer evening in 1987, she was in town for another lesson, and she stood on the practice tee of the deserted old Austin Country Club. Penick, now eighty-two, had relocated to a new club.

This was a sentimental visit to the old course. The driving range meandered off toward the house where the Penicks had once lived. In the twilight the white blossoms on the crepe myrtle trees were barely visible behind the tee where Kathy had learned to play golf.

"Mother and I would drive down from Jal and stay about three days," she reminisced. "I'd take lessons all day, right here. Mother would sit over there making notes about everything Harvey told me. One time she took notes on a paper sack, and I still have it. Even when Harvey was giving another lesson, he'd keep an eye on me and come back to give advice. At night Mother and I would check into a motel. We'd go to a lighted driving range and I'd practice for three or four hours every night. I'd take lessons for two more days, then we'd drive home."

In 1982, when Miss Whitworth won her record eighty-third tournament, she sent a dozen yellow roses to several key people in her life, including Harvey and Helen Penick.

"I couldn't have done it without you," said the card, "Love, Kathy."

As a teenager she was taken to area golf tournaments by her aunt and members of the Jal Ladies' Golf Association. Her hometown gave Kathy recognition, and the handshakes and congratulatory words spurred her on. At seventeen she won her first big tournament, the 1957 New Mexico Women's Amateur.

A few weeks later, an invitation to the Titleholders Championship arrived. The Titleholders was played each spring in Augusta, Georgia, at Augusta Country Club, adjacent to Bobby Jones's great Augusta National layout, and it was considered the women's version of the Masters.

"We thought if you got an invitation, then you had to go," Miss Whitworth said. "So, Mother and I got on the Greyhound bus and rode for two days. I had this little green plaid golf bag that Dad had ordered through the hardware store. When the caddies saw that bag, none of them wanted to caddie for me. They said, 'Not me, I want a pro bag.'"

Kathy repeated in the 1958 New Mexico Amateur, and at nineteen, after one year on a golf scholarship at Odessa (Texas) Junior College, she turned pro.

"I couldn't afford to play a lot of amateur golf," she said. "If I was going to learn the game, I was going to have to learn it on the tour."

Sponsored by her father, Loudermilk and two Jal businessmen, she took off for Florida in her little green Plymouth, accompanied by her mother.

Over the years she would learn all the ins and outs of golf's itinerant lifestyle. The highways and favored motels would become her home, and she would travel by jet and stay in huge, glamorous hotels, but her early frugality remained with her always. Years later I heard Kathy and Patty Berg sharing complaints about shocking motel rates of forty dollars a night. When she was making three hundred thousand dollars a year, only after friends convinced her that it might lengthen her career would she finally fly first class.

She struggled with her game at first. Penick had taught her an effective swing. She had a wonderful natural shoulder turn, good power, and that great touch around the greens, but she was raw. Her scores slopped over into the 80s, even the 90s. After a couple of months on the tour, she hadn't won a dime.

"I wanted to quit," she said. "So I went back home to discuss it with Mother and Dad. They convinced me to give it a little more time, to keep trying. My sponsorship deal was $5,000 a year for three years. So, I went back out feeling a little better. The next week, I won a check for $33 in Ashville, North Carolina. Three of us tied for last place money and I called home, feeling as good as if I'd won the tournament.

"Near the end of the year, Marlene Hagge invited me to spend the off-season in Delray Beach with her and her husband Bob. She was a big star and didn't know me from Adam, but she invited me to stay at her house so that I could spend the winter working on my game. I didn't go, but I'll never forget that she asked."

These are the things she remembers. Little favors. The small acts of friendship.

Her weight was another early hurdle. At five feet nine inches tall, she weighed 215 pounds when she began playing golf. As a rookie she weighed 175 pounds but, using that strong willpower, she knocked off more than thirty-five pounds over the next two years.

She finished fast in that rookie year and managed to win $1,200. In her second season, 1960, she won almost $5,000 and was voted "most improved player."

"But money was never my motivator," she said. "When you start having money as your motivation, you begin to be happy with seventh place or you settle for tenth, just to win a little to help you through the week."

Only winning was enough. In 1962 she won her first event, the Kelley Girl, in Baltimore, Maryland. She would win at least one tournament a year for each of the next seventeen seasons. Some of those years were barnburners: eight victories in 1963, eight in 1966, ten in 1968, seven in 1969. And she was playing against the best: Patty Berg, Louise Suggs, Mickey Wright, Betsy Rawls, Sandra Haynie, and Carol Mann. Today all are members of the LPGA Hall of Fame.

Kathy was named "Player of the Year" seven times and was leading money winner eight times. The Associated Press named her "Woman Athlete of the Year," in 1965 and 1967. Just as it had been Mickey Wright against the field, now it was Kathy Whitworth against the field.

Miss Whitworth was involved with the organizational growth of the LPGA and was elected president three times before 1980. Her interest reflected her family's attitude that you had to give something back. During her later career she settled at the Trophy Club, a golf course development near Dallas, and spoke out on various community causes. But her heart was in Jal. She went home often and each week received *The Jal Record* in the mail.

Through her best years, Kathy remained a modest champion.

Furman Bisher wrote that Miss Whitworth would never cause a stampede of Whitworth adorers. She never caused a commotion, won beauty contests, or was a fashion plate, Bisher said. Rather, he noted hers was the "nice, mild, concerned appearance" of your child's home-room teacher.

I remember her at the 1982 U.S. Women's Open at Tulsa. She was forty-three then and she played a practice round with her old crony, Donna Caponi. They made a poised pairing, both tanned and sleekly dressed, Miss Whitworth a little gray, and they plainly enjoyed playing together. It was a scorcher of a day and the sun was relentless. As they climbed the last hill, I was pleased for them that the round was over. Perhaps they could enjoy a chat over a glass of iced tea in the air-conditioned clubhouse. Then a crowd of reporters descended on them behind the 18th green. For more than an hour, these two cornerstones of the LPGA tour stood, uncomplaining, in the sun. At length, after answering every question, their job was done and they trudged off to the locker room. They looked at this tiresome intrusion as part of their life's work, a stance picked up from the players who had come before them.

For Miss Whitworth, it's a debt of gratitude.

"This is what you *do*," she said. "Patty did it, Betsy did it, it's what you do."

Furman Bisher elaborated. "When the LPGA specified its tour as that of 'ladies,' it had Kathy Whitworth in mind."

As high as she climbed in golf, she was bound to have a long, hard fall when it ended. In 1978 she had tried to change her swing and she fell into bad habits. By 1979 she was over the hill, a sad and broken player who wanted to quit.

"It got worse and worse," she remembered. "It got to where I just hated to go out to the golf course because I knew I couldn't play anymore. There was panic and fear because I didn't know where the ball was going or whether I'd even *hit it*! To actually fear playing golf after having done so well is a horrible experience."

There were painful incidents that ate away at her fierce pride.

In 1980 she was packing her car after the Mixed-Team Championship in Florida, when Ray Floyd walked by.

"Hello, Kathy," nodded Floyd. Then he turned to the seven-time Player of the Year, the winner of more money than anyone in the history of women's golf, and asked casually, "Are you still playing?"

"Yeah. Hi, Ray," Miss Whitworth muttered, looking down and becoming very busy folding her windbreaker.

At each tournament the announcer would give her an elaborate introduction and reel off her illustrious record. After she teed off a few men would drag their wives out to follow, as they might drag their children to a museum, but after one or two holes they would lose interest and she would watch them walk back in. Inevitably reporters would ask her, "When are you going to retire?" And she felt that there was an implication that she had been out there too long, as if she should go quietly now and leave them all to remember her as she once had been.

Jack Nicklaus could tell reporters that he would not answer questions about retirement. Kathy couldn't bring herself to do that. So each week she leaned forward in her chair and carefully and patiently explained that she was still enjoying the tour, that she was working on her game, and maybe, hopefully, she could bring it around before long.

But the tour was changing, and Whitworth's old gang had faded away. Louise Suggs retired and Patty Berg concentrated on exhibitions. Jackie Pung went back to Hawaii and Joyce Ziske got married. Mickey had pretty much quit after 1964 when the strain of being "The Greatest Ever" took the fun out of it.

The new LPGA commissioner, Ray Volpe, was hired and given absolute power. Players like Kathy Whitworth, who had nurtured the tour and kept it alive by running the tournaments, found that they didn't have much to do with it anymore. The new players didn't want to run the tour, but some of the veterans, who had held high office, found it all very hard to take. Kathy had been LPGA president three times. She gritted her teeth.

The warm and happy family had become highly competitive and was now a big, slick business operation, not exactly the place to find solace when your game is going bad. And Miss Whitworth's game was about as bad as it could get.

In 1979 she finished fifty-sixth in the Colgate–Dinah Shore, an event that had given her a huge thrill when she won it in 1977. She was thirty-fourth in the Colgate-European, fortieth in the U.S. Women's Open. For the first time in eighteen years, she didn't win a tournament.

In August she was in a taxi in New York City. She stared out of the window.

"I think I'm gonna retire," she said glumly.

There it was. The dreaded decision. She just couldn't play anymore, she said, and she was tired. No one in the cab was surprised. It had been a year of seeing her slam the ground with her club, of seeing her stomp stonefaced toward the locker room. Kathy Whitworth had been on top for a very long time. Now she was very nearly at the bottom. Discouraged, burned out, the small-town girl headed home.

"Out here it's run, run, run and go, go, go," she said, "and you don't have a chance to sit back and reflect on it. You don't have time to really know where you're going or how you're gonna get there or even to recognize when you get there what you've *got!*"

She went home to sit at the kitchen table and drink coffee with her mother and father. They were her sounding board.

Total concentration was a key to her game.

"Dad has a lot of common sense, he parallels things so I can understand. He never told me what to do, but he made me see both sides and told me what I might think about. I'm still their little girl, you know, and if anything is wrong they're always interested and want to help."

During her winter in Dallas she rested and began to want to play again. At first it was a cautious commitment. She stood in front of a mirror, gripping a yardstick, a tee on the carpet in front of her. Time and again she addressed the tee and swept back the stick in an imaginary takeaway. In a few weeks she began to play with old friends. They pretended not to notice when she banged the ground with her club after a bad shot. The old friends laughed and joked, pretending that it was yet another good winter after another glorious winning season for Kathy Whitworth. But it was not. She had a big bruise on her leg where she had pounded herself with her club shaft and, as she slashed away at the ball, a few times she seemed very close to tears.

In December she went to see Harvey Penick. Her game began to improve, just a little.

The season started slowly. In May, on her way to forty-eighth place in Roswell, Georgia, she told the announcer to introduce her as Kathy Whitworth of Dallas, Texas.

"Leave off all the titles and the records," she said. "That was all in the past."

She missed the cut at the LPGA Championship and at the Women's Open, but in October in San Jose she had a fine closing round, made seven birdies, and tied for ninth. Ahead of her was another winter of hard work.

"I was looking forward to 1981," she said. "I hadn't run out of motivation. I still wanted to play but I hadn't been able to play. Now I felt like I had turned it around. It was just a question of doing it enough times so that I wouldn't fall back into the old habits."

In the first tournament of the year she opened with a 69 and finished third. It was her best start in nearly three years. At Industry Hills, California, she birdied three of the last four holes and tied for second. In the first twelve tournaments she finished in the top ten eight times. She was still having to concentrate and work hard, but she was smiling more now, and she was hopeful.

May 3—the last round of the Women's International at Hilton Head. On the last hole, Miss Whitworth faced a 23-foot birdie putt that would put her in a playoff for the title. She had faced a hundred such putts in her career and in the old days had made more of them than she had missed.

She leaned over the putt. Smoothly she took the putter back and stroked it. The ball went up the incline, slid left, picked up speed, and at the cup turned sharply and dropped into the hole.

The gallery roared and Kathy thrust her arms into the air. She lost the playoff to Sally Little, but she had proved to herself that she could again make the shot when it mattered.

Two weeks later she played in the Coca-Cola Classic at the magnificent old Ridgewood Country Club in New Jersey. It was a fine warm week with the fresh green sparkle of a New England May, and Kathy had a little spring in her step.

"I'm thrilled to be getting closer and closer to winning but it hasn't happened yet," she warned. "I still have a tendency to make some funny swings and get into trouble."

But she shot 69, then 72, and was 5 under par going into the final round. Alice Ritzman, who was twenty-six, was 8 under par and led by three strokes.

In the last round Kathy stumbled early, hitting a ball into a water hazard. Walking back to the tee to replay the shot, she thought, "Stupid, dumb, dumb! Right away my chances of winning are right out the door! You can't make that kind of mistake."

She bogeyed three holes and trailed Miss Ritzman by an overpowering seven shots at the turn. But she had worked too long and too hard to let it get away now. Miss Whitworth birdied the 10th with a fine short iron to the green. On the 15th she made a 10-foot birdie putt, at the 16th a 20-foot birdie putt, and finally she birdied the 17th to make it three in a row. She finished at 8 under. Now she must wait.

She had to hope that Alice would come back to her, and when Miss Ritzman bogeyed four holes on the incoming nine, Kathy had made up seven shots in nine holes. They were tied and would go into a playoff.

During her run of birdies, Kathy had shown her old form.

"I felt very good, very confident at that point," she said. "When we went into the playoff I was very nervous. I hadn't been there in awhile, so it was a good test to see whether I could hold up under pressure."

Hilton Head had been a surprise, she had felt plain lucky to be in that playoff. But this was not a surprise. She had worked for it and had played superbly. She knew only that for three years she had tried to claw her way out of a deep, depressing hole and, if she was to win again, it had to be here, at this place and at this time.

Whitworth versus Ritzman. And who is to say what the win might mean to Alice? She too had struggled. Five times she had failed to win her players' card, and now she had played the best golf of her life.

They teed off in front of a huge gallery and both parred the 10th. The emerald green of the 150-yard par-3 11th hole sat before them in the late-afternoon shadows.

"I knew I had to hit a 7-iron," Kathy said. "I had hit a 7-iron earlier in the day and I knew it was the club."

Miss Ritzman hit first. Perhaps she was too pumped up. She hit her iron too strongly, over the green and to the left. Kathy was up.

"I knew I had to nail it in there. Three years ago I would have stood on the tee, knowing I needed to hit a certain shot and I'd think, How the hell do I *do* it? I can't get the club back. But now I *knew* I could hit that shot because I finally had control over my swing."

The club spanked down cleanly through the ball, sending it soaring at the pin, where it hit, and bit, and stopped nine feet from the hole. Alice chipped short, then chipped again to four feet away. She lay three.

Kathy stood over her birdie putt. She was thinking, she said later, of old friends who had stuck by her. Her eyes moved from the ball to the hole and back to the ball. It all came down to this, this one putt over nine feet of clipped grass. She stroked it smoothly and the ball rolled, then dropped into the hole.

She had won.

She did not thrust her arms into the air as she had done at Hilton Head, but walked quietly to Alice and hugged her.

"My first thought was that I felt sorry for Alice," she said. "But at times last year, and the year before, I thought I could never win again. I really had doubts."

In the pressroom she choked back tears.

"Right now, I don't believe I've won and I can't talk about what this means to me without getting choked up." She stopped and her chin sank down into her chest.

"The win wasn't as important as how I won and the fact that I had been able to play! Playing well is important to me. Winning is important too, but I've won a lot, so it's not that I have to go out and

Nancy Lopez, Debbie Massey, et al., applauded Kathy when Mizuno gave her a strand of pearls for promoting international good will.

prove that I can win. It's just that playing the game is more important now, and playing it well."

That same year Miss Whitworth narrowly lost the United States Women's Open, the one championship she had never won. She led after three rounds and was a great sentimental favorite. Before the final round, she confided to friends that the odds were against her for one reason, it had rained. Once a strapping driver, she could no longer hit it far enough to get to the longest par 4s unless she got roll off the tee. The soggy fairways would suck up her tee shots. No roll.

And so she did not win that year. Pat Bradley made a four-footer on the final hole and was Women's Open Champion. And yet Kathy shone even in defeat. Her third-place finish garnered her $9,000, and she became, at that moment, the first woman to win more than a million dollars in her career. Her fellow players rushed onto the final green with champagne after she holed out.

"She lost the Open, but she never really loses because she's always winning so much respect," said Penny Pulz. "I was proud to be there on the green to toast her."

Pete Axthelm wrote a page about her in *Newsweek*.

"She is the quiet, gracious lady of sport," Axthelm wrote. "Her professional career spans 23 years and 81 tournament victories etched across miles of fairways and highways as she helped women's golf to grow into a thriving business. But Kathy Whitworth has seldom stopped along the route to bask in the spotlight."

She kept playing into her early fifties, years past the age when other great players have retired.

"The press keeps asking me when I'm going to quit," she said. "What's wrong with making golf a lifelong commitment? Why not? I love what I do. Why not continue to do what you love to do, if you're successful at it and get some enjoyment out of it? Even if you're not as successful as some people think you should be, who cares?"

Through sheer tenacity and strength of will, Kathy hung on and began to break the records that we thought were unbreakable. On May 16, 1982, she won the Lady Michelob Classic in Roswell, Georgia, and broke Mickey Wright's LPGA record of eighty-two career victories. In July 1984 at Rochester, New York, she won her eighty-fifth event, breaking Sam Snead's record of eighty-four career victories. She had now won more official professional tournaments than any man or woman in golf.

After that milestone Miss Whitworth returned to Texas and did something she had never done before; she hauled out her scrapbooks.

"I've never looked at them, but I wanted to do it just once," she said.

Near the end of her career, she agreed to serve as LPGA president for a fourth term. One of the issues she faced was the all-exempt tour.

"The LPGA doesn't owe us older players anything," she told me. "The LPGA doesn't owe me anything. All this stuff about what we've done for the LPGA, why, I owe the LPGA everything.

"We've got to make way for these younger players. People don't even know who we are, unless we keep our names in front of the public. You watch, when I quit, after a couple of years people will forget who I ever was."

Kathy was, of course, one of the finest to ever play the game. And yet, when I look beyond her ability, I find her admirable for those qualities that tell a great deal about her character: She is, I think, a more significant person because she watched the younger stars without bitterness and spoke earnestly about the hints of potential greatness that she saw in Nancy Lopez, Betsy King, and Beth Daniel.

Because she submitted to regional qualifying when she first failed to receive an exemption to the U.S. Women's Open, studying the qualifying site, pacing it off and drawing sketches of each hole despite the fact that it was her home course. Because she hid her disappointment when she failed to qualify, answered reporters' questions about that failure, and sent flowers to her friend Bettye Dayton, who drove her golf cart.

Because she hated an easy golf course, or a boring one. Because she refused to play in the LPGA Championship when she felt the site dishonored the tournament.

Because she was a pioneer and drove the narrow highways, helped run the tournaments, and loved her fellow players. Because she never forgot a kindness nor friends who endured when her career began to wane. Because she never turned down an interview or autograph request. Because she tried to learn new shots when she was fifty years old and would not let age chase her from the tour.

Because she wanted to be the best player in the world, and admitted it. Because she loved the game.

The Boom Begins

The Ladies Professional Golf Association enjoyed a number of high points on the hazardous road to prosperity: In 1954 the USGA gave women professionals credibility by assuming sponsorship of the U.S. Women's Open. In the early 1960s, many critics of distaff skill joined the ranks of believers after watching Mickey Wright's ball-striking.

"Mickey got the outside world to take a second look at women's golf," said Judy Rankin, "and when they looked, the discovered the rest of us."

In the late 1970s, Nancy Lopez prompted new interest in the tour. It might even be said that a couple of Japanese stars, 1977 LPGA champion Chako Higuchi and 1987 Player of the Year Ayako Okamoto, helped lure Japanese sponsors to the LPGA. There's little doubt, however, that the LPGA was boosted into the major league sports world of big purses largely through the support of David Foster, the forward-thinking CEO of the Colgate-Palmolive Company.

In 1972 the average LPGA tournament purse was about $30,000. Premier events, like the association's own championship and the Women's Open, offered purses of $50,000 and $40,000 respectively.

Foster, meanwhile, was seeking a new marketing concept for his rapidly expanding conglomerate. Foster, an amateur golfer with a single-digit handicap, sought to appeal to Colgate's natural market—women. Foster approached Bud Erickson, the LPGA's executive director, offering a massive infusion of money.

Colgate, Foster said, would sponsor rich international tournaments and a splashy, celebrity-packed event near Palm Springs, the $110,000 Colgate–Dinah Shore Winner's Circle. He would even hire LPGA players as Colgate spokesmen in television commercials.

Naturally, Erickson accepted.

Foster was a hands-on sponsor. With his attention to detail, the innaugural Colgate–Dinah Shore in 1972 was a grand success. Dinah's show business friends played in the pro-am, and the gra-

Ayako Okamoto, 1989 LPGA Player of the Year.

cious Miss Shore acted as hostess. The tournament was telecast on network television, an occasion prompting sportscaster Heywood Hale Broun to announce that Colgate had pulled the LPGA out of "the sisterhood of the semi-solvent."

Colgate would also sponsor women's tennis and track-and-field events, but golf remained its focus. In 1974 Foster kicked off the Colgate-European Open at Sunningdale Golf Club in England, a $50,000 event for a limited field, and the $72,500 Colgate–Far East Open in Melbourne, Australia. In 1975 Foster started the Colgate–Triple Crown, a $50,000 event for ten players at Doral Country Club in Miami.

Colgate owned Ram Golf Company, a golf equipment manufacturing firm in suburban Chicago, and by 1979 Foster had signed

*Part of the Ram Team on the 1978 Colgate Far East Trip. **(Left to right)** Pam Higgins, Susan O'Conner, Marlene Floyd, Rhonda Glenn, Marlene Hagge, Sandra Post.*

twenty-six women to the Ram advisory staff. He paid them large salaries, prompting other companies, most notably Wilson Sporting Goods Company, to hike the salaries of their own stars to keep them in the fold.

After Foster took the lead, other companies jumped on the LPGA bandwagon. By 1977 the tour had ten events offering purses of $100,000 or more. Colgate's Dinah Shore Winner's Circle still led the way with prize money of $240,000.

David Foster was the LPGA's patron saint, and his company remained involved with the women's tour for a decade.

In 1979 Foster retired from Colgate. Without his driving impetus, the company lost enthusiasm for an LPGA of international scope. The company dropped the foreign tournaments and the Triple Crown, but ran the Dinah Shore Winner's Circle through 1981, when sponsorship was yielded to Nabisco.

Foster, however, had shown the women professionals a grand time, setting a new standard of what the tour might become. He flew players to foreign events by first-class air travel, had them picked up in chauffered luxury cars, and housed them in fabulous hotels. Thanks to Foster, a number of players who had never before traveled the world now visited London, Bangkok, Kuala Lumpur, Melbourne, and Manila. It was a heady time.

Foster signed a number of good and personable players to the Ram staff. He hired stars, of course, but he also hired nonwinners who consistently made a good appearance for the company. In turn, the Ram salaries prompted great loyalty.

Marlene Hagge played in the big leagues of women's golf during five decades.

No one was more appreciative than Marlene Bauer Hagge. "The Gremlin," as she was known, was a founding member of the LPGA. In 1950 Marlene, sixteen, and her sister Alice, eighteen, had turned professional and played lucrative exhibitions. They were graceful and petite, the tour's first glamour girls, and their fresh beauty attracted new male fans to women's golf.

Their golf skills were considerable. Taught by their father, Dave, the Bauer sisters had very long, limber swings. Alice was good enough to be a contender in several major events, and Marlene was a champion. In 1949, at fifteen, she had won the first U.S. Girls' Junior Championship and the Western Girls' title. The Associated Press named her "Woman Athlete of the Year."

The Bauer sisters and Babe Zaharias were golf's most famous

Judy Rankin was the first player to win more than $100,000 in a season.

women, and *Life* magazine named Marlene as one of the year's top teenagers, putting her on a list with Elizabeth Taylor.

Between 1952 and 1972, Miss Hagge won twenty-five tournaments. In 1956 she won the LPGA Championship and was the tour's leading money winner. In 1972 she captured the Burdines Invitational, her last victory.

In the 1970s and 1980s Marlene's ball-striking remained superb. She was one of the few women who could generate the clubhead speed to produce a fine *"Crack!"* when she made contact, but her concentration and putting began to waver. The Ram contract was a nice bonus.

Foster had also signed Judy Rankin. At the age of fifteen, as

Sandra Post, a Canadian, won the LPGA Championship and two Dinah Shore Championships.

Judy Torluemke, her face had graced the cover of *Sports Illustrated*. An interesting sidelight is that, from 1956 through 1987, Judy was one of eight women golfers to appear on the *Sports Illustrated* cover. While the LPGA's official record book notes that in 1987 Patty Sheehan became the first woman golfer to be so honored, women golfers had made many appearances on the *SI* cover. Barbara Romack, at the height of her amateur powers, was the first, in 1956. "Curtis Cup Golfer," noted the cover blurb. Miss Romack was followed, in 1959, by Anne Quast, "Amateur Golf Champ," and in 1960 by Barbara McIntire, "Girl Golf Star."

Judy's cover came in 1961. In 1962 *SI* put Mickey Wright on the cover to promote her article, "How to Hit as Far as a Man." Betsy Rawls was next, in 1964, with an accompanying article on fairway woods.

Nancy Lopez's momentum was recognized with a *Sports Illustrated* cover appearance in 1978. Patty Sheehan was one of eight "Athletes Who Care" in 1987. Althea Gibson, a future LPGA player, was on the cover in 1957, but the great tennis champion appeared as a result of her outstanding tennis skills.

Anyway, the youngest of these cover girls, Judy Rankin, turned pro at seventeen, but seemed unable to take advantage of her natural ability until 1967, when she married Walter "Yippy" Rankin of Midland, Texas.

If there was a man behind the woman, it was Yippy Rankin. A successful insurance agent, he chose to spend most of his time on the tour. Until her marriage, an imperturbable Judy seemed to lack fire.

No longer "The Great Gundy," JoAnne Carner was now "Big Mama."

Yippy, in turn cajoling and encouraging, made her focus on winning.

Yippy suffered as Judy played. His habit of occasionally kicking a tree whenever she missed a shot became a tour joke. But Judy cared a great deal about her husband's opinion. The year after their marriage, Judy won for the first time. In 1976 she was the LPGA's number-one player, the first to crack $100,000 for a year's effort. She led the tour again in 1977. By 1978 she had won twenty-five tournaments.

Judy's grip was unorthodox at best, a hooker's grip of startling severity. At the same time, her swing was very upright. Those factors possibly combined to cause the severe back problems that would eventually lead to back surgery and her retirement from competition. During the mid-1970s, however, from tee to green Judy Rankin was one of the tour's best.

There were a number of good players during the Colgate era. Sandra Post, a fiery young Canadian, was a popular and consistent professional who would capture the LPGA Championship, two Colgate–Dinah Shore titles, and a great deal of money before returning to her native Canada when she tired of the grind.

Debbie Austin, after plodding along for several years, burst through 1977 with five victories. Donna Caponi, the two-time Women's Open champion, nurtured her slow, rhythmical swing to good performances and regularly finished among the top ten on the money list.

JoAnne Gunderson Carner, still going for broke on every shot, was in her prime. She had won the Women's Open in 1971 and 1976. In 1978, on her way to the LPGA Hall of Fame, JoAnne became the first to win $100,000 three years in a row.

Sally Little holed a bunker shot to win the 1977 Women's International at Hilton Head, South Carolina.

Sandra Palmer, a leading money winner, won the U.S. Women's Open in 1975.

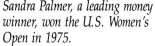

Pat Bradley instantly impressed her colleagues with her talent in the 1970s.

Though young and strong, Pat Bradley was just beginning to develop into the fine player she would become in the next decade. Sandra Palmer, Debbie Massey, and Sally Little were enjoying some great years, while the colorful Amy Alcott, though still a youngster, was one of the tour's top players.

Reporters were again turning to the women's tour for stories. Undeniably, beauty always attracted the press to a woman athlete, and in the 1970s Jan Stephenson was the tour's glamour girl. Turning professional in 1973, Jan joined petite Laura Baugh as the tour's beauties of the decade. Miss Stephenson, however, was more outspoken, posed in suggestive clothing for magazine photographs, and soon got most of the ink.

Susie Maxwell Berning's eleven tour victories included three U.S. Women's Opens.

Jan Stephenson was a big gallery attraction and won three major championships.

Jan had the game to back it up. In 1974 she was "Rookie of the Year." A great fairway wood player and a better putter than she liked to admit, she would soon win tournaments. Despite a number of injuries, she remained a winner through the 1980s and into the 1990s, capturing the U.S. Women's Open, the LPGA Championship, and the du Maurier, among her other titles. Men wrote about her wherever she played, and she was a great asset to the tour.

Hollis Stacy, on the other hand, resembled Shirley Temple. Hollis went into the record books as a mere moppet when she won the U.S. Girls' Junior three straight times, in 1969, 1970, and 1971. In one of those finals she had battled with Amy Alcott in a duel that many remember as the best match-play contest in history.

274

The eternally youthful Hollis Stacy won three U.S. Women's Opens.

Hollis giggled. Hollis told jokes. Hollis was just—well—cute. Well into her thirties she would still look like the U.S. Girls' Junior champion, but Miss Stacy wanted to win the big ones. In fact, they seemed to be the only tournaments to capture her attention. Although she would win quite a few events, her career is remarkable because she won the U.S. Women's Open three times.

Like Susie Maxwell Berning, whose eleven wins included three Women's Open titles, Hollis played her best in the Open. Her first win came at Hazeltine National Golf Club in 1977, when she outlasted new professional Nancy Lopez.

In 1978, through a long, dark afternoon of rain delays at Country Club of Indianapolis, Hollis battled powerful JoAnne Carner. JoAnne had won five U.S. Women's Amateur titles and two Women's Opens. Hollis had her three Girls' Junior titles. Both were so-called "USGA brats." Unlike so many players who suffered nerve attacks at the sight of the USGA flag, they welcomed a USGA championship. That Women's Open came down to the last hole. In the dusk, JoAnne missed a curling putt, Hollis made one, and Miss Stacy jumped into her caddie's arms.

In 1984 Hollis would outlast her old rival Amy Alcott and Rosie Jones in Salem, Massachusetts, to win her third Open title and her sixth USGA championship.

As the 1978 season began, the tour had a fresh infusion of stars as well as continuing good play by veterans like Kathy Whitworth, Sandra Palmer, and Sandra Haynie. With a huge boost from David Foster and Colgate, the LPGA seemed to have broken through to riches and star status.

Indeed, the tour's best days were ahead. Galleries and media attention were growing, and a good share of credit must go to a young woman from New Mexico who would soon dazzle all of golf.

The New Age

After the 1960s, golf, overall, was growing, but the momentum of women's amateur golf shifted: Women's senior golf boomed. College golf grew, spurred by a federal ruling of the 1970s, Title IX, that forced colleges to boost spending for women's sports and led to a big increase in women's golf scholarships. Interest increased in midamateur golf, for women twenty-five and older, prompting the USGA to begin the U.S. Women's Mid-Amateur in 1987.

Serious lifetime amateurs were a vanishing breed, a decline keyed by a combination of factors: Travel became so expensive that most good young amateurs now headed for the pro tours, where expenses were at least deductible. Meanwhile, changing social mores had softened attitudes that professional games were somehow less genteel than amateur competition. Newspapers geared their headlines to pro sports, and amateur results, especially *women's* amateur results, were relegated to the agate type. Television golf coverage exploded and, at home, fans could watch professional golf rather than traipsing after women amateurs.

There were plenty of new golfers, but they were young and unfamiliar. The old stars vanished, many to senior golf and a few, like JoAnne Gunderson Carner, to the LPGA tour.

The Florida Orange Blossom Circuit nearly disappeared. Henry Flagler's railroad route no longer entertained wealthy winter visitors; they flew in on jets. Several of the huge hotels, like the Ponce de Leon and Harder Hall, were shut down.

And so the old tournaments dwindled. After fifty years, more than half were discontinued; the venerable Florida East Coast Championship, the International Mixed Two-Ball, the International Mixed-Foursomes, and the great old Palm Beach Championship bit the dust.

Southern pro events, which had welcomed amateurs, couldn't match the purses and political considerations of the new LPGA Tour. The Sea Island Invitational, the Tampa Open, and the Titleholders faded away. To be sure, they were replaced by glitzy new events, but the LPGA Tour now had to support more than one hundred young pros. In its early, struggling, days, the LPGA had counted on amateurs, some more famous than the pros themselves, to fill out the fields and draw crowds. Now, sadly, there was no longer room for amateurs. They could play in an LPGA event, but only by battling it out with young pros to win a rare qualifying spot.

At the end of the 1980s, the survival of the Orange Blossom

Circuit hinged on four events. The Doherty, the Hollywood Four-Ball, and the South Atlantic remained. The Harder Hall Invitational was saved by the efforts of one woman, Wilma Gilliland, a member of the USGA Women's Committee and the board of the Trans-National Golf Association.

In 1988 the Harder Hall Hotel was in bankruptcy. With her husband, Bruce, Mrs. Gilliland mailed the invitations from her home in Nebraska and collected entry fees on the first tee. Pairings, rulings, and scoring were handled by the pro shop staff. Wilma bought prizes, delicate figures of birds carved by Curtis Cup player Lancy Smith, at Miss Smith's generous discount, and the Harder Hall Invitational staggered into its fifth decade.

Caddies were rare, and players now drove motorized golf carts, which discouraged galleries. Except at the South Atlantic Championship, the crowds dwindled and even final-round matches drew only a hundred or so fans.

The Sally, however, was now sponsored by Oceanside Country Club, and it remained a good place for women amateurs. In 1988 Oceanside was one of the few clubs in the nation with a woman president, a dynamo named Kit Martin. Oceanside members remained boosters of women's amateur golf, and the South Atlantic was run as slickly as a pro event. Gallery ropes lined the fairways. Huge banners welcomed the players. It was a week of great parties, the defending champion had the use of a courtesy Cadillac, and prizes stretched the rules of amateur status to the limit.

Flagsticks for the Sally, appliquéd with the names of past champions—Van Wie, Berg, Zaharias, Romack, Riley, Quast, McIntire, and Bell—struck a poignant note, but the old days were gone. Women's amateur golf had entered a new era.

12

The Lopez Phenomenon

In 1975 the LPGA needed a star.

Without Babe Zaharias the organization would have never gotten off the ground. After Babe died there was Mickey Wright. And then Wright retired. Without at least one dominant personality, an attractive player who could play her way into weekly contention, the tour wouldn't grow.

"We don't have the flash," said Gloria Ehret. "There has to be a Jack Nicklaus or Johnny Miller among us.

"We need more images, more Laura Baughs, more Marilynn Smiths," Miss Ehret said, referring to Laura's beauty and Marilynn's gregarious personality.

Women's professional golf was a perennial underdog, always in need of new fans, new sponsors, and new tournaments. There had been steady growth in LPGA prize money, but "steady" wasn't fast enough. At the same time, men's golf was booming and women tennis players were getting rich—a televised tennis match between Billy Jean King and a male challenger, Bobby Riggs, drew astronomical ratings in prime time.

In 1975 LPGA prize money totaled $1.8 million, while the PGA Tour played for almost $7.9 million. The women professionals were disturbed enough about their purse at the U.S. Women's Open—$55,000 compared to the men's U.S. Open purse of $236,300—to threaten a boycott of the national championship.

They backed off from the boycott, but the emotional issue continued.

"I guess it's a matter of impatience when you get down to it," Carol Mann said that year. "We think we should be farther along. I think the pressure of other women's activities in sports—namely tennis—has shaken all of us up. The publicity that other women's sports has gained has also shaken us up."

The LPGA board fired executive director Bud Erickson and hired a new chief executive, Ray Volpe, a former hockey marketing man.

"Bud is a nice guy who works hard," said Maria Astrologes, a new player. "But he isn't the type of person you want hustling money for tournaments."

In two seasons Volpe managed to hustle LPGA prize money up to $3 million. Over the next few years, the LPGA's purses and television coverage increased, and Volpe took much of the credit. But he had the good fortune to come into office shortly after the Colgate-Palmolive Company, under CEO David Foster, had decided to back the LPGA by sponsoring big-money tournaments. In 1972 Colgate had kicked off the Colgate–Dinah Shore Winner's Circle for an unheard of purse of $110,000.

In 1974 Foster devised two new tournaments, the $50,000 Colgate–European Open in England and the $72,500 Colgate–Far East Open in Australia, flying the entire LPGA field to the events via first-class tickets. In 1975 he added the Colgate–Triple Crown, a limited-field event with a $50,000 purse. Foster even hired LPGA players to star in commercials pitching Colgate products. He put the LPGA on the map.

Colgate's support of the tour prompted other large corporations to jump in with big purses; Kent, Honda, Michelob, Strohs, and J.C. Penney began sponsoring tournaments in 1978. Volpe had signed up the tournaments, but his luck was in his timing—it was Foster's lead that prompted corporate America to boost the LPGA into the big time.

Then, from 1978 through the late 1980s, the LPGA made giant steps into the realm of big money because of one individual—a charismatic young brunette with a dazzling smile: Nancy Lopez. It's no coincidence that from Miss Lopez's rookie year, 1978, through her last year as the tour's number-one player, 1985, LPGA purses jumped to $9 million.

Nancy didn't just arrive on the tour, she burst upon it. She won nine tournaments in 1978 and set a new money-winning mark with $189,813. Nancy became the first professional golfer in history to be named "Player of the Year" as well as "Rookie of the Year." She won the Vare Trophy with a scoring average of 71.76, the first time an LPGA player had averaged less than 72 strokes a round.

Nancy Lopez burst upon the scene when the LPGA tour badly needed a star.

It's difficult to comprehend the impact of a single individual on an entire sport. Miss Lopez had more pure charisma than any player since the Babe, and the game to go with it.

The big splash started after Nancy won her second tournament and second event in a row, the Sunstar Classic in Los Angeles. She would win three tournaments in a row that year, then, following a week off, she would win two more in a row. Public reaction was no less than incredulous.

At that time I represented a golf equipment company in its dealings with a staff of twenty-five LPGA players, including Nancy, and saw firsthand how the world of golf responded to that charisma: fans by the thousands trailed in Nancy's wake. Tournament sponsors prayed that she would win their event. They offered her the use of luxury cars and gave her reserved parking places next to the locker room door. Reporters and photographers swarmed her. Headlines sometimes blared NANCY LOSES BY A STROKE rather than proclaiming the winner.

She appeared on Dinah Shore's television show and the "Tonight Show." Her picture ran on the front page of *The New York Times,* and she graced the cover of *Sports Illustrated*. When she walked down a New York City street on her way to an appearance on "Good Morning America," fans yelled good-luck wishes through their car windows. At the 1979 Women's Open, after an autograph hound accidentally stabbed Nancy's hand with a pen, armed guards were assigned to protect her.

At one tournament she nailed a tee shot into the crowd, and her ball struck a galleryite in the head. Nancy rushed to the scene, bursting

Miss Lopez in her fantastic rookie year.

into tears when she saw blood on the man's forehead. She reached out to hold his hand. The man looked up and said to a friend, "At least I'm going to get a chance to meet her!"

It was the first time anything like it had happened on the LPGA Tour.

Great athletes need strong egos as well as great skills. Golfers are not exempt. The players had been clamouring for a superstar. Now they had one, but some weren't sure they liked it. There's a sort of unspoken rule on the tour: one for all and all for one. Most of the time the players observed it. But many were unsure of Nancy's loyalty to the group, and there was strong grumbling about the attention directed at their new media darling.

One of my favorite angry comments came from a player who had captured her own share of headlines: "Did you hear? The tournament sponsor offered Nancy a reserved parking place, and she took it!"

The grumbling wasn't universal, but Nancy might have enjoyed more peer support had she turned down some of the perks that set her above the others.

However, at twenty-one she handled the uproar very, very well. She ignored any hostility, was gracious, and never turned down an autograph request.

Her appearances for our equipment firm puts her popularity into perspective. In the spring of 1978 I scheduled an appearance at a sporting goods store in a San Diego shopping mall. For two hours the store was packed, and we had some trouble protecting Nancy from her fans. In contrast, two other staff members, both former LPGA Players of the Year, had made a Los Angeles store appearance the previous week, and three people had shown up.

Not all Lopez appearances were boffo. In New Jersey I took several staff players to give a golf clinic at a country club. The players chatted amicably with the members during a luncheon. Minutes before the clinic, Nancy and Sally Little pulled me into the ladies' locker room.

"We want to ask you something," Nancy said. "How do you give a golf clinic?"

I gave them a crash course. They weren't Patty Berg up there, but they got through it.

Miss Lopez was impressive in a remote South Dakota town. She drew about 150 people, mostly school children, to a sporting goods store in the middle of a weekday. Nancy usually made a little speech. This time she instinctively absorbed the audience demographics and spoke with warmth and conviction about the importance of staying in school.

That warmth, her innate feel for people, was a key to Nancy's startling popularity. After all, she wasn't beautiful in the conventional way—she battled a slight weight problem throughout much of her career—but her appearance offered a lot of pluses, lovely hair, glowing skin, and sparkling brown eyes. Her smile was spellbinding, prompting a television film crew to put together a dazzling sequence of Nancy's smiles played to the song "When You Smile." She dressed well, in clothes that were always neat and well-ironed, and had more poise than any young woman I've met.

On the golf course she seldom chatted with fans. She was no showboat. Rather, she walked sedately down the fairway with great dignity, "the Spanish Queen," said one reporter.

People loved her, but not for her manner and appearance alone—Nancy was a winner. Her poise under pressure was one of her greatest assets. Her swing was unorthodox. She addressed the ball with her hands set low, then raised them oddly as she took the club back. But, from the top of her backswing, through the ball, to her finish she was in perfect position.

She hit the ball a long way with her irons, and her driving distance came from a low draw that produced overspin and gave her a lot of roll.

She wasn't merely a good putter, she was a great one, especially on slower greens, and such an intense competitor that she made many, many putts when they mattered most.

She almost never discussed the technical aspects of golf, leading many reporters to believe that she was simply a natural player who automatically, and successfully, fired every shot at the hole.

She *was* a natural player, but she also had a fine golf mind, as I discovered in a discussion at the 1985 Women's Open. One hole, a dogleg to the right, had challenged her, she said.

"That tee has a little right-to-left slope in it," Nancy said, "and you have to be careful; the ball is slightly above your feet, and if you make a normal swing you're going to hook the ball away from the dogleg. Then you have to make sure that you don't block it into the trees on the right."

Despite her seeming innocence about golf's subtleties, she knew the game.

Part of her appeal was in the story of her background. Nancy was born in 1957 in Torrance, California, the daughter of a Mexican-American couple.

The family moved to Roswell, New Mexico, a town of about forty thousand residents, where Domingo Lopez opened an auto-body repair shop.

Both Nancy's parents played golf, and her father had a 3 handicap. When she was eight, Domingo introduced her to the game. Throughout her career he was her only instructor, although pros gave her occasional tips. Nancy's ability was immediately apparent. While she loved golf, she also ran for the track team at Mesa School.

Marina and Domingo Lopez were a hard-working couple, and Domingo spent many long hours in his shop to give Nancy and her older sister, Delma, as many advantages as possible. The family wasn't poor, but money was tight and golf was expensive. Nancy's mother believed there wasn't enough money for three golfers in the family, so she quit playing to allow Nancy to play. It was a sacrifice, because her mother loved to play.

In a 27-hole junior tournament, Nancy won by a margin of 110 strokes. At twelve she captured the New Mexico Women's Amateur Championship. She was now showing great potential, and the Lopezes worked hard to encourage her talent, Domingo doling out his weekly earnings in three piles: "This money is for the house, this money is for Nancy's golf, and this money is for my job."

Nancy played at a municipal course in Roswell. While her parents could not have afforded to join the city's private club, she says as Mexican-Americans they wouldn't have been welcomed as members. Nancy had great pride in her heritage, saying later that she would not have joined the club had she been invited. After playing at the private club in a city tournament, she said she was happy to leave the course, noting "a polite frostiness" that made her glad to return to municipal golf.

Miss Lopez won the U.S. Girls' Junior Championship in 1972 and 1974.

Nancy won the U.S. Girls' Junior in 1972 and 1974, and captured the Western Junior three times. She was reluctant to go to college, believing that her parents couldn't afford the expense. Fortunately, she was awarded a $10,000, four-year golf scholarship by Colgate-Palmolive and entered the University of Tulsa, where she played on the women's golf team. In 1975, as an amateur, she finished second in the Women's Open. In 1976 she won the Trans, the Western, and AIAW Women's Collegiate titles, and was named to the Curtis Cup team and Women's World Amateur team.

After her sophomore year she turned professional, in July 1977. Miss Lopez finished as runner-up in the 1977 U.S. Women's Open, her first tournament as a pro. After waltzing through the LPGA Qualifying School, she played in five LPGA events, finishing second in the Colgate-European and the Long Island Charity Classic.

Nancy Lopez was on her way. In 1978, her first full season of professional golf, she won nine of the twenty-five tournaments she entered, including the LPGA Championship. In 1979 she won eight tournaments and was Player of the Year for the second year in a row.

By 1987 she had won enough tournaments to qualify for the LPGA Hall of Fame. She was inducted into the World Golf Hall of Fame in 1989.

Married to baseball star Ray Knight in 1982, she has two daughters—Ashley, who was born in 1983, and Erin, born in 1986.

She continued to be a consistent winner on the LPGA Tour, adding more victories to her outstanding record. But Nancy's legacy is that she joined the LPGA when the tour most needed a superstar and became a greater star than anyone could have possibly imagined. In her wake, parents encouraged their daughters to play the game, and more young women became interested in a career in professional golf.

Nancy Lopez was a once-in-a-lifetime phenomenon.

More Than a Game

By the last decade of the century, the improved status of women in golf was taken in stride: Breaking all predictions, women made up 40 percent of America's new golfers. They held positions as head professionals, were respected as instructors and golf executives, and even had their own national magazine, *Golf For Women*.

Such gains, however, were hard-won. It took forty years for a women's golf magazine to gain a national foothold. The first effort had been in the 1950s and 1960s, when Dorothy Pease had written and published the *Lady Golfer*, a chatty publication fondly regarded by tournament players that floundered through a lack of advertising dollars. In 1977 publisher William Golden added *Woman Golfer* to his list of sports magazines. A slick, four-color publication, *Woman Golfer* attracted nearly one hundred thousand readers but few advertisers. It folded after eighteen months.

In the late 1980s, women were hailed as golf course architects although they had been designing courses for decades. Marion Hollins, 1921 U.S. Women's Amateur champion, had been the driving force behind Alister Mackenzie's 1929 design of Pasatiempo Golf Club in Santa Cruz, California. Helen Dettweiler, a founder of the Ladies Professional Golf Association, planned and laid out the first golf course totally designed by a woman, Cochran Ranch Golf Course near Palm Springs, California, in the 1950s.

Beginning in the 1970s, Betty Peter drew plans for noted golf architect Joe Lee and was involved in the planning of many of Lee's courses.

A decade later three women had careers in golf course architecture. Alice Dye, an amateur golfer of national stature in the 1960s, began working on course design with her husband, Pete Dye. Mrs. Dye became a crusader for a new two-tee system for women, advocating a set of forward tees for women golfers of lesser skill.

Jan Beljan, daughter of a Pittsburgh-area golf professional, was a course architect/senior designer for Tom Fazio's design company of Jupiter, Florida, and worked on the designs of some notable golf courses, including Wild Dunes in Isle of Palms, South Carolina, and the Vintage Club in Indian Wells, California.

"Respect," said Miss Beljan, "can only be earned. That was achieved on daily supervisory jobs by being there as long and working as hard as everyone else—every day, daylight to dusk."

Rachel M. Therrien, a former golf shop worker at Bangor (Maine) Municipal Golf Course, became a golf architect with the firm of Geoffrey S. Cornish and Brian M. Silva of Amherst, Massachusetts. She had been a member of the green crew at hallowed Winged Foot Golf Club, then assistant superintendent at Westchester Country Club while studying related subjects at several universities.

Judy Bell (with glasses) with her victorious 1988 U.S. Women's World Amateur Team.

"I have seen golf course management and design work change from much manual effort to skills highly mechanized and technical," Miss Therrien said. "More surprisingly, perhaps, I've witnessed a male-focused culture give way to a more cosmopolitan one."

One of the most noteworthy advances, however, came among the ranks of golf's volunteers.

Judy Bell, the daughter of Mr. and Mrs. Carl Bell of Wichita, Kansas, was born in 1936, the youngest of four children and the only girl. At the age of twelve her picture had graced *Golf World* magazine as a promising young golfer. She caused quite a stir. When she won Helen Lengfeld's California Girls' Junior, an open tournament, at the age of fifteen, Judy's homecoming in Wichita was greeted by the local high school band.

Miss Bell developed into a very fine amateur, capturing the Trans-Mississippi Championship, the Broadmoor Ladies' Invitational, and a number of titles on the Florida winter circuit. In 1960 and 1962, during the reign of amateur stalwarts JoAnne Gunderson, Anne Quast, and Barbara McIntire, she was named to the American Curtis Cup team.

In the 1964 U.S. Women's Open at San Diego Country Club, a par-73 layout of 6,470 yards, she fired 31-36—67, which tied the lowest Women's Open score in history and set a record for amateurs.

A long hitter, Judy had a fluid swing that, while technically correct, was more impressive for its natural grace. She was capable of phenomenal scoring and, but for a chipping disability rather like the "yips" in putting, many thought she would have won every amateur title.

But Miss Bell had other talents. With Barbara McIntire she started a mail-order clothing business and at amateur tournaments sold Bermuda shorts out of the trunk of her car. The enterprise flourished, and they eventually opened several fine clothing shops at the posh Broadmoor Hotel in Colorado Springs, Colorado.

Colorado Springs, where her family had summered when she was a child, became Miss Bell's home. With Miss McIntire she opened offices in a charmingly renovated cottage. The two women signed on as volunteers with the United States Golf Association, and for many years the constant ringing of the telephone and the flurry of mail at their offices signaled that Colorado might well become the center of women's amateur golf.

Judy—chairman of the USGA's Women's Committee from 1981 though 1984, permanent chairman of the Broadmoor Ladies' Invitational, twice captain of the American Curtis Cup team—devoted herself to improving the status of women's championships.

From the USGA's expert on rules and competitions, P.J. Boatwright, she learned to set up competition courses and at most USGA women's championships could be seen pacing the course in sneakers, rain suit, and a rather eccentric straw hat, paint can in hand, as she set the hole and tee placements.

A woman of keen intellect and a tireless worker who thrived on responsibility, Miss Bell easily vaulted the barriers placed on many women, yet it was a startling development when, in 1987, she became the first woman to crack the all-male bastion of the Executive Committee of the United States Golf Association, the rule-making body that also runs all American championships.

The following year she was appointed to the Rules Committee of the annual Masters tournament at Augusta National Golf Club in Georgia.

Such responsibilities, never before assumed by a woman, clearly made her an exception to all previous rules, and Miss Bell had gone further in golf administration than she had ever expected.

However, in 1990, at the age of fifty-three, she was elected Treasurer of the USGA, the only woman ever elected as an officer.

Miss Bell was perhaps the only person in golf surprised at her election. In the following months various golf magazines speculated that she would one day be USGA president, an idea she was quick to scotch. Nevertheless, the speculation seemed justified and, considering that the first president of the first women's golf organization, the Ladies Golf Union, had been a man, women's golf appeared to have come full circle.

Vicki Goetz, 1989 U.S. Women's Amateur Champion.

The Amateurs

The century's last decade saw the arrival of new amateur stars and elevated the status of one older one. Anne Quast Sander remained a phenomenon, playing fine golf into her mid-fifties and performing well enough to be named to the 1990 American Curtis Cup team.

Vicki Goetz of Hull, Georgia, on the other hand, was a teenager. With Brandie Burton of San Bernardino, California, Miss Goetz was the newest remarkable amateur. She won the 1989 U.S. Women's Amateur, finished as low amateur in the Women's Open in 1989 and 1990, and was an easy Curtis Cup selection. A remarkable short game, accurate driving and iron play, and emotional discipline were her greatest assets.

Brandie Burton, at eighteen, was one of the longest hitters in quite some time, often nailing her drives well over 250 yards. A powerful five feet seven inches, she was able to generate the clubhead speed of a man and thrilled galleries with her rifling shots. Winning the U.S. Girls' Junior in 1989, runner-up to Miss Goetz in the 1989 Women's Amateur, she was a student at Arizona State. In seven collegiate tournaments, she was medalist in six and was named to the Curtis Cup team in 1990.

Carol Semple Thompson winning the 1990 Women's Mid-Amateur Championship.

At the end of the year, friends urged her to turn professional. She frankly had overpowered most amateur opponents, but a nagging injury gave emphasis to the decision. Brandie had injured her knee in a swimming accident several years before, and the injury often made it difficult for her to swing, even walk. Most were concerned that she would be unable to play golf for long and might as well test her talents on the professional tour. She joined the LPGA in October 1990 and placed very well in her first tournaments. If the knee holds up, her future has great promise.

Carol Semple Thompson of Sewickley, Pennsylvania, remained a class act. Her fine record included victories in the 1973 U.S. Women's Amateur and the 1974 British Amateur. She was a member of six Curtis Cup teams. One of her finest qualities was her longevity as a good player. Carol rededicated herself to competition in the 1980s and continued to record fine finishes, winning several key Florida events and finishing as low amateur in the 1988 U.S. Women's Open.

The veteran player with the long graceful swing became the heart of the 1990 American Curtis Cup team. Her quiet dedication was an inspiration to all, and no one enjoyed the American victory more than Mrs. Thompson.

In 1990 she captured the U.S. Women's Mid-Amateur Championship on her home course, Allegheny Country Club in Sewickley. With her mother, Phyllis Semple, a fine amateur of the 1960s, on hand for the presentation, Carol's win was an emotional and popular victory.

Juli Simpson Inkster's record in the Women's Amateur boggles the mind. After marrying golf professional Brian Inkster in 1980, she won the Women's Amateur on her honeymoon. She repeated in 1981 and 1982, the first woman since Virginia Van Wie to capture three state Women's Amateur championships.

Mrs. Inkster joined the LPGA Tour in 1983. She won two majors the very next year, the Nabisco–Dinah Shore and the du Maurier Classic. A seemingly laid-back person, she was a fierce competitor, and few were surprised that she won thirteen events, including four in 1986, her best season.

After the birth of daughter Hayley in February, Juli's 1990 season was, naturally, something of a comeback year, and she played in only eighteen events, but the swing that took her to the top of all of amateur golf promises to take her to a fine record as a professional.

In the Eye of the Storm

By the late 1980s the old days of camaraderie and caravans were gone, but prosperity had arrived. In 1989 Betsy King led all money winners on the LPGA Tour with $654,000. Beth Daniel won $863,000 in 1990.

Miss Daniel, a native of Charleston, South Carolina, had been through several ups and downs. Turning professional in 1979 after winning the 1975 and 1977 U.S. Women's Amateur, she was hailed as a rival for Nancy Lopez. The comparison did not sit well with Beth. A sensitive, highly strung individual, she resented predictions of greatness. Potential is a terrible burden and Beth, despite an unorthodox grip that caused her to sometimes block shots to the right, was considered by many to have the best golf swing since Mickey Wright.

In the early years she felt that she wasn't able to live up to such predictions.

"I've always felt that I had to prove myself," Miss Daniel said in 1983. "I've never felt people thought that much of me, I guess. I think anyone who has a lot of given talent probably has more pressure on them. I get mad when people say I'm a waste of talent. They don't realize how hard I work. But, I don't know, I've been put in a tough situation."

At the beginning of her rookie season, a sportswriter signed on

Beth Daniel, 1990 LPGA
Player of the Year.

as her caddie. Beth Daniel was going to be the subject of a book before she even stepped on the first tee. It all boiled over in her first tournament. She finished in a tie for seventh, hurled four clubs, and on the final hole heaved her ball into a lake.

"I had just come out on the Tour and all of a sudden I was being compared to Lopez," Beth said. "It was like walking around with a 500-pound weight on my shoulders."

Nevertheless, Miss Daniel was Rookie of the Year, winning a tournament and nearly $100,000. In 1980 and 1981 she led all money winners. While she had great success, it was disappointment that she most remembered. Like losing the 1981 U.S. Women's Open to Pat Bradley by one stroke after finishing the championship at 8 under par. That one sent her to the back benches of the locker room in tears.

In the 1982 Women's Open she seemed more relaxed and led the championship going into the final round. At the eighth hole Beth led by a stroke. She hit a fine iron shot to the green and faced a birdie putt that would give her a two-shot edge. She addressed the putt, then looked up and said, "The ball moved!"

No one had seen the ball move, not her fellow competitors, not the USGA officials, not even Beth Daniel. "But I was positive it

Betsy King winning the 1990 U.S. Women's Open. She also won in 1989.

moved," Beth said later. "I always set my putter down with a certain amount of space between the blade and the ball and the space wasn't there. I knew it had rolled. Why did it have to happen in the Open?"

Was there any doubt that she would call the penalty on herself? "No, I knew."

She failed to win, but such conduct, in the best traditions of the game, can make you pull for a player, and Beth's fans looked forward to the future. For the next few years she was a consistent winner and won at least one tournament a year through 1985. In 1986, hampered by a bad back, she dropped to twenty-first on the money list and to twenty-ninth in 1987. In 1988 she was absent for thirteen weeks with a bout of mononucleosis.

The illness caused her to take stock. She had paid a price for her bad attitude, and she believed she had gotten lazy.

"I lay on the couch all that time and thought about how much I love golf and how much I missed the competition," she said. "I came back on tour with new determination."

Returning in 1989, Miss Daniel had something to prove. "I had to show people, and myself, that I wasn't going to quit, that I could still play this game."

In 1989 she won four events. In 1990 she won more money than anyone in history and shot nine consecutive rounds in the 60s. There were personal bests as well: She shot a 63, a career low, and won the 1990 LPGA Championship, her first major. From August 1989 through the end of the 1990 season, she won eleven tournaments and more than $1 million.

At the age of thirty-six, Miss Daniel had come into her own.

Unlike Beth Daniel's, Betsy King's early years were fraught with winless frustration. But she had shown potential as an amateur—she finished eighth in the 1976 Women's Open, the best amateur finish in a decade—and she had talent.

Through the first seven years of her pro career Betsy finished no higher than fourteenth on the money list. The problem was a swing flaw. She was a long hitter but had a reverse pivot, keeping too much weight on her left side on the backswing, then falling back on her right foot through the area of impact. The flaw caused inconsistency, but Miss King, like Miss Daniel, is a hard worker.

Teaching professional Ed Oldfield pointed out the flaw, and Betsy's constant practice paid off. From 1984 through 1986 she won seven tournaments. In 1987 her four victories included two of the tour's most prestigious events, the Nabisco–Dinah Shore and the McDonald's Championship, and she vaulted to second on the money list. The following year she won three tournaments. But Betsy's banner year was 1989—she captured the U.S. Women's Open and finished the season with more than $600,000 in winnings, a new record.

While Beth Daniel dominated the tour in 1990, Miss King captured world attention with her second straight U.S. Women's Open victory and another major, the Nabisco–Dinah Shore.

Betsy was a quiet person who showed little emotion, but she was a great perfectionist, a fine striker of the ball, and a wonderful putter. Since 1983 her scoring average had been slightly over 71 strokes.

Like Miss Daniel, Miss King was a graduate of Furman University. While the two women were highly competitive, it was a friendly rivalry that could spur each to new heights and, of all modern players, Betsy King and Beth Daniel may eventually have careers of historic proportion.

Only one player, Mickey Wright, has ever held four major championship titles in the same year. But Pat Bradley almost equalled history in 1986, when she won the LPGA Championship, the du Maurier Classic, and the Nabisco–Dinah Shore. Only the U.S. Women's Open escaped her. It was a remarkable achievement.

Miss Bradley looked like a winner from the first minute she joined the tour in 1974. A strong young woman, she was a former skier and could hit the ball a very long way. She had a natural, smooth swing with a long arc, and there were many predictions that Miss Bradley would become a truly fine player.

Pat Bradley won three of the four majors in 1986.

A native New Englander, she was part of a large, close family.

"I cannot repay what they've done," she said. "My brothers and parents sacrificed. It was always, Make sure Pat gets to a tournament, make sure Pat has the best equipment. The only way I can repay them is in my career, which we can all share."

Pat had always known what she wanted, and that was to be a great player.

"When I joined the tour I went right to the sources, right to the great players," she said. "I didn't hang out with my contemporaries. I wanted to get to know players like Kathy Whitworth, Judy Rankin, Marlene Hagge, Sandra Post, Donna Caponi, the top players. I played practice rounds with them. They were winners and I wanted to see how they operated.

"I played with Marlene Hagge for the first time in England," Pat recalled. "I remember being told she was the fastest player on tour. 'Don't hold up Marlene,' I was told. On the first hole, I took a 9 but I

Miss Bradley (shown here in 1990) bounced back from an illness to again be a dominant player.

was in the hole before Marlene made her 4. I didn't want to hold her up.

"The tour was smaller then, we were dealing with a total field of 75 to 80 players. The first tee time was 10 A.M. and the last tee time was noon. We were all prime time."

Miss Bradley's first instruction came from John Wirbal of Nassua, New Hampshire, who gave her the basics. In the late 1970s she began taking lessons from former LPGA touring professional Gail Davis. Miss Davis eased her out of a tendency to aim to the right, helped her develop a proper setup for each shot, and provided the less tangible morale boost that Pat needed. A thumb injury also made some swing changes unavoidable, and Miss Bradley's swing lost its rich fullness, but she became a more controlled player. She had always been an excellent putter. She began a steady march up the money list, second in 1978 and 1985, third in 1981 and 1983.

In 1986 she enjoyed a golden season, winning three major titles

Patty Sheehan, a leading professional and a fan favorite, at the 1988 U.S. Women's Open.

and two regular tour events. The following season wasn't quite up to her newly set standards, she won but one tournament. In 1988 Pat's career seemed to bottom out. She won only $15,000 and spent the year in misery. When she was diagnosed as having hyperthyroidism, the cause was discovered. After treatment she rebounded and in the next two seasons won more than $900,000.

"It's tremendous truth that if you set your mind to something, if the will is there, you will find a way," she said. "But it's something you have to go through, the trials and tribulations."

The year Pat Bradley joined the professional ranks, Patty Sheehan of Middlebury, Vermont, was a high school student. One of the top junior skiers in the nation, Patty switched to golf and had a brilliant college career at San Jose State, where she won the 1980 AIAW National Championship.

She turned professional that same year and was an instant success. Competing in only six events, she averaged nearly $3,000 a tournament. In 1981, her first full season, Miss Sheehan won a tournament and finished eleventh on the money list. She has not been out of the top ten since and has won twenty-five tournaments with an average of just over 71 strokes per round.

Capturing the LPGA Championship in 1983 and 1984, she seemed destined for great things and was the tour's 1983 Player of the Year. In 1984 she won the Vare Trophy. She crossed the million-dollar mark in 1985, the fastest player to do so, in just four years and nine months.

Barely topping five feet three inches, Miss Sheehan was remarkably strong for her size. She had tremendous leg drive and a fine, efficient, natural swing. On occasion her swing became somewhat flippy, a slight looseness that resulted in her only bad strokes, but she had a good short game and was an excellent bunker player. Her game had few flaws.

Patty was one of those unique players who dare to be different. When everyone else sported tailored shorts, she began wearing plus fours, or "knickers," as we Americans call them, and her colorful wardrobe became her trademark.

An effervescent young woman, she liked to chat and joke with the crowd, but her jovial spirit went hand-in-hand with an emotional personality. Sometimes Patty wanted so much to win that she pressured herself right out of a seeming victory. Her downfall in the 1990 U.S. Women's Open, where she lost a nine-stroke lead after 36 holes, would haunt her for many months.

She was a many-faceted personality. Of a sometimes serious nature, she was deeply affected by the plight of abused youngsters and provided the financial backing for a California home for teenaged girls called "Tigh Sheehan." She invested a great deal of time and money in this cause and, for her concern, was featured as one of *Sports Illustrated* magazine's Sportsmen of the Year in 1987, as one of eight "athletes who care." In 1985 she won the Founders Cup and in 1986 was the Samaritan Award winner for her commitment to improving the lot of others.

Miss Sheehan went through her own difficult time in 1989. A massive California earthquake nearly leveled her newly built house, which was uninsured. For Patty, a great natural athlete to whom success came easily, it was a personal tragedy, but the loss exposed a certain steely side of her character and spurred her to great achievements in 1990.

Under great financial pressure, she felt as if she were starting over and yet played the best golf of her career. For the first time, her yearly scoring average dipped below 71, to 70.62 strokes per round, and she won five tournaments and $732,000. She had not only secured her bank account, she had proven that she could play fine golf in adverse circumstances. I would not be surprised if her performance under pressure spurs her to even greater play in future years.

Laura Davies, 1987 U.S. Women's Open Champion.

Other talented players emerged on the LPGA Tour: Laura Davies, the longest hitter in women's golf, was from England. Regularly belting her tee shots nearly 280 yards, and often further, she captured the 1987 U.S. Women's Open in a playoff with JoAnne Carner and Ayako Okamoto and went on to win several regular tour events.

Miss Okamoto, a star softball pitcher in Japan, had a natural, fluid swing. While hampered by a bad back, she remained a champion and was the LPGA's 1987 Player of the Year. Ayako focused the attention of the Japanese media on American professional golf, following in the footsteps of Chacko Higuchi, one of the most accomplished of international players who, in 1977, won the LPGA Championship and during her career captured dozens of tournaments in Japan.

Colleen Walker, a native of Florida, won the Vare Trophy in 1988 and contended in several major championships. With Sherri Turner, Rosie Jones, Liselotte Neumann, and Dottie Mochrie, she was one of the era's more promising players.

In 1990 women's professional golf had grown to truly international stature. The LPGA Tour was strong and was complemented by women's pro tours in Europe and Japan as well as several satellite tours in the United States. It was appropriate that the great growth of women's golf should be celebrated by a truly international event, and

Liselotte Newman winning the 1988 U.S. Women's Open.

the pros kicked off a noteworthy international team competition.

It was called the Solheim Cup, and the inaugural was staged at Lake Nona Golf Club in Orlando, Florida. An American team headed by captain Kathy Whitworth trounced a European team captained by former British Amateur champion, Michelle Walker, 11½ points to 4½. The Americans simply overpowered their opposition but, as in the Curtis Cup Match, the international rivalry was intense.

The event shows much promise. It will increase international interest in women's golf and add to the distaff game's competitive lustre.

The New Amateurs

The world largely ignored the first U.S. Women's Mid-Amateur Championship when it was played at Southern Hills Country Club in Tulsa, Oklahoma, in October 1987.

There was no admission charge, yet through the first rounds there was also virtually no gallery, just a few idle club members following women golfers who were their house guests for the week.

A club waiter taped some of the tournament on a home video camera. The local newspaper sent one reporter to Southern Hills. The only other press representative on hand was George Eberl, managing editor of *Golf Journal*. The *Journal*, published by the USGA, naturally covered all USGA championships, but Eberl also had a proprietory interest in the Women's Mid-Am.

He looked kindly upon women's golf. A native Californian, Eberl won awards as an investigative reporter for *Stars & Stripes* in Germany before finding a pleasant niche with the USGA. At golf he was a self-confessed hacker and on a good day shot around 100 with his antiquated clubs. But the game's language and lore delighted his literary nature, and Eberl was something of a crusader. He found the old game ripe for his efforts to promote two decidedly liberal causes. One was the environment, a passion that he pursued in articles about coastline preservation, water conservation, and toxic fertilizers. Eberl's second interest was equality for women. He had lobbied hard for a women's mid-amateur and was now on hand to observe the event that, with several key USGA officials, his persistence had helped to create.

Saturday, the first day of 36-hole qualifying, was bitterly cold. At dusk Friday a long line of blue clouds had formed on the northern horizon and rolled ominously southward. This strange front, a "blue norther," plunged temperatures into the forties, and a stinging north wind threatened to upend the starter's tent on the first tee.

It was a bitter beginning for the new tournament.

A thin, pert-looking California player with long black hair tossed her golf bag onto the first tee.

"Anybody want to caddie?" she said.

A man in a windbreaker picked up the bag.

"Understand, this is a volunteer job," the young woman said. "I can't pay you."

The man nodded. At the end of nine holes he bought a soft drink and crackers and shared them with his golfer. She had no money, he knew, but she had charm and courage.

Earlier in the year, what was left of the amateur ranks had begun to prepare: Polly Riley's decision to play was a big commitment. Competition would take a physical toll. Her hair was gray and she squinted at her scorecard through bifocals. She had endured several

Polly Riley, a fierce competitor since the 1940s, returned to tournament play in 1987.

painful medical problems in recent years, and while she looked fit, a nagging injury to her Achilles' tendon had caused her to ride electric golf carts. No golf carts would be allowed in the Mid-Amateur or in the qualifying rounds.

Miss Riley, however, brushed off suggestions that she include walking in her training regime for the upcoming tournament.

"I won't walk until I have to," she smirked, "I know how to walk—you put one foot in front of the other. Left, right. Left, right."

The prospect of a new national match-play championship tickled a long-dormant competitive streak, and Polly attacked the tournament with all her savvy. On the eve of the Dallas qualifying round, she went far out onto the course to survey the 13th hole. Like a commander surveying a battlefield on the eve of conflict, she paced the yardage and peered at a water hazard that had swallowed her tee shot earlier that day. She practiced putting until dark and discovered that if she moved her hands slightly forward at address, her stroke became smooth and consistent. She had prepared for the qualifier for nearly two months.

Barbara Fay Bodie drove to Dallas from Louisiana. Mrs. Bodie was the mother of four sons, the youngest of whom was twelve. Two decades earlier, as Barbara Fay White, she had been a Curtis Cup player, a tall, slender woman whose startling accuracy and determination had helped her win a number of important titles. Barbara Fay was a great match player, somber and stoic, but she was good at stroke play, too, and had set several scoring records.

She had turned professional for a short time, then regained her amateur status. Now she was literally building her own golf course in Louisiana. Mrs. Bodie had hired a golf architect to design the layout, but she and her sons were doing the construction work. For several years she had been wheeling bulldozers and trucks around the property, shoving earth into mounds for greens and tees, and sculpting fairways and bunkers with the same sinewy strength and iron-jawed will that had once defeated human opponents.

Like Polly Riley, she was facing her first USGA competition in many years.

The USGA had kicked off a mid-amateur championship for men in 1980, limiting the field to players twenty-five years old and older and deliberately excluding vast numbers of college players who used amateur golf merely as a stepping stone to the professional tour.

Organizers of these mid-am championships sought the true amateur golfer. Finding such players seemed a Diogenic task. Modern golf was geared for profit: corporations offered point money to the leading professionals, real estate developments hosted pro tournaments in order to sell homesites, foreign corporations flew planeloads of players to Japan and Britain to promote products.

On the flip side of amateur golf, colleges vied for the best young players and offered scholarships worth tens of thousands of dollars.

In the 1980s one more amateur tournament might seem inconsequential, but it was the beginning of a needed revival.

The amateur ideal was handed down by the English in the days of the leisure class, when sport was pursued for its own sake, mostly in the spring and summer. The old idea was that an amateur was a lady or a gentleman, but that a professional, who pursued sport as a trade, was a notch below that.

Modern amateurs found it increasingly expensive to compete, yet the Rules of Golf barred players from accepting expense money.

As early as 1929, Glenna Collett, America's great woman amateur, had warned that the original amateur code was on the brink of oblivion.

"We have strayed far from the amateur ideal just as we have from armoured knights and fainting ladies," Miss Collett wrote in her memoirs. "America has no place for the gentleman of leisure."

Glenna Collett, America's first great amateur star, predicted tough times for future amateur competitors.

Glenna favored creating a special category of "tournament players," skilled amateurs who, like amateur tennis players of that era, would be allowed to accept tournament expenses and entry fee money. Miss Collett in no way saw this as the demise of playing games strictly for fun.

"The great majority, who are less skilled, will form the backbone and sinew of sport. The real amateurs will use the courts of private residences, will crowd the private country-club links and municipal courses, will play polo far from cheering crowds," she wrote.

Her idea never caught on.

Financial pressure created tension among the top amateurs. Some privately accused others of violating amateur rules by secretly accepting expense money from unknown sponsors. There was seldom any concrete evidence of these violations, but amateurs who competed frequently without any visible means of support were regarded with suspicion.

In 1962 Anne Quast Decker, the reigning U.S. Women's Amateur champion, wrote a letter to the USGA complaining that some players were known to accept financial help. Mrs. Decker contended that the honest amateur should not be penalized for honesty. She said the USGA should consider changing the rules to allow skilled amateurs to accept expense money.

Philip H. Strubing, a lawyer from Philadelphia, was chairman of the USGA's Amateur Status and Conduct Committee. Strubing eloquently outlined the USGA's position in his answer.

> To define "expenses" would be difficult. Logically, "expenses" could include not only money for travel, board and lodging, but expenditures for golf clubs, balls, clothing, etc. Even if "expenses" were limited to travel, board and lodging, it would be difficult, if not impossible, to fix the amount.
>
> You indicate that a number of "amateurs" now violate the existing rule on expenses. If "expenses" were permitted, we believe the same players would and could cheat. For example, it would be easy to accept money for first class travel, but use cheaper facilities.
>
> Inevitably a class of player would come into existence who would spend his time going from tournament to tournament on "expense" money supplied by others. Such players would make golf their primary interest,—a vocation, in fact. As such, they should compete against professionals, not against those for whom golf is a secondary interest, played solely for pleasure.
>
> In the long run, it would be found that only the better amateur players would be able to obtain expense money from outside sources. This would indeed be unfair to other amateurs of less proficiency. The latter group would soon tire of competing against the former.
>
> . . . What it comes down to is really this: Most if not all of us are unable to do some things we'd like to do for want of funds with which to do them. That is the natural order. To distort the natural order in such an activity as golf is to distort both the activity and those who participate in it. . . .
>
> One final point. You ask if the USGA is really "blind" to all that goes on in the matter of financing of individuals' golf expenses. The USGA is not and does not attempt to be a policing organization. We have neither the means nor the desire to play detective on players holding themselves out as amateurs. The same principle applies to the Rules of Golf, which must be enforced by the player himself. Golf, above all other games, is a game of self-discipline. We do not expect any player consciously to violate the Rules of Golf; neither do we expect any player to violate the Rules of Amateur Status.

A decade later, a loophole in the amateur status rules had combined with a federal law to create an entirely new class of amateur—the college player. College golfers spent much of their time going from tournament to tournament on expense money supplied by their colleges and universities.

In the 1970s women's college golf boomed to near-parity with men's college golf because of the Title IX provision of federal law that required colleges and universities to increase spending for women's sports programs. Colleges boosted their tennis, track, and golf programs, pumped new money into women's sports scholarships, and budgeted for women's golf teams to travel to competition.

The Rules of Amateur Status allowed golfers to accept such

START	LEADERS	HOLE	1	2	3	4	5	6	7	8	9	10	11	12	13	14	15	16	17	18	MESSAGES
		PAR	4	4	3	4	4	5	4	3	5	3	4		5	4	3	5	4	4	
5	ALCOTT		6	5	5	4	4	4	4	4	4	4	5		5	5	4	5	5		
3	STACY H		3	3	3	4	4	3	3	4	4	4	4		4	3	4	4	5		
10	GARBACZ		10	10	9	9	10	9	11	11	11	11	10		10	10	10	9	9	10	OLIVER
4	DANIEL		3	3	4	4	5	5	6	6	6	6	7		7	8	8	8	10	11	LOW AMATEUR
8	CLARK		8	8	8	9	10	10	10	10	9	8	8		8	8	8	8	8	8	+ 22
5	McMULLEN		4	4	5	5	6	7	7	7	7		7		7	7	7	8	7		USGA OPEN
5	BLALOCK		5	5	5	5	5	5	6	6		6	6		6	6	8	8	10		RECORD
7	BRUCE		7	7	7	8	9	8	9	9		7			8	9	9	9	9		284
6	YOUNG D		6	6	6	7	6	6	7	8					10	10	10	9	8		
4	LOPEZ		4	5	6	7	8	9	10	10	9	9			11	11	10	10	10		

Amy Alcott, here winning the 1980 U.S. Women's Open, has helped lead women's golf toward a bright future.

scholarships, grant-in-aid, and college tournament expenses.

College players, gearing up for the pro ranks, became tournament tough. Their college tournament schedules gave them an edge over women who pursued careers, raised children, and chose not to take golf so seriously as to spend life soaking their golf socks in the bathroom sinks of remote motel rooms on the pro tour.

At any rate, the changing face of amateur golf inspired changes, and in September 1986 the USGA's executive committee approved the first U.S. Women's Mid-Amateur Championship for players of at least age twenty-five. Regional qualifying rounds were staged at thirty sites the following August.

Wind came up the morning of the Dallas qualifying round but did little to ease the searing heat. Older players suffered, becoming light-headed and faint as their aging cardiovascular systems pumped with creaky inefficiency. Women club members in electric carts dashed from one group to the next, dispensing Gatorade, salt tablets, ice, and wet towels like ambulance nurses at the front.

Barbara Fay Bodie's legs were giving out and her concentration drifted in the heat. Polly Riley was struggling as well. Miss Riley draped a wet towel around her neck and damp strands of gray hair wreathed her face. When a friend passed, she raised her hand in a weak salute and trudged on. Head down. Resolute.

In the end, Mrs. Bodie's score was too high and Barbara Fay lounged in the locker room, sipping a beer and contemplating the unfamiliar sensation of defeat.

"It's the walking," she said. "When we play at the Broadmoor, in the mid-am division, we ride carts and I shoot in the 70s and it's just fine. But I don't have time to walk and play golf any more."

Polly Riley shot 83, knocking out players nearly forty years her junior to grab the last Dallas qualifying spot. Her nephew, Mike Riley, had caddied for her, and the two stood in front of the scoreboard with their arms around each other. Polly, a lifelong amateur, would be going to the first U.S. Women's Mid-Amateur Championship.

It has been nearly one hundred years since the very first women's championship was staged in Great Britain. As women's golf moves into its second century, competition is keen and there are more tournaments, more fine players, and a larger cast of golfers of all skill levels than ever before. The first one hundred years of women's golf produced historic players who developed despite adverse circumstances. Hundreds of remarkable women have promoted the game, and the future looks very bright indeed.

Appendix

The Record Book of Women's Golf

British Women's Open Amateur Championship

Year	Winner, Runner-up	Year	Winner, Runner-up	Year	Winner, Runner-up
1893	Lady Margaret Scott Issette Pearson	1903	Rhona Adair F. Walker-Leigh	1913	Muriel Dodd Evelyn Chubb
1894	Lady Margaret Scott Issette Pearson	1904	Lottie Dod May Hezlet	1914	Cecil Leitch Gladys Ravenscroft
1895	Lady Margaret Scott E. Lythgoe	1905	Bertha Thompson M.E. Stuart	1915–19	No Championship (World War I)
1896	Amy Pascoe Lena Thomson	1906	Mrs. W. Kennion Bertha Thompson	1920	Cecil Leitch Molly Griffiths
1897	Edith C. Orr N. Orr	1907	May Hezlet Florence Hezlet	1921	Cecil Leitch Joyce Wethered
1898	Lena Thomson Elinor Neville	1908	Maud Titterton Dorothy Campbell	1922	Joyce Wethered Cecil Leitch
1899	May Hezlet J. Magill	1909	Dorothy Campbell Florence Hezlet	1923	Doris Chambers Mrs. Muriel Dodd MacBeth
1900	Rhona Adair Elinor Neville	1910	Elsie Grant-Suttie Lily Moore	1924	Joyce Wethered Mrs. Beryl Hawtrey Cautley
1901	Mary Graham Rhona Adair	1911	Dorothy Campbell Violet Hezlet	1925	Joyce Wethered Cecil Leitch
1902	May Hezlet Elinor Neville	1912	Gladys Ravenscroft Stella Temple		

Year	Winner, Runner-up	Year	Winner, Runner-up	Year	Winner, Runner-up
1926	Cecil Leitch Mrs. Percy Garon	1952	Moira Paterson Frances Stephens	1972	Michelle Walker Claudine Cros Rubin
1927	Simone Thion de la Chaume Dorothy Pearson	1953	Marlene Stewart Philomena Garvey	1973	Ann Irvin Michelle Walker
1928	Nanette le Blan S. Marshall	1954	Frances Stephens Elizabeth Price	1974	Carol Semple Angela Bonallack
1929	Joyce Wethered Glenna Collett	1955	Jessie Valentine Barbara Romack	1975	Nancy Roth Syms Suzanne Cadden
1930	Diana Fishwick Glenna Collett	1956	Margaret "Wiffi" Smith Mary Patton Janssen	1976	Catherine Panton Allison Sheard
1931	Enid Wilson Wanda Morgan	1957	Philomena Garvey Jessie Valentine	1977	Angela Uzielli Vanessa Marvin
1932	Enid Wilson C. Purvis-Russell Montgomery	1958	Jessie Valentine Elizabeth Price	1978	Edwina Kennedy Julia Greenhalgh
1933	Enid Wilson Diana Plumpton	1959	Elizabeth Price Belle McCorkindale	1979	Maureen Madill Jane Lock
1934	Helen Holm Pam Barton	1960	Barbara McIntire Philomena Garvey	1980	Anne Quast Sander Liv Wollin
1935	Wanda Morgan Pam Barton	1961	Marley Spearman Diana Robb	1981	Belle Robertson Wilma Aitken
1936	Pam Barton Bridget Newell	1962	Marley Spearman Angela Bonallack	1982	Kitrina Douglas Gillian Stewart
1937	Jessie Anderson Doris Park	1963	Brigitte Varangot Philomena Garvey	1983	Jill Thornhill Regine Lautens
1938	Helen Holm Elsie Corlett	1964	Carol Sorenson Bridget Jackson	1984	Jody Rosenthal Julie Brown
1939	Pam Barton Mrs. T. Marks	1965	Brigitte Varangot Belle McCorkindale Robertson	1985	Lillian Behan Claire Waite
1940–45	No Championship (World War II)	1966	Elizabeth Chadwick Vivien Saunders	1986	Marnie McGuire Louise Briers
1946	Jean Hetherington Philomena Garvey	1967	Elizabeth Chadwick Mary Everard	1987	Janet Collingham Susan Shapcott
1947	Mildred "Babe" Zaharias Jacqueline Gordon	1968	Brigitte Varangot Claudine Cros Rubin	1988	Joanne Furby Julie Wade
1948	Louise Suggs Jean Donald	1969	Catherine Lacoste Claudine Cros Rubin	1989	Helen Dobson Elaine Farquharson
1949	Frances Stephens Val Reddan	1970	Dinah Oxley Belle McCorkindale Robertson	1990	Julie Wade Hall
1950	Lally de St. Sauveur Jessie Valentine	1971	Michelle Walker Beverley Huke		
1951	Catherine MacCann Frances Stephens				

U.S. Women's Amateur Championship

Year	Winner, Runner-up	Year	Winner, Runner-up	Year	Winner, Runner-up
1895	Mrs. C.S. Brown Miss N.C. Sargent	1898	Beatrix Hoyt Maude Wetmore	1901	Genevieve Hecker Lucy Herron
1896	Beatrix Hoyt Mrs. Arthur Turnure	1899	Ruth Underhill Mrs. Caleb F. Fox	1902	Genevieve Hecker Louisa A. Wells
1897	Beatrix Hoyt Miss N.C. Sargent	1900	Frances C. Griscom Margaret Curtis	1903	Bessie Anthony Miss J.A. Carpenter

Year	Winner, Runner-up	Year	Winner, Runner-up	Year	Winner, Runner-up
1904	Georgianna M. Bishop Mrs. E.F. Sanford	1928	Glenna Collett Virginia Van Wie	1955	Patrica A. Lesser Jane Nelson
1905	Pauline Mackay Margaret Curtis	1929	Glenna Collett Mrs. Leona Pressler	1956	Marlene Stewart JoAnne Gunderson
1906	Harriot Curtis Mary B. Adams	1930	Glenna Collett Virginia Van Wie	1957	JoAnne Gunderson Mrs. Ann Casey Johnstone
1907	Margaret Curtis Harriot Curtis	1931	Helen Hicks Mrs. Glenna Collett Vare, Jr.	1958	Anne Quast Barbara Romack
1908	Katherine C. Harley Mrs. T.H. Polhemus	1932	Virginia Van Wie Mrs. Glenna Collett Vare, Jr.	1959	Barbara McIntire Joanne Goodwin
1909	Dorothy I. Campbell Mrs. Nonna Barlow	1933	Virginia Van Wie Helen Hicks	1960	JoAnne Gunderson Jean Ashley
1910	Dorothy I. Campbell Mrs. G.M. Martin	1934	Virginia Van Wie Dorothy Traung	1961	Mrs. Anne Quast Decker Phyllis Preuss
1911	Margaret Curtis Lillian B. Hyde	1935	Mrs. Glenna Collett Vare, Jr. Patty Berg	1962	JoAnne Gunderson Anne Baker
1912	Margaret Curtis Mrs. Nonna Barlow	1936	Pamela Barton Maureen Orcutt	1963	Mrs. Anne Quast Welts Peggy Conley
1913	Gladys Ravenscroft Marion Hollins	1937	Mrs. Estelle Lawson Page, Jr. Patty Berg	1964	Barbara McIntire JoAnne Gunderson
1914	Mrs. Katherine Harley Elaine V. Rosenthal	1938	Patty Berg Mrs. Estelle Lawson Page, Jr.	1965	Jean Ashley Mrs. Anne Quast Welts
1915	Mrs. Florence Vanderbeck Mrs. William A. Gavin	1939	Betty Jameson Dorothy Kirby	1966	Mrs. JoAnne Gunderson Carner Mrs. Marlene Stewart Streit
1916	Alexa Stirling Mildred Caverly	1940	Betty Jameson Jane S. Cothran	1967	Mary Lou Dill Jean Ashley
1917-18	No Championship (World War I)	1941	Mrs. Betty Hicks Newell Helen Sigel	1968	Mrs. JoAnne Gunderson Carner Mrs. Anne Quast Welts
1919	Alexa Stirling Mrs. William A. Gavin	1942-45	No Championship (World War II)	1969	Catherine Lacoste Shelley Hamlin
1920	Alexa Stirling Mrs. Dorothy Campbell Hurd	1946	Mildred "Babe" Zaharias Mrs. Clara Sherman	1970	Martha Wilkinson Cynthia Hill
1921	Marion Hollins Alexa Stirling	1947	Louise Suggs Dorothy Kirby	1971	Laura Baugh Beth Barry
1922	Glenna Collett Mrs. William A. Gavin	1948	Grace S. Lenczyk Helen Sigel	1972	Mary Budke Cynthia Hill
1923	Edith Cummings Alexa Stirling	1949	Mrs. Dorothy Germain Dorothy Kielty	1973	Carol Semple Mrs. Anne Quast Sander
1924	Mrs. Dorothy Campbell Hurd Mary K. Browne	1950	Beverly Hanson Mae Murray	1974	Cynthia Hill Carol Semple
1925	Glenna Collett Mrs. Alexa Stirling Fraser	1951	Dorothy Kirby Claire Doran	1975	Beth Daniel Donna Horton
1926	Mrs. G. Henry Stetson Mrs. Wright D. Goss, Jr.	1952	Jacqueline Pung Shirley McFedters	1976	Donna Horton Marianne Bretton
1927	Miriam Burns Horn Maureen Orcutt	1953	Mary Lena Faulk Polly Riley	1977	Beth Daniel Mrs. Cathy Sherk
		1954	Barbara Romack Mary K. (Mickey) Wright		

The Illustrated History of Women's Golf

Year	Winner, Runner-up	Year	Winner, Runner-up	Year	Winner, Runner-up
1978	Mrs. Cathy Sherk Mrs. Judith Oliver	1982	Mrs. Juli Simpson Inkster Cathy Hanlon	1986	Kay Cockerill Kathleen McCarthy
1979	Carolyn Hill Patty Sheehan	1983	Joanne Pacillo Sally Quinlan	1987	Kay Cockerill Tracy Kerdyk
1980	Mrs. Juli Simpson Inkster Patti Rizzo	1984	Deb Richard Kim Williams	1988	Pearl Sinn Karen Noble
1981	Mrs. Juli Simpson Inkster Mrs. Lindy Goggin	1985	Michiko Hattori Cheryl Stacy	1989	Vicki Goetze Brandie Burton
				1990	Pat Hurst Stephanie Davis

Women's Western Amateur Championship

Year	Winner	Year	Winner	Year	Winner
1901	Bessie Anthony	1934	Leona Pressler Cheney	1968	Catherine Lacoste
1902	Bessie Anthony	1935	Marion Miley	1969	Jane Bastanchury
1903	Bessie Anthony	1936	Dorothy Traung	1970	Jane Bastanchury
1904	Frances Everett	1937	Marion Miley	1971	Beth Barry
1905	Mrs. C.L. Dering	1938	Patty Berg	1972	Debbie Massey
1906	Mrs. C.L. Dering	1939	Edith Estabrooks	1973	Mrs. Carol Falk
1907	Lilian French	1940	Betty Jameson	1974	Lancy Smith
1908	Mrs. W.F. Anderson	1941	Mrs. Russell Mann	1975	Debbie Massey
1909	Vida Llewellyn	1942	Betty Jameson	1976	Nancy Lopez
1910	Mrs. Thurston Harris	1943	Dorothy Germain	1977	Lauren Howe
1911	Caroline Painter	1944	Dorothy Germain	1978	Beth Daniel
1912	Caroline Painter	1945	Phyllis Otto	1979	Mary Hafeman
1913	Myra B. Helmer	1946	Louise Suggs	1980	Kathy Baker
1914	Mrs. H.D. Hammond	1947	Louise Suggs	1981	Amy Benz
1915	Elaine V. Rosenthal	1948	Dot Kielty	1982	Lisa Stanley
1916	Mrs. F.C. Letts, Jr.	1949	Helen Sigel	1983	Tammy Welborn
1917	Mrs. F.C. Letts, Jr.	1950	Polly Riley	1984	Joanne Pacillo
1918	Elaine V. Rosenthal	1951	Marjorie Lindsay	1985	Kathleen McCarthy
1919	Mrs. Perry W. Fiske	1952	Polly Riley	1986	Leslie Shannon
1920	Mrs. F.C. Letts, Jr.	1953	Claire Doran	1987	Kathleen McCarthy
1921	Mrs. Melvin Jones	1954	Claire Doran	1988	Anne Quast Sander
1922	Mrs. David Gaut	1955	Pat Lesser	1989	Katie Peterson
1923	Miriam Burns	1956	Anne Quast	1990	Pat Cornett-Iker
1924	Edith Cummings	1957	Meriam Bailey		
1925	Elaine Rosenthal Reinhardt	1958	Barbara McIntire		
1926	Dorothy Page	1959	JoAnne Gunderson		
1927	Leona Pressler	1960	Ann Casey Johnstone		
1928	Leona Pressler	1961	Anne Quast Decker		
1929	Opal Hill	1962	Carol Sorenson		
1930	Miriam Tyson	1963	Barbara McIntire		
1931	Opal Hill	1964	Barbara Fay White		
1932	Opal Hill	1965	Barbara Fay White		
1933	Lucille Robinson	1966	Peggy Conley		
		1967	Dorothy Porter		

Women's Canadian Open Amateur Championship

Year	Winner	Year	Winner	Year	Winner
1901	L. Young	1933	Ada Mackenzie	1966	Helene Gagnon
1902	M. Thomson	1934	Alexa Stirling Fraser	1967	Bridget Jackson
1903	F. Harvey	1935	Ada Mackenzie	1968	Marlene Stewart Streit
1904	M. Thomson	1936	Mrs. A.B. Darling	1969	Marlene Stewart Streit
1905	M. Thomson	1937	Mrs. J. Rogers		
1906	M. Thomson	1938	Mrs. F.J. Mulqueen	1970	Mrs. G.H. Moore
1907	M. Thomson	1939-46	No tournament (World War II)	1971	Jocelyn Bourassa
1908	M. Thomson			1972	Marlene Stewart Streit
1909	V.H. Anderson	1947	Grace Lenczyk		
1910	Dorothy Campbell	1948	Grace Lenczyk	1973	Marlene Stewart Streit
1911	Dorothy Campbell	1949	Grace DeMoss		
1912	Dorothy Campbell	1950	Dorothy Kielty	1974	Debbie Massey
1913	M. Todd	1951	Marlene Stewart	1975	Debbie Massey
1914-18	No tournament (World War I)	1952	Edean Anderson	1976	Debbie Massey
		1953	Barbara Romack	1977	Cathy Sherk
1919	Ada Mackenzie	1954	Marlene Stewart	1978	Cathy Sherk
1920	Alexa Stirling	1955	Marlene Stewart	1979	Stacey West
1921	Cecil Leitch	1956	Marlene Stewart	1980	Edwina Kennedy
1922	Mrs. William A. Gavin	1957	Betty Stanhope	1981	Jane Lock
		1958	Marlene Stewart Streit	1982	Cindy Pleger
1923	Glenna Collett			1983	Dawn Coe
1924	Glenna Collett	1959	Marlene Stewart Streit	1984	Kimberly Williams
1925	Ada Mackenzie			1985	Kimberly Williams
1926	Ada Mackenzie	1960	Judy Darling	1986	Marilyn O'Connor
1927	Helen Payson	1961	Judy Darling	1987	Tracy Kerdyk
1928	Virginia Wilson	1962	Gayle Hitchens	1988	Michiko Hattori
1929	Helen Hicks	1963	Marlene Stewart Streit	1989	Cheryl Damphouse
1930	Maureen Orcutt			1990	Sarah LeBrun Ingram
1931	Maureen Orcutt	1964	Margie Masters		
1932	Margery Kirkham	1965	Jocelyn Bourassa		

North and South Women's Amateur Championship

Year	Winner	Year	Winner	Year	Winner
1904	Mrs. Myra D. Paterson	1914	Florence Harvey	1923	Glenna Collett
1905	Mary H. Dutton	1915	Nonna Barlow	1924	Glenna Collett
1906	Mrs. Myra D. Paterson	1916	Nonna Barlow	1925	Mrs. M. Jones
1907	Molly B. Adams	1917	Elaine Rosenthal	1926	Louise Fordyce
1908	Julia Mix	1918	Mrs. Dorothy Campbell Hurd	1927	Glenna Collett
1909	Mary Fownes	1919	Nonna Barlow	1928	Opal Hill
1910	Florence Vanderbeck	1920	Mrs. Dorothy Campbell Hurd	1929	Glenna Collett
1911	Louise Elkins	1921	Mrs. Dorothy Campbell Hurd	1930	Glenna Collett
1912	Mrs. J.R. Price			1931	Maureen Orcutt
1913	Lillian Hyde	1922	Glenna Collett	1932	Maureen Orcutt
				1933	Maureen Orcutt

Year	Winner	Year	Winner	Year	Winner
1934	Charlotte Glutting	1954	Joyce Ziske	1973	Beth Barry
1935	Estelle Lawson	1955	Margaret "Wiffi" Smith	1974	Marlene Stewart Streit
1936	Deborah Verry	1956	Marlene Stewart	1975	Cynthia Hill
1937	Estelle Lawson Page	1957	Barbara McIntire	1976	Carol Semple
1938	Jane Cothran	1958	Carolyn Cudone	1977	Marcia Dolan
1939	Estelle Lawson Page	1959	Ann Casey Johnstone	1978	Cathy Sherk
1940	Estelle Lawson Page	1960	Barbara McIntire	1979	Julie Gumlia
1941	Estelle Lawson Page	1961	Barbara McIntire	1980	Charlotte Montgomery
1942	Louise Suggs	1962	Clifford Ann Creed	1981	Patti Rizzo
1943	Dorothy Kirby	1963	Nancy Roth	1982	Anne Quast Sander
1944	Estelle Lawson Page	1964	Phyllis Preuss	1983	Anne Quast Sander
1945	Estelle Lawson Page	1965	Barbara McIntire	1984	Susan Pager
1946	Louise Suggs	1966	Nancy Roth Syms	1985	Lee Ann Hammack
1947	Mildred Didrikson Zaharias	1967	Phyllis Preuss	1986	Leslie Shannon
1948	Louise Suggs	1968	Alice Dye	1987	Carol Semple Thompson
1949	Peggy Kirk	1969	Barbara McIntire	1988	Donna Andrews
1950	Pat O'Sullivan	1970	Hollis Stacy	1989	Page Marsh
1951	Pat O'Sullivan	1971	Barbara McIntire	1990	Brandie Burton
1952	Barbara Romack	1972	Jane Bastanchury Booth		
1953	Pat O'Sullivan				

Women's Eastern Amateur Championship

Year	Winner	Year	Winner	Year	Winner
1906	Fanny Osgood	1927	Glenna Collett	1951	Pat O'Sullivan
1907	Mary B. Adams	1928	Maureen Orcutt	1952	Helen Sigel
1908	Fanny Osgood	1929	Maureen Orcutt	1953	Mary Ann Downey
1909	Mary B. Adams	1930	Frances Williams	1954	Mae Murray Jones
1910	Fanny Osgood	1931	Helen Hicks	1955	Mary Ann Downey
1911	Mrs. Nonna Barlow	1932	Glenna Collett Vare	1956	Mrs. Norman Woolworth
1912	Mrs. Nonna Barlow	1933	Charlotte Glutting	1957	Joanne Goodwin
1913	Mrs. Nonna Barlow	1934	Maureen Orcutt	1958	Mary Patton Janssen
1914	Mrs. H.A. Jackson	1935	Glenna Collett Vare	1959	Mrs. Edward McAuliffe
1915	Mrs. Florence H. Vanderbeck	1936	Edith Quier	1960	Carolyn Cudone
1916	Mrs. William A. Gavin	1937	Charlotte Glutting	1961	Marge Burns
1917–18	No tournament (World War I)	1938	Maureen Orcutt	1962	Helen Sigel Wilson
1919	Mrs. Nonna Barlow	1939	Mrs. H. Warren Beard	1963	Phyllis Preuss
1920	Mrs. Nonna Barlow	1940	Grace Amory	1964	Nancy Roth
1921	Mrs. Nonna Barlow	1941	Marion McNaughton	1965	Nancy Roth
1922	Glenna Collett	1942–45	No tournament (World War II)	1966	Nancy Roth Syms
1923	Glenna Collett	1946	Laddie Irwin	1967	Phyllis Preuss
1924	Glenna Collett	1947	Maureen Orcutt	1968	JoAnne Gunderson Carner
1925	Maureen Orcutt	1948	Pat O'Sullivan	1969	Dorothy Germain Porter
1926	Mrs. G. Henry Stetson	1949	Maureen Orcutt		
		1950	Peggy Kirk		

Year	Winner	Year	Winner	Year	Winner
1970	Lancy Smith	1977	Noreen Uihlein	1984	Tina Tombs
1971	Lancy Smith	1978	Julie Green	1985	Kimberly Williams
1972	Alice Dye	1979	Kathy Baker	1986	Nancy Porter
1973	Lancy Smith	1980	Patti Rizzo	1987	Christina Barrett
1974	Lancy Smith	1981	Mary Hafeman	1988	Katie Peterson
1975	Debbie Massey	1982	Kathy Baker	1989	Katie Peterson
1976	Judy Oliver	1983	Mary Ann Widman	1990	Carol McKenzie

Women's Southern Amateur Championship

Year	Winner	Year	Winner	Year	Winner
1911	Mrs. Roger Smith	1937	Dorothy Kirby	1966	Nancy Roth Syms
1912	Mrs. Frank G. Jones	1938	Marion Miley	1967	Barbara Fay White Boddie
1913	Mrs. E.W. Daley	1939	Marion Miley	1968	Phyllis Preuss
1914	Mrs. Frank G. Jones	1940	Aniela Gorczyca Goldthwaite	1969	Mary Ann Rathmell
1915	Alexa Stirling	1941	Louise Suggs	1970	Katherine Hite
1916	Alexa Stirling	1942–45	No tournament (World War II)	1971	Beth Barry
1917	Mrs. K.G. Duffield	1946	Estelle Lawson Page	1972	Beth Barry
1918	No tournament (World War I)	1947	Louise Suggs	1973	Beth Barry
1919	Alexa Stirling	1948	Polly Riley	1974	Martha Jones
1920	Mrs. Dave Gaut	1949	Margaret Gunther	1975	Beth Barry
1921	Mrs. Dave Gaut	1950	Polly Riley	1976	Brenda Goldsmith
1922	Helen D. Lowndes	1951	Polly Riley	1977	Cecile Maclaurin
1923	Mrs. Dave Gaut	1952	Katherine McKinnon	1978	Mrs. Sam Furrow
1924	Helen D. Lowndes	1953	Polly Riley	1979	Brenda Goldsmith
1925	Mrs. John Armstrong	1954	Polly Riley	1980	Martha Jones
1926	Marion Turpie	1955	Betty Probasco	1981	Toni Wiesner
1927	Ruth Raymond	1956	Mary Ann Downey	1982	Beth Barry
1928	Marion Turpie	1957	Clifford Ann Creed	1983	Lynda Brown
1929	Margaret Maddox	1958	Mary Ann Reynolds	1984	Robin Weiss
1930	Mrs. Dave Gaut	1959	Judy Eller	1985	Kim Williams
1931	Marion Turpie Lake	1960	Judy Eller	1986	Kim Williams
1932	Mrs. Ben Fitz-Hugh	1961	Polly Riley	1987	Virginia Derby
1933	Aniela Gorczyca	1962	Clifford Ann Creed	1988	Robin Weiss
1934	Betty Jameson	1963	Mrs. Paul Hendrix	1989	Mary Schmidt
1935	Mary Rogers	1964	Nancy Roth	1990	Martha Wilkinson Kirouac
1936	Mrs. Mark McGarry	1965	Phyllis Preuss		

Women's South Atlantic Golf Championship

Year	Winner	Year	Winner	Year	Winner
1926	Dorothy Klotz	1929	Virginia Van Wie	1932	Frances Williams
1927	Mrs. Dorothy Klotz Pardue	1930	Virginia Van Wie	1933	Frances Williams
1928	Virginia Van Wie	1931	Martha Parker	1934	Virginia Van Wie

Year	Winner	Year	Winner	Year	Winner
1935	Marion Miley	1955	Pat Lesser	1973	Lancy Smith
1936	Lucille Robinson	1956	Anne Quast	1974	Debbie Massey
1937	Katherine Hemphill	1957	Barbara Romack	1975	Cynthia Hill
1938	Patty Berg	1958	Judy Bell	1976	Pat Meyers
1939	Patty Berg	1959	Evelyn Glick	1977	Cynthia Hill
1940	Betty Hicks	1960	Barbara McIntire	1978	Debbie Rasso
1941	Jane Cothran	1961	Doris Phillips	1979	Lancy Smith
1942	Georgia Tainter	1962	Clifford Ann Creed	1980	Sherrie Ann Keblish
1943–46	No Championship (World War II)	1963	Phyllis Preuss	1981	Patti Rizzo
1947	Mildred Didrikson Zaharias	1964	Barbara Fay White	1982	Lisa Stanley
1948	Carol Diringer	1965	Phyllis Preuss	1983	Claire Hourihane
1949	Marge Lindsay	1966	Phyllis Preuss	1984	Claire Waite
1950	Mary Agnes Wall	1967	Phyllis Preuss	1985	Lancy Smith
1951	Polly Riley	1968	Sandra Post	1986	Leslie Shannon
1952	Barbara Romack	1969	Phyllis Preuss	1987	Cindy Scholefield
1953	Barbara Romack	1970	Lancy Smith	1988	Caroline Keggi
1954	Pat Lesser	1971	Lancy Smith	1989	Vicki Goetz
		1972	Nancy Hager	1990	Katie Peterson

Women's Trans National Amateur Championship

(formerly the Trans. Mississippi)

Year	Winner	Year	Winner	Year	Winner
1927	Miriam Burns Horn	1952	Carol Bowman	1974	Barbara Barrow
1928	Opal Hill	1953	Edean Anderson	1975	Beverley Davis
1929	Opal Hill	1954	Vonnie Colby	1976	Nancy Lopez
1930	Mrs. Hulbert Clarke	1955	Polly Riley	1977	Catherine Reynolds
1931	Opal Hill	1956	Margaret "Wiffi" Smith	1978	Nancy Roth Syms
1932	Patti Beyer	1957	Marge Ferrie	1979	Brenda Goldsmith
1933	Phyllis Buchanan	1958	Marjorie Lindsay	1980	Patti Rizzo
1934	Opal Hill	1959	Ann Casey Johnstone	1981	Amy Benz
1935	Marion Miley	1960	Sandra Haynie	1982	Cindy Figg
1936	Marion Miley	1961	JoAnne Gunderson	1983	Sherri Steinhauer
1937	Betty Jameson	1962	Jeannie Thompson	1984	Claire Waite
1938	Patty Berg	1963	Judy Bell	1985	Leslie Shannon
1939	Patty Berg	1964	Carol Sorenson	1986	Carol Semple Thompson
1940	Betty Jameson	1965	Sharon Miller	1987	Pearl Sinn
1941	Lucille Mann	1966	Roberta Albers	1988	Nanci Bowen
1942–45	No tournament (World War II)	1967	Jane Bastanchury	1989	Karen Noble
1946	Mildred "Babe" Zaharias	1968	Carole Jo Skala	1990	Cathy Mockett
1947	Polly Riley	1969	Jane Bastanchury		
1948	Polly Riley	1970	Martha Wilkinson		
1949	Betsy Rawls	1971	Jane Bastanchury		
1950	Marjorie Lindsay	1972	Michelle Walker		
1951	Mary Ann Downey	1973	Liana Zambresky		

Broadmoor Ladies' Invitation Golf Tournament

Year	Winner
1928	Anna Monsted Fowler
1929–41	No Championship
1942	Mrs. Murray Gose
1943	Mrs. Murray Gose
1944	Betty Jean Rucker
1945	Mildred Didrikson Zaharias
1946	Mildred Didrikson Zaharias
1947	Mildred Didrikson Zaharias
1948	Mary Sargent
1949	Patty Blanton
1950	Betsy Rawls
1951	Mrs. Russell Mann
1952	Bee McWane
1953	Lesbia Lobo
1954	No Championship
1955	Jean Ashley
1956	Patty Blanton
1957	Judy Bell
1958	Judy Bell
1959	Natasha Matson
1960	Judy Bell
1961	Natasha Matson Fife
1962	Barbara McIntire
1963	Natasha Matson Fife
1964	Barbara Fay White
1965	Barbara McIntire
1966	Dorothy Germain
1967	Carmen Piasecki
1968	Jane Bastanchury
1969	Jane Bastanchury
1970	Jane Bastanchury
1971	Phyllis Preuss
1972	Nancy Roth Syms
1973	Cynthia Hill
1974	Judy Oliver
1975	Nancy Roth Syms
1976	Debbie Massey
1977	Cynthia Hill
1978	Phyllis Preuss
1979	Mari McDougall
1980	Mary Beth Zimmerman
1981	Chris Monaghan
1982	Dana Howe
1983	Jody Rosenthal
1984	Danielle Ammaccapane
1985	Kim Gardner
1986	Kim Saiki
1987	Cindy Scholefield
1988	Kim Saiki
1989	Toni Wiesner
1990	Brandie Burton

Helen Lee Doherty Invitational

Year	Winner
1933	Opal S. Hill
1934	Maureen Orcutt
1935	Jean Bauer
1936	Patty Berg
1937	Patty Berg
1938	Patty Berg
1939	Patty Berg
1940	Patty Berg
1941	Betty Hicks
1942	Georgia Tainter
1943	Billie Hartung
1944	Marjorie Row
1945	Louise Suggs
1946	Louise Suggs
1947	Mildred Didrikson Zaharias
1948	Louise Suggs
1949	Dorothy Kirby
1950	Polly Riley
1951	Claire Doran
1952	Mary Lena Faulk
1953	Mary Lena Faulk
1954	Grace DeMoss Smith
1955	Pat Lesser
1956	Joanne Goodwin
1957	Anne Quast
1958	Mary Ann Downey
1959	Marlene Stewart Streit
1960	Marlene Stewart Streit
1961	Marlene Stewart Streit
1962	Phyllis Preuss
1963	Nancy Roth
1964	Nancy Roth
1965	Marlene Stewart Streit
1966	Nancy Roth Syms
1967	Alice Dye
1968	JoAnne Gunderson Carner
1969	Barbara McIntire
1970	Martha Wilkinson
1971	Phyllis Preuss
1972	Jane Bastanchury Booth
1973	Jane Bastanchury Booth
1974	Debbie Massey
1975	Cynthia Hill
1976	Phyllis Preuss
1977	Lancy Smith
1978	Carolyn Hill
1979	Lancy Smith
1980	Nancy Rubin
1981	Leslie Shannon
1982	Laurie Rinker
1983	Gina Hull
1984	Leslie Shannon

Year	Winner	Year	Winner	Year	Winner
1985	Kimberly Williams	1988	Michelle McGann	1990	Katie Peterson
1986	Cindy Scholefield	1989	Vicki Goetze		
1987	Carol Semple Thompson				

Hollywood Women's International Four-Ball

Year	Winning Team	Year	Winner	Year	Winner
1946	Louise Suggs, Jean Hopkins	1960	Doris Phillips, Joanne Goodwin	1976	Phyllis Preuss, Cindy Hill
1947	Peggy Kirk, Mildred Didrikson Zaharias	1961	Phyllis Preuss, Barbara Williams	1977	Nancy Roth Syms, Marcia Dolan
1948	Marge Lindsay, Pat Devany	1962	Cookie Swift Berger, Carolyn Cudone	1978	Lancy Smith, Jeanne Marie Boylan
1949	Bee McWane, Polly Riley	1963	Nancy Roth, Margo Michaelis	1979	Cookie English, Alice Dye
1950	Alice Bauer, Marlene Bauer	1964	Jane Woodworth, Gloria Ehret	1980	Reggie Hawes, Barbara Charles
1951	Betsy Rawls, Betty Dodd	1965	Nancy Roth, Maureen Crum	1981	Diane Headings, Renee Headings
1952	Bee McWane, Polly Riley	1966	Jan Ferraris, Jeanie Butler	1982	Sandra Stubbe, Penney Hammel
1953	Mary Lena Faulk, Mary Ann Downey	1967	Sharon Moran, Roberta Albers	1983	Lancy Smith, Leslie Shannon
1954	Cookie Swift Berger, Vonnie Colby	1968	Jane Bastanchury, Martha Wilkinson	1984	Michelle Berteotti, Gina Hull
1955	Joyce Ziske, Margaret "Wiffi" Smith	1969	Jane Bastanchury, Martha Wilkinson	1985	Deborah McHaffie, Donna Bender Moir
1956	Anne Quast, Ruth Jessen	1970	Jane Bastanchury, Martha Wilkinson	1986	Leslie Shannon, Robin Weiss
1957	Marge Lindsay, Mary Ann Downey	1971	Marcia Dolan, Nancy Roth Syms	1987	Carol Semple Thompson, Toni Wiesner
1958	Marge Lindsay, Mary Ann Downey	1972	Marilyn Palmer, Dale Shaw	1988	Leslie Shannon, Robin Weiss
1959	Marlene Stewart Streit, Ann Casey Johnstone	1973	Jane Bastanchury Booth, Cindy Hill	1989	Leslie Shannon, Robin Weiss
		1974	Jane Bastanchury Booth, Cindy Hill	1990	Sara Ingram, Kiernan Prechtl
		1975	Dale Shaw, Lancy Smith		

U.S. Girls' Junior Championship

Year	Winner	Year	Winner	Year	Winner
1949	Marlene Bauer	1953	Mildred Meyerson	1957	Judy Eller
1950	Patricia A. Lesser	1954	Margaret "Wiffi" Smith	1958	Judy Eller
1951	Arlene Brooks	1955	Carole Jo Kabler	1959	Judy Rand
1952	Mary K. "Mickey" Wright	1956	JoAnne Gunderson	1960	Carol Sorenson

Year	Winner	Year	Winner	Year	Winner
1961	Mary Lowell	1972	Nancy Lopez	1983	Kim Saiki
1962	Mary Lou Daniel	1973	Amy Alcott	1984	Cathy Mockett
1963	Janis Ferraris	1974	Nancy Lopez	1985	Dana Lofland
1964	Peggy Conley	1975	Dayna Benson	1986	Pat Hurst
1965	Gail Sykes	1976	Pilar Dorado	1987	Michelle McGann
1966	Claudia Mayhew	1977	Althea Tome	1988	Jamille Jose
1967	Elizabeth Story	1978	Lori Castillo	1989	Brandie Burton
1968	Margaret Harmon	1979	Penny Hammel	1990	Sandrine Mendiburu
1969	Hollis Stacy	1980	Laurie Rinker		
1970	Hollis Stacy	1981	Kay Cornelius		
1971	Hollis Stacy	1982	Heather Farr		

Women's Harder Hall Invitational

Year	Winner	Year	Winner	Year	Winner
1956	Evelyn Glick	1969	Phyllis Preuss	1981	Patti Rizzo
1957	Evelyn Glick	1970	Martha Wilkinson	1982	Lancy Smith
1958	Marge Burns	1971	Phyllis Preuss	1983	Lancy Smith
1959	Marge Burns	1972	Jane Bastanchury Booth	1984	Kim Gardner
1960	Marge Burns	1973	Jane Bastanchury Booth	1985	Lancy Smith
1961	Marge Burns	1974	Debbie Massey	1986	Adele Lukken
1962	Ellen Gery	1975	Nancy Hager	1987	Robin Weiss
1963	Phyllis Preuss	1976	Judy Oliver	1988	Caroline Keggi
1964	Barbara Fay White	1977	Debbie Rasso	1989	Katie Peterson
1965	Marge Burns	1978	Mary E. Murphy	1990	Carol Semple Thompson
1966	Phyllis Preuss	1979	Debbie Rasso		
1967	Phyllis Preuss	1980	Lancy Smith		
1968	JoAnne Gunderson Carner				

U.S. Senior Women's Amateur Championship

Year	Winner	Year	Winner	Year	Winner
1962	Maureen Orcutt	1972	Mrs. Carolyn Cudone	1983	Mrs. Dorothy Porter
1963	Mrs. Sis Choate	1973	Mrs. Gwen Hibbs	1984	Mrs. Constance Guthrie
1964	Mrs. Loma Smith	1974	Mrs. Justine B. Cushing	1985	Mrs. Marlene Stewart Streit
1965	Mrs. Loma Smith	1975	Mrs. Alberta Bower	1986	Mrs. Constance Guthrie
1966	Maureen Orcutt	1976	Mrs. Cecile Maclaurin	1987	Mrs. Anne Quast Sander
1967	Mrs. Marge Mason	1977	Mrs. Dorothy Porter	1988	Mrs. Lois Hodge
1968	Mrs. Carolyn Cudone	1978	Mrs. Alice Dye	1989	Mrs. Anne Quast Sander
1969	Mrs. Carolyn Cudone	1979	Mrs. Alice Dye	1990	Mrs. Anne Quast Sander
1970	Mrs. Carolyn Cudone	1980	Mrs. Dorothy Porter		
1971	Mrs. Carolyn Cudone	1981	Mrs. Dorothy Porter		
		1982	Mrs. Edean Ihlanfeldt		

U.S. Women's Public Links Championship

Year	Winner	Year	Winner	Year	Winner
1977	Kelly Fuiks	1982	Nancy Taylor	1986	Cindy Schreyer
1978	Kelly Fuiks	1983	Kelli Antolock	1987	Tracy Kerdyk
1979	Lori Castillo	1984	Heather Farr	1988	Pearl Sinn
1980	Lori Castillo	1985	Danielle Ammaccapane	1989	Pearl Sinn
1981	Mary Enright			1990	Cathy Mockett

U.S. Women's Mid-Amateur Championship

Year	Winner	Year	Winner
1987	Cindy Scholefield	1989	Robin Weiss
1988	Martha Jones Lang	1990	Carol Semple Thompson

The Curtis Cup Match

1932:

Great Britain and Ireland: 3½	United States: 2½
Wanda Morgan	Opal Hill
Enid Wilson	Virginia Van Wie
Mrs. J.B. Watson	Helen Hicks
Molly Gourlay	Maureen Orcutt
Doris Park	Leona Pressler Cheney
Diana Fishwick	Dorothy Higbie, Reserve
Elsie Corlett	
Captain: Joyce Wethered	Captain: Glenna Collett Vare

1934:

Great Britain and Ireland: 2½	United States: 6½
Molly Gourlay	Virginia Van Wie
Pam Barton	Charlotte Glutting
Diana Fishwick	Maureen Orcutt
Wanda Morgan	Leona Cheney
Diana Plumpton	Opal Hill
Mrs. J.B. Walker	Lucile Robinson
Mrs. George Coats, Reserve	Aniela Goldthwaite
	Marion Miley, Reserve
Captain: Doris Chambers	Captain: Glenna Collett Vare

1936:

Great Britain and Ireland: 4½	United States: 4½
Wanda Morgan	Patty Berg
Marjorie Garon	Maureen Orcutt
Pam Barton	Leona Pressler Cheney
Mrs. J.B. Walker	Opal Hill
Jessie Anderson	Charlotte Glutting
Helen Holm	Marion Miley, Reserve
Phyllis Wade, Reserve	Aniela Goldthwaite, Reserve
Bridget Newell, Reserve	
Captain: Doris Chambers	Captain: Glenna Collett Vare

1938: Great Britain and Ireland: 3½   United States: 5½

Helen Holm   Estelle Lawson Page
Clarrie Tiernan   Maureen Orcutt
Jessie Anderson   Glenna Collett Vare
Elsie Corlett   Patty Berg
Mrs. J.B. Walker   Marion Miley
Phyllis Wade   Kathryn Hemphill
Nan Baird   Charlotte Glutting

Captain: Mrs. R.H. Wallace-   Captain: Frances E. Stebbins
   Williamson

1940–46 No Matches (World War II)

1948: Great Britain and Ireland: 2½   United States: 6½

Jacqueline Gordon   Louise Suggs
Jean Donald   Grace Lenczyk
Philomena Garvey   Dorothy Kirby
Zara Bolton   Dorothy Kielty
Maureen Ruttle   Estelle Lawson Page
Val Reddan   Polly Riley
Helen Holm
Mrs. A.C. Critchley, Reserve

Captain: Doris Chambers   Captain: Glenna Collett Vare

1950: Great Britain and Ireland: 1½   United States: 7½

Jean Donald   Dorothy Germain Porter
Jessie Valentine   Beverly Hanson
Frances Stephens   Helen Sigel
Elizabeth Price   Peggy Kirk
Philomena Garvey   Dorothy Kielty
Jeanne Bisgood   Dorothy Kirby
                                          Polly Riley
                                          Grace Lenczyk

Captain: Mrs. A.C. Critchley   Captain: Glenna Collett Vare

1952: Great Britain and Ireland: 5   United States: 4

Jean Donald   Dorothy Kirby
Elizabeth Price   Grace DeMoss
Frances Stephens   Claire Doran
Jessie Valentine   Marjorie Lindsay
Moira Paterson   Polly Riley
Philomena Garvey   Pat O'Sullivan
Jeanne Bisgood   Mae Murray
Mrs. P.J. McCann, Reserve

Captain: Lady Katherine Cairns   Captain: Aniela Goldthwaite

1954: Great Britain and Ireland: 3   United States: 6

Frances Stephens   Mary Lena Faulk
Elizabeth Price   Polly Riley
Jessie Valentine   Claire Doran
Philomena Garvey   Pat Lesser
Mrs. R.T. Peel   Dorothy Kirby
Janette Robertson   Barbara Romack
Jeanne Bisgood   Grace DeMoss Smith

Captain: Mrs. John B. Beck   Captain: Mrs. Harrison F. Flippin

1956: Great Britain and Ireland: 5   United States: 4

Jessie Valentine   Pat Lesser
Philomena Garvey   Margaret "Wiffi" Smith
Frances Stephens Smith   Polly Riley
Elizabeth Price   Barbara Romack
Janette Robertson   Mary Ann Downey
Veronica Anstey   Carolyn Cudone
Angela Ward   Jane Nelson
Mrs. Nigel Howard, Reserve

Captain: Mrs. Sloan Bolton   Captain: Mrs. Harrison Flippin

1958: Great Britain and Ireland: 4½   United States: 4½

Angela Ward Bonallack   Barbara Romack
Elizabeth Price   Polly Riley
Janette Robertson   JoAnne Gunderson
Frances Stephens Smith   Anne Quast
Bridget Jackson   Barbara McIntire
Jessie Valentine   Ann Casey Johnstone
Dorothea Sommerville, Reserve   Meriam Bailey, Reserve
                                          Anne Richardson, Reserve

Captain: Daisy Ferguson   Captain: Mrs. Charles Dennehy

1960: Great Britain and Ireland: 2½   United States: 6½

Angela Ward Bonallack   JoAnne Gunderson
Elizabeth Price   Barbara McIntire
Belle McCorkindale   Judy Eller
Janette Robertson   Anne Quast
Ruth Porter   Joanne Goodwin
Frances Smith   Ann Casey Johnstone
Philomena Garvey   Judy Bell

Captain: Maureen R. Garrett   Captain: Mrs. Mildred Prunaret

1962: Great Britain and Ireland: 1   United States: 8

Angela Ward Bonallack   Anne Quast Decker
Marley Spearman   Barbara McIntire
Ann Irvin   Clifford Ann Creed
Sheila Vaughn   JoAnne Gunderson
Mrs. Alastair Frearson   Jean Ashley
Ruth Porter   Ann Casey Johnstone
Jean Roberts   Judy Bell
Sally Bonallack   Phyllis Preuss

Captain: Frances Stephens Smith   Captain: Polly Riley

1964: Great Britain and Ireland: 7½   United States: 10½

Marley Spearman   Barbara McIntire
Angela Ward Bonallack   Phyllis Preuss
Bridget Jackson   Carol Sorenson
Susan Armitage   Barbara Fay White
Sheila Vaughn   JoAnne Gunderson
Ruth Porter   Nancy Roth
Joan Lawrence   Peggy Conley
Julia Greenhalgh   Carol Sorenson

Captain: Elsie Corlett   Captain: Mrs. T.W. Hawes

1966:   Great Britain and Ireland: 5

Angela Ward Bonallack
Susan Armitage
Belle McCorkindale Robertson
Joan Hastings
Elizabeth Chadwick
Pamela Tredinnick
Ita Burke
Marjory Fowler

Captain: Mrs. Sloan Bolton

United States: 13

Jean Ashley
Phyllis Preuss
Anne Quast Welts
Barbara McIntire
Barbara Fay White Boddie
Carol Flenniken
Nancy Roth Syms
Helen Sigel Wilson

Captain: Dorothy Germain Porter

1968:   Great Britain and Ireland: 7½

Belle Robertson
Ann Irvin
Margaret Pickard
Vivien Saunders
Ann Howard
Pamela Tredinnick
Bridget Jackson
Dinah Oxley

Captain: Mrs. Sloan Bolton

United States: 10½

Shelley Hamlin
Anne Quast Welts
Mary Lou Dill
Peggy Conley
Phyllis Preuss
Jean Ashley
Roberta Albers

Captain: Evelyn Monsted

1970:   Great Britain and Ireland: 6½

Dinah Oxley
Mary McKenna
Belle Robertson
Ann Irvin
Mary Everard
Julia Greenhalgh
Margaret Pickard

Captain: Jeanne Bisgood

United States: 11½

Shelley Hamlin
Jane Bastanchury
Phyllis Preuss
Martha Wilkinson
Cynthia Hill
Jane Fassinger
Nancy Hager
Alice Dye

Captain: Carolyn Cudone

1972:   Great Britain and Ireland: 8

Beverly Huke
Mary Everard
Belle Robertson
Diane Frearson
Michelle Walker
Mary McKenna
Dinah Oxley
Kathryn Phillips

Captain: Frances Stephens Smith

United States: 10

Laura Baugh
Martha Wilkinson Kirouac
Jane Bastanchury Booth
Barbara McIntire
Beth Barry
Hollis Stacy
Lancy Smith

Captain: Jean Ashley Crawford

1974:   Great Britain and Ireland: 5

Jennifer Lee-Smith
Carol LeFeuvre
Mary McKenna
Julia Greenhalgh
Mary Everard
Maureen Walker
Tegwen Perkins

Captain: Belle Robertson

United States: 13

Anne Quast Sander
Jane Bastanchury Booth
Carol Semple
Cynthia Hill
Mary Budke
Bonnie Lauer
Beth Barry
Debbie Massey

Captain: Mrs. Allison Choate

1976:

Great Britain and Ireland: 6½	United States: 11½
Dinah Oxley-Henson	Debbie Massey
Suzanne Cadden	Donna Horton
Mary McKenna	Beth Daniel
Julia Greenhalgh	Cynthia Hill
Ann Irvin	Nancy Roth Syms
Tegwen Perkins	Carol Semple
Ann Stant	Nancy Lopez
Jennifer Lee Smith	Barbara Barrow
Captain: Belle Robertson	Captain: Barbara McIntire

1978:

Great Britain and Ireland: 6	United States: 12
Julia Greenhalgh	Beth Daniel
Vanessa Marvin	Brenda Goldsmith
Mary Everard	Cynthia Hill
Muriel Thompson	Lancy Smith
Tegwen Perkins	Pat Cornett
Mary McKenna	Carolyn Hill
Angela Uzielli	Noreen Uihlein
Carole Caldwell	Judy Oliver
Captain: Carol Comboy	Captain: Helen Sigel Wilson

1980:

Great Britain and Ireland: 5	United States: 13
Mary McKenna	Lancy Smith
Claire Nesbitt	Terri Moody
Tegwen Perkins Thomas	Patty Sheehan
Gillian Stewart	Lori Castillo
Maureen Madill	Judy Oliver
Carole Caldwell	Carol Semple
Jane Connachan	Lancy Smith
Lynda Moore	Brenda Goldsmith
	Mary Hafeman
Captain: Carol Comboy	Captain: Nancy Roth Syms

1982:

Great Britain and Ireland: 3½	United States: 14½
Belle Robertson	Juli Inkster
Mary McKenna	Carol Semple
Kitrina Douglas	Kathy Baker
Janet Soulsby	Lancy Smith
Gillian Stewart	Amy Benz
Jane Connachan	Cathy Hanlon
Belle Robertson	Mari McDougall
Wilma Aitken	Judy Oliver
Vicki Thomas	
Captain: Maire O'Donnell	Captain: Betty Probasco

1984:

Great Britain and Ireland: 8½	United States: 9½
Claire Waite	Joanne Pacillo
Beverly New	Anne Quast Sander
Jill Thornhill	Lancy Smith
Penny Grice	Jody Rosenthal
Mary McKenna	Mary Anne Widman
Laura Davies	Heather Farr
Claire Hourihane	Penny Hammel
Vicki Thomas	Dana Howe
Captain: Diane Bailey	Captain: Phyllis Preuss

1986:   Great Britain and Ireland: 13

Lillian Behan
Jill Thornhill
Patricia Johnson
Karen Davies
Belle Robertson
Mary McKenna
Vicki Thomas
Claire Hourihane

Captain: Diane Bailey

United States: 5

Kandi Kessler
Cindy Schreyer
Danielle Ammaccapane
Dottie Mochrie
Kim Gardner
Kathleen McCarthy
Kim Williams
Leslie Shannon

Captain: Judy Bell

1988:   Great Britain and Ireland: 11

Linda Bayman
Julie Wade
Karen Davies
Susan Shapcott
Jill Thornhill
Vicki Thomas
Shirley Lawson

Captain: Diane Bailey

United States: 7

Tracy Kerdyk
Kathleen McCarthy Scrivner
Cindy Scholefield
Carol Semple Thompson
Leslie Shannon
Caroline Keggi
Pat Cornett
Pearl Sinn

Captain: Judy Bell

1990:   Great Britain and Ireland: 4

Helen Dobson
Elaine Farquharson
Linzi Fletcher
Julie Wade Hall
Kathryn Imrie
Catriona Lambert
Vicki Thomas
Helen Wadsworth

Captain: Jill Thornhill

United States: 14

Brandie Burton
Vicki Goetz
Karen Nobel
Katie Peterson
Margaret Platt
Anne Quast Sander
Carol Semple Thompson
Robin Weiss

Captain: Leslie Shannon

Women's Western Open

The Western Open was considered a major championship in women's professional golf until it was discontinued after the 1967 tournament.

Year	Winner	Year	Winner	Year	Winner
1930	Mrs. Lee Mida	1942	Betty Jameson	1952	Betsy Rawls
1931	June Beebe	1943	Patty Berg	1953	Louise Suggs
1932	Jane Weiller	1944	Mildred "Babe" Zaharias	1954	Betty Jameson
1933	June Beebe			1955	Patty Berg
1934	Marian McDougall	1945	Mildred "Babe" Zaharias	1956	Beverly Hanson
1935	Opal Hill			1957	Patty Berg
1936	Opal Hill	1946	Louise Suggs*	1958	Patty Berg
1937	Betty Hicks*	1947	Louise Suggs*	1959	Betsy Rawls
1938	Bea Barrett*	1948	Patty Berg	1960	Joyce Ziske
1939	Helen Dettweiler	1949	Louise Suggs	1961	Mary Lena Faulk
1940	Mildred "Babe" Zaharias	1950	Mildred "Babe" Zaharias	1962	Mickey Wright
1941	Patty Berg	1951	Patty Berg	1963	Mickey Wright
				1964	Carol Mann

*denotes amateur

Year	Winner	Year	Winner
1965	Susie Maxwell	1967	Kathy Whitworth
1966	Mickey Wright		

Titleholders Championship 1937-1972

The Titleholders was considered a major championship until it was discontinued after the 1972 tournament.

Year	Winner	Year	Winner	Year	Winner
1937	Patty Berg*	1949	Peggy Kirk*	1959	Louise Suggs
1938	Patty Berg*	1950	Mildred Didrikson Zaharias	1960	Fay Crocker
1939	Patty Berg*	1951	Pat O'Sullivan*	1961	Mickey Wright
1940	Betty Hicks*	1952	Mildred Didrikson Zaharias	1962	Mickey Wright
1941	Dorothy Kirby*	1953	Patty Berg	1963	Marilynn Smith
1942	Dorothy Kirby*	1954	Louise Suggs	1964	Marilynn Smith
1943-45	No Championship (World War II)	1955	Patty Berg	1965	Kathy Whitworth
1946	Louise Suggs*	1956	Louise Suggs	1966	Kathy Whitworth
1947	Mildred Didrikson Zaharias*	1957	Patty Berg	1967-71	No tournament
1948	Patty Berg	1958	Beverly Hanson	1972	Sandra Palmer

*denotes amateur

U.S. Women's Open Championship

The U.S. Women's Open was initiated in 1946 by an organization that no longer exists, the Women's Professional Golfers Association. In 1950 the newly formed Ladies Professional Golf Association assumed sponsorship. In 1953 the United States Golf Association became the sponsor at the request of the LPGA. The first U.S. Women's Open was conducted at match play.

Year	Winner, Runner-up	Year	Runner-up	Year	Runner-up
1946	Patty Berg Betty Jameson	1952	Louise Suggs Marlene Bauer, Betty Jameson	1958	Mickey Wright Louise Suggs
1947	Betty Jameson Sally Sessions,* Polly Riley*	1953	Betsy Rawls Jacqueline Pung	1959	Mickey Wright Louise Suggs
1948	Mildred Didrikson Zaharias Betty Hicks	1954	Mildred Didrikson Zaharias Betty Hicks	1960	Betsy Rawls Joyce Ziske
1949	Louise Suggs Mildred Didrikson Zaharias	1955	Fay Crocker Louise Suggs, Mary Lena Faulk	1961	Mickey Wright Betsy Rawls
1950	Mildred Didrikson Zaharias Betsy Rawls	1956	Kathy Cornelius Barbara McIntire*	1962	Murle Lindstrom Ruth Jessen, JoAnn Prentice
1951	Betsy Rawls Louise Suggs	1957	Betsy Rawls Patty Berg	1963	Mary Mills Sandra Haynie, Louise Suggs
				1964	Mickey Wright Ruth Jessen

Year	Runner-up	Year	Runner-up	Year	Runner-up
1965	Carol Mann Kathy Cornelius	1974	Sandra Haynie Beth Stone, Carol Mann	1982	Janet Alex JoAnne Gunderson Carner, Beth Daniel, Donna White, Sandra Haynie
1966	Sandra Spuzich Carol Mann	1975	Sandra Palmer Nancy Lopez,* JoAnne Gunderson Carner, Sandra Post	1983	Jan Stephenson JoAnne Gunderson Carner, Patty Sheehan
1967	Catherine Lacoste* Susie Maxwell, Beth Stone	1976	JoAnne Gunderson Carner Sandra Palmer	1984	Hollis Stacy Rosie Jones
1968	Susie Maxwell Berning Mickey Wright	1977	Hollis Stacy Nancy Lopez	1985	Kathy Baker Judy Clark
1969	Donna Caponi Peggy Wilson	1978	Hollis Stacy JoAnne Gunderson Carner, Sally Little	1986	Jane Geddes Sally Little
1970	Donna Caponi Sandra Haynie, Sandra Spuzich	1979	Jerilyn Britz Debbie Massey, Sandra Palmer	1987	Laura Davies Ayako Okamoto, JoAnne Gunderson Carner
1971	JoAnne Gunderson Carner Kathy Whitworth	1980	Amy Alcott Hollis Stacy	1988	Liselotte Neumann Patty Sheehan
1972	Susie Maxwell Berning Kathy Ahern, Pam Barnett, Judy Rankin	1981	Pat Bradley Beth Daniel	1989	Betsy King Nancy Lopez
1973	Susie Maxwell Berning Shelley Hamlin, Gloria Ehret			1990	Betsy King Patty Sheehan

*denotes amateur

LPGA Championship

Year	Winner	Year	Winner	Year	Winner
1955	Beverly Hanson	1968	Sandra Post**	1980	Sally Little
1956	Marlene Hagge*	1969	Betsy Rawls	1981	Donna Caponi
1957	Louise Suggs	1970	Shirley Englehorn***	1982	Jan Stephenson
1958	Mickey Wright	1971	Kathy Whitworth	1983	Patty Sheehan
1959	Betsy Rawls	1972	Kathy Ahern	1984	Patty Sheehan
1960	Mickey Wright	1973	Mary Mills	1985	Nancy Lopez
1961	Mickey Wright	1974	Sandra Haynie	1986	Pat Bradley
1962	Judy Kimball	1975	Kathy Whitworth	1987	Jane Geddes
1963	Mickey Wright	1976	Betty Burfeindt	1988	Sherri Turner
1964	Mary Mills	1977	Chako Higuchi	1989	Nancy Lopez
1965	Sandra Haynie	1978	Nancy Lopez	1990	Beth Daniel
1966	Gloria Ehret	1979	Donna Caponi		
1967	Kathy Whitworth				

*1956: Hagge d. Patty Berg in sudden death.
**1968: Post (68) d. Kathy Whitworth (75) in 18-hole playoff.
***1970: Englehorn d. Kathy Whitworth in sudden death.

Nabisco–Dinah Shore Winner's Circle

Formerly known as the Colgate–Dinah Shore Winner's Circle from 1972 through 1981.

Year	Winner	Year	Winner	Year	Winner
1972	Jane Blalock	1979	Sandra Post	1986	Pat Bradley
1973	Mickey Wright	1980	Donna Caponi	1987	Betsy King
1974	Jo Ann Prentice	1981	Nancy Lopez	1988	Amy Alcott
1975	Sandra Palmer	1982	Sally Little	1989	Juli Inkster
1976	Judy Rankin	1983	Amy Alcott	1990	Betsy King
1977	Kathy Whitworth	1984	Juli Inkster		
1978	Sandra Post	1985	Alice Miller		

Du Maurier Classic

Formerly known as La Canadienne in 1973 and the Peter Jackson Classic from 1974 through 1983.

Year	Winner	Year	Winner	Year	Winner
1973	Jocelyne Bourassa	1979	Amy Alcott	1985	Pat Bradley
1974	Carole Jo Skala	1980	Pat Bradley	1986	Pat Bradley*
1975	JoAnne Carner	1981	Jan Stephenson	1987	Jody Rosenthal
1976	Donna Caponi	1982	Sandra Haynie	1988	Sally Little
1977	Judy Rankin	1983	Hollis Stacy	1989	Tammi Green
1978	JoAnne Carner	1984	Juli Inkster	1990	Cathy Johnston

*Bradley d. Ayako Okamoto in a sudden-death playoff

LPGA All-Time Records

9 Holes

28, Mary Beth Zimmerman, 1984, Par 36; Pat Bradley, 1984, Par 35; Muffin Spencer-Devlin, 1985, Par 35

18 Holes

62 (30-32) by Mickey Wright, Hogan Park GC, Midland, Texas, in the first round of the 1964 Tall City Open, Par 71
62 (32-30) by Vicki Fergon at Almaden G & CC, San Jose, California, in the second round of the 1984 San Jose Classic, Par 73
62 (32-30) by Laura Davies, Rail GC, Springfield, Illinois, in the first round of the 1991 Rail Charity Classic, Par 72

36 Holes

129 (64-65) by Judy Dickinson at Pasadena Yacht & CC, St. Petersburg, Florida, in the 1985 S&H Golf Classic, Par 72

54 Holes

197 (67-65-65) by Pat Bradley at the Rail GC, Springfield, Illinois, in the 1991 Rail Charity Classic, Par 72

72 Holes

268 (66-67-69-66) by Nancy Lopez at the Willow Creek GC, High Point, North Carolina, in the 1985 Henredon Classic. Par 72

Consecutive Wins

4, by Mickey Wright in 1962; by Mickey Wright in 1963; by Kathy Whitworth in 1969

Victories in One Year

13, by Mickey Wright in 1963

Official Money in One Year

$863,578, by Beth Daniel in 1990

Most Official Career Victories

88, by Kathy Whitworth

Lowest Season Scoring Average

70.38, Beth Daniel, 1989

Margin of Victory

14 strokes, Louise Suggs in 1949 Women's Open; Cindy Mackey in 1986 MasterCard International Pro-Am

Birdies in One Round

11, by Vicki Fergon, at Almaden CC, San Jose, California, in 1984 San Jose Classic (she shot a 62)

Consecutive Birdies

8, by Mary Beth Zimmerman at Rail GC in Springfield, Illinois, in the 1984 Rail Charity Classic (she shot a 64)

Quickest Win as a Professional

3rd event, Amy Alcott, 1975 Orange Blossom Classic

Career Holes in One

11, Kathy Whitworth

Consecutive Rounds in 60s

8, Beth Daniel, 1990, beginning with 68-68 in the last two rounds of the JAL Big Apple Classic, August 18 and 19, all three rounds of the Northgate Classic (66-69-68), August 24, 25, 26, through all three rounds of the Rail Charity Golf Classic (67-69-67), Septmeber 1, 2, 3

LPGA Vare Trophy Winners

The Vare Trophy, named for six-time U.S. Women's Amateur Champion Glenna Collett Vare, was donated by LPGA founding member Betty Jameson. It is awarded annually to the tour leader in scoring average.

Year	Player	Scoring Avg.	Year	Player	Scoring Avg.
1953	Patty Berg	75.00	1972	Kathy Whitworth	72.38
1954	Mildred Didrikson Zaharias	75.48	1973	Judy Rankin	73.08
1955	Patty Berg	74.47	1974	JoAnne Gunderson Carner	72.87
1956	Patty Berg	74.57	1975	JoAnne Gunderson Carner	72.40
1957	Louise Suggs	74.64	1976	Judy Rankin	72.25
1958	Beverly Hanson	74.92	1977	Judy Rankin	72.16
1959	Betsy Rawls	74.03	1978	Nancy Lopez	71.76
1960	Mickey Wright	73.25	1979	Nancy Lopez	71.20
1961	Mickey Wright	73.55	1980	Amy Alcott	71.51
1962	Mickey Wright	73.67	1981	JoAnne Gunderson Carner	71.75
1963	Mickey Wright	72.81	1982	JoAnne Gunderson Carner	71.49
1964	Mickey Wright	72.46	1983	JoAnne Gunderson Carner	71.41
1965	Kathy Whitworth	72.61	1984	Patty Sheehan	71.40
1966	Kathy Whitworth	72.60	1985	Nancy Lopez	70.73
1967	Kathy Whitworth	72.74	1986	Pat Bradley	71.10
1968	Carol Mann	72.04	1987	Betsy King	71.14
1969	Kathy Whitworth	72.38	1988	Colleen Walker	71.26
1970	Kathy Whitworth	72.26	1989	Beth Daniel	70.38*
1971	Kathy Whitworth	72.88	1990	Beth Daniel	70.54

*Record

LPGA Player of the Year

Year	Player	Year	Player	Year	Player
1950–65	No award	1978	Nancy Lopez	1990	Beth Daniel
1966	Kathy Whitworth	1979	Nancy Lopez		
1967	Kathy Whitworth	1980	Beth Daniel		
1968	Kathy Whitworth	1981	JoAnne Gunderson Carner		
1969	Kathy Whitworth	1982	JoAnne Gunderson Carner		
1970	Sandra Haynie	1983	Patty Sheehan		
1971	Kathy Whitworth	1984	Betsy King		
1972	Kathy Whitworth	1985	Nancy Lopez		
1973	Kathy Whitworth	1986	Pat Bradley		
1974	JoAnne Gunderson Carner	1987	Ayako Okamoto		
1975	Sandra Palmer	1988	Nancy Lopez		
1976	Judy Rankin	1989	Betsy King		
1977	Judy Rankin				

LPGA Hall of Fame

Year	Honoree	Year	Honoree	Year	Honoree
1951	Patty Berg	1960	Betsy Rawls	1982	JoAnne Gunderson Carner
1951	Betty Jameson	1964	Mickey Wright	1987	Nancy Lopez
1951	Louise Suggs	1975	Kathy Whitworth		
1951	Mildred Didrikson Zaharias	1977	Sandra Haynie		
		1977	Carol Mann		

Bob Jones Award

Since 1955 the United States Golf Association has presented the Bob Jones Award honoring a person who, by a single act or over the years, emulates Jones's sportsmanship, respect for the game and its rules, generosity of spirit, sense of fair play, self-control, and perhaps even sacrifice.

Seven women have received the award.

Year	Honoree	Year	Honoree	Year	Honoree
1957	Mildred Didrikson Zaharias	1963	Patty Berg	1983	Maureen Garrett
1958	Margaret Curtis	1965	Glenna Collett Vare	1989	Peggy Kirk Bell
		1981	JoAnne Gunderson Carner		

References

Barton, Pam. *A Stroke a Hole*. London: Blackie & Son, 1937.

Berg, Patty. *Inside Golf for Women*. Chicago: Contemporary, 1977.

Collett, Glenna. *Golf for Young Players*. Boston: Little, Brown & Co., 1926.

———. *Ladies in the Rough*. New York: Alfred A. Knopf, 1929.

Corcoran, Fred, with Bud Harvey. *Unplayable Lies*. New York: Duell, Sloan & Pearce, 1965.

Cornish, Geoffrey S., and Ronald E. Whitten. *The Golf Course*. New York: Rutledge Press, 1981.

Cossey, Rosalynde. *Golfing Ladies*. London: Orbis, 1984.

Darwin, Bernard. *Golf Between Two Wars*. London: Chatto & Windus, 1944.

Dobereiner, Peter. *The World of Golf*. New York: Atheneum, 1981.

Flexner, Eleanor. *Century of Struggle, The Women's Rights Movement in the United States*. Cambridge: Harvard University Press, Belknap Press, 1980.

Gibson, Nevin H. *Great Moments in Golf*. Cranbury, N.J.: A.S. Barnes & Co., 1973.

Goodner, Ross. *Golf's Greatest*. Norwalk, Conn.: Golf Digest, 1978.

Helme, Eleanor E. *After the Ball*. London: Hurst & Blackett, 1931.

Hicks, Betty. *Travels with a Golf Tour Gourmet*. Palo Alto: Group Fore Productions, 1986.

Leahy, Patrick J. *The Curtis Cup: Aunt Pedge and Aunt Hat*. Bernardsville, N.J.: Somerset Hills Country Club, 1990.

Lees-Milne, Alvilde, and Rosemary Verey, eds. *The Englishwoman's Garden*. London: Chatto & Windus, 1983.

Leitch, Cecil. *Golf for Girls*. New York: American Sports Publishing Co., 1916.

Lerner, Gerda. *The Majority Finds Its Path, Placing Women in History*. Oxford: Oxford University Press, 1979.

Lopez, Nancy, with Peter Schwed. *The Education of a Woman Golfer*. New York: Simon & Schuster, 1979.

Mair, Lewine. *Lady Heathcoat-Amory*. London: Golf Monthly, 1984.

Ross, John M., ed. *Golf Magazine's Encyclopedia of Golf*. New York: Harper & Row, 1979.

Steel, Donald. *Golf Records, Facts, and Champions*. Middlesex, England: Guinnes Superlatives, 1987.

Stringer, Mabel A. *Golfing Reminiscences*. London: Mills & Boon, 1924.

United States Golf Association. *USGA Record Book, 1895–1959*. Far Hills, N.J.: United States Golf Association, 1981.

———. *USGA Record Book, 1960–1980*. Far Hills, New Jersey: United States Golf Association, 1981.

Ward-Thomas, Pat. *The Lay of the Land*. London: Ailsa, 1990.

Ward-Thomas, Pat, Herbert Warren Wind, Charles Price, and Peter Thomson. *The World Atlas of Golf*. London: Mitchell Beazley, 1976.

Wethered, Joyce. *Golfing Memories and Methods*. London: Hutchinson & Co., 1934.

Whitworth, Kathy, with Rhonda Glenn: *Golf for Women*. New York: St. Martin's Press, 1990.

Wilson, Enid. *A Gallery of Women Golfers*. London: Country Life, 1961.

Wind, Herbert Warren. *The Story of American Golf*. New York: Alfred A. Knopf, 1975.

Wright, Mickey. *Play Golf the Wright Way*. Garden City, N.Y.: Doubleday & Co., 1962.

Zaharias, Mildred Didrickson Babe. *This Life I've Led: My Autobiography*. New York: A.S. Barnes, 1955.

Index

A

Abbott, Elizabeth, **xii**
ABC Sports, 179
Adair, Rhona, **37,** 37-39
Addams, Jane, 32
Alcott, Amy, 273, 275, **306**
Allen, Eleanor W., 45
Allen, Margaret, 206
Amateur status, 137, 152-53, 303-06
Anthony, Bessie, 38
Anthony, Susan B., 32
Armour, Tommy, 142
Armstrong, Gloria, 167
Arnaz, Desi, 169
Ashley, Jean, 220, **222**
Astor, John Jacob, 30
Astor, Mrs. John Jacob, 33
Astrologes, Maria, 280
Auchterlonie, William, 16
Austin, Debbie, 192, 272
Australian Ladies Golf Union, 115

B

Babe Zaharias Cancer Fund, 144, 146
Babe Zaharias Hall of Fame, 146
Bahey, Rosamond, **ii**
Bailey, Miriam, 220
Baird, Nan, **108**
Ball, Lucille, 169
Barber, Amzi L., 33
Barlow, Nonna, **29,** 43, 44, **224**
Barrett, Bea, 128, 157

Barton, Mervyn, 109, 111, 113-14
Barton, Pam, 48, 88, 102, **104,**
    105-14, **107, 113**
Bauer, Alice, 156, **157,** 159, 161, 167,
    169, **194,** 269
Bauer, Jean, **124, 152**
Bauer, Marlene. *See* Hagge.
Baugh, Laura, 273, 279
Bednarsky, Karen, 219
Belante, Johnny, 201, 207
Beljan, Jan, 286
Bell, Bonnie, 196
Bell, Carl, 287
Bell, Mrs. Carl, 287
Bell, Judy, 49, 50, 73, 119, 220, **287,**
    287-88
Bell, Peggy Kirk, 115, **116,** 129, **140,**
    141, 156-57, 161-62, 167, 177
Belmont, Oliver, 30
Benny, Jack, 169
Berg, Herman, 124, 126-27
Berg, Patty, 47, 57, **108,** 110, 121-31,
    123, 124, 125, 129, 131, 141-43,
    146, 149-52, **152,** 154, 156-59, **161,**
    162-63, 165-67, **166, 168,** 169, 171,
    186, 192, 196, 207-08, 211, 232,
    251, 257-59, 283
Berger, Cookie Swift, 220
Berning, Susie Maxwell, 179, 182,
    274, 275
Berthelynn Cup, 70
Bird, May, 31

Bisgood, Jeanne, 112-13, 115, 116, **120**
Bishop, Georgianna **35,** 41, 44
Boddie, Barbara Fay White, **230,** 303, 306
Boit, Florence, 30
Bolstad, Les, 122, 125, 207
Bonallack, Angela Ward, **106,** 119
Booth, Jane Bastanchury, 184
Bowen, Bertha, 133, 136-37, 142-44, 146
Bowen, R.L., 133
Bradley, Pat, 253, 264, 273, **273,** 292, 294-97, **295, 296**
Breer, Murle, 196
Britz, Jerilyn, 192
Browne, Mary K., 54-55
Browne, Mrs. Charles S., 31, **32**
Burke, Jack, Jr., 208
Burns, Marge, 220
Burton, Brandie, 289-90
Bush, Betty, 129, **164**

C

Cairns, Katherine, **118**
Campbell, Dorothy, 42, 50-55, **52,** 110, 225
Caponi, Donna, 180, 259, 272, 295
Carnegie, Andrew, 25
Carner, JoAnne Gunderson, 58, 72, 119, 177, **178,** 192, **193,** 214, 220, **233,** 234, 236-37, **238,** 239, 240-43, **240, 241, 242, 243,** 245-47, 272, **272,** 275-76, 287, 299
Cassatt, Mary, 32
Catherine of Aragon, 6
Catterall, Mrs. Ernest, 17
Chandler, Peggy, 136
Cheney, Leona, 46, 48, 96, **97**
Chicago Women's Golf Association, 215
Chrysler, Miss, 44
Chrysler, Walter P., 94
Churchill, Winston, 121
Cleveland District Women's Golf Assoc., 115
Cochran Ranch Golf Course, 169, 286
Colbert, Claudette, 95
Colgate-Palmolive Co., 266-68, 272, 275, 280, 285

Collett, Glenna, *See* Vare.
Compston, Archie, 109
Congdon, Chuck, 246
Conley, Peggy, 247
Cooper, Lady Diana, 105
Corcoran, Fred, 141, 159-63, 169, 187-88
Corlett, Elsie, 46
Cornelius, Bill, 254
Cornelius, Karen, 196-97, 234
Cornelius, Kathy, 179, 182, 196
Cornelius, Kay,
Cornish, Geoffrey S., 286
Cox, Robert, 28
Creed, Clifford Ann, 204, 220
Crenshaw, Ben, 256
Critchley, Diana, 115
Crocker, Mary Lou, 188-91
Cros, Claudine. *See* Rubin.
Crosby, Bing, 231
Cudone, Carolyn, 216-20
Cullen, Betsy, 194-95
Cummings, Edith, 61, **62,** 63, 70-71, **71,** 72, 225, 227
Curie, Marie, 32
Curtis Cup, 41-50, **47, 49,** 82, 88, 91, **106,** 114-19
Curtis, Greely S., 35
Curtis, Greely S., Jr., 36
Curtis, Harriot, 36, 41-50, **43, 49**
Curtis, James, 44
Curtis, Laurence, 30, 44
Curtis, Margaret, 35-36, 38, **40,** 41-43, **43,** 115
Cuthell, Mrs. *See* Adair.
Cypress Point Club, 93

D

Daniel, Beth, 265, 291-94, **292**
Danoff, Bettye Mims, 154-55, 159, 162, 167, 169, 195-96
Darwin, Bernard, 80
Davies, Laura, 299, **299**
Davis, Gail, 296
Day, Connie, 220
de la Chaume, Simone Thion. *See* Lacoste.
Dennehy, Mrs. Charles, **168**
DeMoss, Grace, xiv, 116-19, **117,** 220
Dettweiler, Helen, 128, 137, 150, **152,** 153-55, 159-60, 164, 169, 286

Dey, Joseph C., Jr., 196, 216-17, 243
Dickinson, Gardner, 172
Didricksen, Ole, 133
Didrickson, Babe. *See* Zaharias.
Dod, Lottie, 17, 42
Dodd, Betty, 161-62, **164**
Dodd, Muriel, 44
Donald, Jean, 115, **118**
Doran, Claire, xiv, 177, 220
Downey, Mary Ann, 220
Draper, Dorothy, 179
Draper, Tom, **228**
Dreyspool, Joan Flynn, 160, 209
Dummet, Robin, 196
Dunn, May, 151-52
Durocher, Leo, 138
Dwyer, Mary, 253
Dye, Alice, 220, 286
Dye, Pete, 286
Dyer, Braven, 135

E
Eberl, George, 86-86, 301
Ehret, Gloria, 279
Eisenhower, Dwight D., 169
Elizabeth I, 3
Eller, Judy, 220
Ellinor, Merrill, F., 229
Elkins, Louise, **29,** 61
Englehorn, Shirley, 167, 179
English Ladies' Closed
    Championship, 66, 83, 88
Erickson, Bud, 266, 280
Everard, H.S.C., 10

F
Fair, Talbot, 10
Faulk, Mary Lena, 220, 232-33
Fazio, Tom, 286
Fenn, Bessie, 151-52, 227-28
Ferraris, Jan, 191
Fishwick, Diana, 46
Fiske, Gertrude, **28**
Findlay, Alexander, 228
Fitton, Barbara, 220
Fitzgerald, F. Scott, 63
Flagler, Henry Morrison, 25, 227,
    276
Floyd, Marlene, **268**
Floyd, Ray, 259
Fontaine, Joan, 95

Foster, David, 266-68, 270, 275, 280
Fownes, Mary, **224**
Fox, Mrs. Caleb, 60, 220
Fraser, Alexa Stirling. *See* Stirling.
Fraser, Madge Neill, 60
French Golf Union, 45
French Open, 77, 109
Friedan, Betty, 222

G
Gallico, Paul, 135
Garaialde, Jean, 181
Garrett, Maureen, 105-07, **106,** 112,
    115, 229, 231
Garson, Greer, 169
Garvey, Mrs. Cash, 160
Garvey, Philomena, **106,** 115, **118,**
    119
Gavin, Mrs. Willam A., 71
Gibson, Althea, 188, 213, 271
Gilliland, Wilma, 277
Gilroy, T., 10
Glen Head Country Club. *See*
    Women's National Golf and
    Country Club.
Glenn, Rhonda, **228, 268**
Glover, Alexa, 42
Glutting, Charlotte, 96
Goetz, Vicki, 289, **289**
Goldthwaite, Aniela, xiv, 96, **97**
Golden, William, 286
Golf for Women (GFW) magazine, 286
Goodwin, Joanne, 220
Gourlay, Molly, 46, **46, 48,** 75, 114
Graham, Mary, 42
Gregory, Ann, 212-219, **213, 215, 216**
Gregory, Percy, 215, 217-18
Griffin, Ellen, 155
Griffiths, Molly, 66
Griscom, Frances, 35, 36, 41, **42**

H
Hagen, Walter, 126
Hagge, Marlene Bauer, 149, **157,** 159,
    161-62, 169, 192-93, **194,** 235, 254,
    258, **268,** 269-70, **269,** 295-96
Hagge, Bob, 254, 258
Hamlin, Shelley, 184
Hammond, Joan, 115
Handmacher, Alvin, 161-63
Hanson, Beverly, 115, 160, 192

Harley, Katherine, 44
Harlow, Jean, 95, **95**
Harrison, Mabel, 44
Harvey, F.J., 29, 44
Haynie, Sandra, 180, 182, 211, **253,** 258, 275
Heathcoat-Amory, Lady Joyce. *See* Wethered.
Heathcoat-Amory, Sir John, 82
Hecker, Genevieve, 36, **37**
Helme, Eleanor, 160
Hemphill, Kathryn, 96, **152,** 155-56, 160
Henie, Sonja, 136
Henry, VIII, 6
Hezlet, Florence, 42, 51
Hezlet, May, 42
Hicks, Betty, 128, 155, 159-60
Hicks, Helen, 46, 96, **124,** 128, **129,** 151-52, **151**
Higbie, Dorothy, 46
Higgins, Pam, **268**
Higuchi, Chako, 266, 299
Hill, Opal, 46, 96, 128, 152, 159, 169, 229
Hillerich & Bradsby Sporting Goods, 152
Hilton, Harold, 22, 24
Hogan, Ben, 141, 171, 201-02
Hoke, Diana, 218
Holderness, Sir Ernest, 46
Hollins, Harry P., 93
Hollins, Marion, 44, 46, **46,** 60-61, 70, 89, **89,** 92-96, **92, 94,** 98, 286
Holm, Mrs. A.M., 139
Homestead, The, 179
Hopkins, Mrs. Henry, 27
Howe, Dorothy Campbell Hurd. *See* Campbell.
Howland, Cornelia, 27, 28
Hoyt, Beatrix, **4, 20,** 32-37
Hulton, Blanche Martin, 10
Hurd, J.B., 54
Hurd, Dorothy. *See* Campbell.
Hyde, Lillian, 44

I

Icely, L.B., 150, 153, 159
Ihlanfeldt, Edean, 219-20
Indian Palms Country Club. *See* Cochran Ranch.

Inkster, Brian, 291
Inkster, Hayley, 291
Inkster, Juli Simpson, 291

J

Jackson, Kay, 72
Jameson, Betty, 99-102, **100, 101,** 110, 129, 149, 155, 159, 169
Jamison, Jane Cothran, **152**
Janssen, Mary Patton, 220
Johnstone, Ann Casey, 220
Jones, Bobby, 55-57, **56,** 58-59, 66, 69, 73, 93, 201
Jones, Ernest, 89
Jones, Robert Trent, 229
Jones, Rosie, 275, 299
Jordan, Mrs. Curtis, 217

K

Kabler, Carole Jo, 240
Kazmierski, Joyce, 205
Kertes, Stan, 208, 231
Kielty, Dorothy, 115, 220
Kimball, Judy, 180
King, Betsy, 265, 291, **293,** 294
King, Billy Jean, 279
King, Martin Luther, Jr., 214
Kirby, Dorothy, 115, 161, 220
Kirk, Peggy. *See* Bell.
Kite, Tom, 256
Klotz, Dot, 229
Knight, Ashley, 285
Knight, Erin, 285
Knight, Ray, 285

L

Lacoste, Catherine, **176,** 177-85, **181, 183, 184,** 220, 242
Lacoste, Rene, 180, **180**
Lacoste, Simone, 180, **180**
Ladies Golf Union, 6, 10, 21, 44-46, 82, 89, 111, 115
Ladies Professional Golf Assoc., 159-60
Lady Golfer magazine, 286
Lapham, Roger, 93
Lee, Joe, 286
Leitch, Cecil, xiv, 22-24, **23,** 45, 53, 61, 66-67, 70, 98, 181
Lenczyk, Grace, 115, 116, 140, 164, 220

Lengfeld, Helen, 161, 287
Lesser, Pat, 220
Letts, Mrs. F.E., 53
Lexington Country Club, 102
L.G.U. *See* Ladies Golf Union.
Lifur, Mrs. Gregg, 96
Lindsay, Marge, 116, **129,** 220
Little, Sally, 262, 273, **273,** 283
Littleton, Tommy, 128
Lopez, Domingo, 284
Lopez, Marina, 284
Lopez, Nancy, 123, **264,** 265-66, 271,
    275, **278,** 279-85, **281, 282, 285,**
    291-92
LoPresti, Tom, 231
Loudermilk, Harvey, 256-57
L.P.G.A., *See* Ladies Professional
    Golf Association.
Lythgoe, E., 18

M
MacDougall, Marion, **152**
MacGregor Sporting Goods, 153
MacLaurin, Ceil, 220
Mackenzie, Ada, 99-100, 110
Mackenzie, Alister, 93, 286
Mademoiselle magazine, 156
Maiden, Stewart, 57
Manice, Dorothy, 161
Manley, Hobart, **228**
Mann, Carol, 180, 190, **190, 253,** 258,
    280
Marble, Alice, 95
Martin, Kit, 277
Martin, Mrs. G.M., 54
Martinez, Cha Cha, 229
Mary, Queen of Scots, 1-3, **2,** 6
Massey, Debbie, **264,** 273
Mather, Hilday, 53
Matson, Natasha, 220
Matthews, Fee Fee, 220
Maxwell, Louise, 35
Maxwell, Susie. *See* Berning.
May, George S., 129, 215
McCann, Kitty, **118**
McCorkindale, Belle. *See* Robertson.
McCormack, Mark, 236
McDonald's Corporation, 170
McDonald, Helen, 151-52
McInnis, Gordon, 238-39

McIntire, Barbara, 119, 122, 182, 214,
    220, **230,** 234-36, **234,** 245, 247,
    271, 287-88
McKenna, Mary, 119
McKinnon, Betty, **161, 164**
Meadow Brook Club, 31
Merion Cricket Club, 54
Metropolitan Women's Golf Assoc.,
    44
Miley, Marion, 48, 102-3, 110
Milland, Ray, 169
Miller, Issette Pearson. *See* Pearson.
Miller, Johnny, 279
Miller, Sharon, 189-90, 192
Mills, Mary, 191, 196
Mingola, Cuzzy, 191
Minikahda Country Club, 121
Minneapolis City Championship,
    125
Mobley, Mary Ann, 254
Mochrie, Dottie, 299
Moore, Henry, 214
Moore, Myra, 214
Morgan, J.P., 25, 93
Morgan, Wanda, 46, 112
Morris County Golf Club, 27-28, 31,
    31, 33
Morse, S.F.B., 93
Morris, Old Tom, 53
Mozel, Mary, 156-57
Muir, Mrs. H. Howie, 25
Musial, Stan, 141
Murray, Mae, 116, 220

N
Nabisco Brands, 268
Nelson, Byron, 202
Nelson, Jane, 220
Neumann, Liselotte, 299, **300**
Niclaus, Barbara, 75
Nicklaus, Jack, 75, 201, 260, 279
North and South Women's Amateur,
    29, 70, 72

O
O'Connor, Susan, **268**
Ogilvie, Isabel, **152**
Okamoto, Ayako, 266, **267,** 299
Oldfield, Ed, 247, 294
Olympic Games, 135
Orcutt, Maureen, 46, **49,** 55, 96, 98,
    110-11, 128, 157-58, 160, 227

O'Reilly, Nan, 160
Osgood, Fanny, 45
O'Sullivan, Pat, 220, 221
Owings, Mrs. Thaddeus, 217

P

Page, Estelle Lawson, **49,** 96, 110
Palmer, Sandra, **195,** 273, **273,** 275
Pam Barton Fund, 115
Park, Doris, 46, 79
Pasatiempo Country Club, 93-96, **98,**
    286
Paterson, Moira, **118**
Pearson, Issette, 6, 8, **8,** 10, 15-16,
    18-19, 41
Pease, Dorothy, 286
Peter, Betty, 286
Penick, Harvey, 174, 233, 256-57, 261
P. Goldsmith & Sons Sporting
    Goods Co., 153
Phelps, Miss M., 23
Phillips, Candy, 189-90
Phillips, Doris, 220
Phillips, Miss M.E., 18
Pickford, Mary, 95
Pooley, Violet, 44
Porter, Dorothy Germain, 115, **116,**
    128, 158, 220
Porter, Ruth, **106**
Post, Sandra, **269, 271,** 272, 295
Postlewait, Kathy, 192
Powell, Renee, 188, 213
Prentice, JoAnne, 179
Preuss, Tish, 119, 220, **221**
Pressler, Harry, 206-07
Pressler, Leona. See Cheney.
Price, Elizabeth, **106,** 115, 116-19,
    117, 118
Price, Jrs. J.R., **29**
Pringle, Jim, 125
Probasco, Betty, 220
Pultz, Penny, 264
Pung, Jackie, 260
Purves, Laidlaw, 9-10

Q

Quast, Anne. See Sander.
Quast, Joan, 244
Quast, Tom, 244
Quier, Edith, 223

R

Ram Golf Company, 267-68
Rankin, Judy, 196, 266, 270-72, **271,**
    295
Rankin, Tuey, 196
Rankin, Yippy, 271-72
Ravenscroft, Gladys, **25,** 44, 110
Rawls, Betsy, 129, 131, 143-44, **148,**
    161, 162, 164-67, **166, 168,** 170-75,
    173, 186, 192, 200, 208, 210-11,
    251, 256, 258-59, 271
Raynor, Helen, 128, 158
Reid, John, 30
Revere, Paul, 28
Rice, Grantland, 135
Richardson, Ann, 220
Richardson, Mrs. Ryder, 18
Riggs, Bobby, 279
Riley, Polly, xiii, xiv, 48, 115, **118,**
    119, 128, 143, 156-57, 160, 164-65,
    213-14, 220, 232, 301-03, **302,**
    306-07
Ritzman, Alice, 262-63
Robert Cox Cup, 28
Robertson, Belle, **106,** 119
Robertson, Janette, **106**
Robichaux, Jolyn, 216
Rockefeller, John D., 25, 229
Rogers, Will, 95
Roosevelt, Franklin D., 121
Romack, Barbara, 146, 179, 185, **186,**
    188, 192-93, 195, 208, 220, 225,
    229, 232, 271
Rosenthal, Elaine, 58
Ross, Donald, 222, 228
Rubin, Claudine Cros, 177-78, **181,**
    184
Russell, Rosalind, 169
Ruttle, Maureen. See Garrett.

S

Sanchez, Wanda, **90**
Sander, Anne Quast, 119, 180, 214,
    220, 234, 244-47, **245,** 271, 287,
    289, 304
Sands, W.H., 32-33
Sarazen, Gene, 82, 128
Sargent, Mrs. N.C., 32
Scott, F.B., 44
Scott, Lady Louisa, 14-15
Scott, Lady Margaret, 12-18, **13,** 33

Scott, Lord Eldon, 14, 16
Scottish Fishwives, 7
Scottish Women's Amateur
    Championship, 5
Sears, Evelynn, 44
Semple, Phyllis, 220, 291
Seignious, Hope, 128-29, 155-57,
    159-60
Sessions, Sally, 156, 159, 169
Sheehan, Patty, 271, 297-98, **297**
"Shell's Wonderful World of Golf,"
    177
Shore, Dinah, 266-67, 281
Sigel, Helen. *See* Wilson.
Silva, Brian M., 286
Sitwell, Lady Ida, 6
Smith, Alex, 69-70
Smith, Frances Stephens, **90,** 91,
    106, 115, 116, **118,** 119
Smith, Lancy, 119, 277
Smith, Marilynn, **158,** 159, 161-62,
    168-69, 190-91
Smith, Wiffi, 220
Snead, Sam, 141, 171-72, 265
Solheim Cup, 300
Sorenson, Carol, 220, **230**
Spearman, Marley, **106**
Spork, Shirley, 155, 159, 162, 167,
    169, 191
Sports Illustrated magazine, 271
Stacy, Hollis, 274-75, **275**
Stanton, Elizabeth Cady, 32
Steegman, Monica, 229
Stephens, Frances. *See* Smith.
Stephenson, Jan, 273-74, **274**
Stetson, Mrs. G. Henry, **59,** 60
Stewart, Earl, Jr., 208
Stewart, Harold, 238-39
Stewart, Marlene. *See* Streit.
Stewart, Mary, 238
Stirling, Alexa, viii, xiv, 55-63, **56,
    57, 62,** 70, 77, 93
Stirling, Dr. Alexander, 55-56
Stirling, Mrs. Alexander, 55
Stout, Mrs. Charles T., **35**
Stone, Beth, 179, 183
Stranahan, Frank, 156, 217
Streit, J. Douglas, 239
Streit, Marlene Stewart, **90,** 184, 214,
    220, **228, 237,** 234, 236-39, **238,**
    240, 245, 247

Stringer, Mabel, 160
Strubing, Philip H., 304-05
St. Andrews Ladies Golf Club, 7
Suggs, John, 162, 172
Suggs, Louise, 143, **154,** 155-56, 159,
    162-64, 167, 169, **170,** 171-75, 179,
    183, 186, 189, 192, 208, 211, 258,
    260
Sullivan, Ed, 229
Syms, Nancy Roth, 180, 220

T
Taylor, Elizabeth, 270
Taylor, J.H., 66
Temple, Stella, 60
Therrien, Rachel M., 286-87
Thompson, Bea, 137
Thompson, Carol Semple, 290-91,
    290
Thornton, Eoline, 213
Tillinghast, A.W., 38
Titterton, Maud, 23-24, 53
"Tonight Show," 281
Toski, Bob, 171
Tournaments, tours, international
    matches, origins of,
    British Ladies Open Amateur,
        10-16
    Broadmoor Ladies Invitational, 225
    Colgate-European Open, 267
    Colgate-Far East Open, 267
    Colgate Triple Crown, 267
    Curtis Cup match, 42-47
    Eastern Women's Amateur, 225
    Florida East Coast Championship,
        228
    Florida Orange Blossom Circuit,
        225
    Harder Hall Invitational, 229
    Helen Lee Doherty Invitational,
        229
    Hollywood Four-Ball, 229
    International Mixed Two-Ball, 229
    L.P.G.A. Tour, 141, 149-63
    Louise Suggs Invitational, 171
    Nabisco-Dinah Shore
        Championship, 266
    National Mixed Foursomes, 229
    North & South Championship,
        225

Pacific Northwest Ladies Championship, 225
Palm Beach Championship, 227
South Atlantic Championship, 228
Solheim Cup, 300
Southern Women's Amateur Championship, 225
Titleholders Championship, 155, 161
Trans-National Championship, 225
U.S. Girls' Junior Championship, 225
U.S. Women's Amateur Championship, 31-32, 266
U.S. Women's Mid-Amateur Championship, 276, 301-03, 306-07
U.S. Women's Open Championship, 130
Weathervane Transcontinental Tournament, 161-62
Western Junior Girls Championship, 225
Women's Canadian Open Amateur, 225
Women's National Collegiate Championship, 225
Women's Texas Open, 137
Women's Western Amateur Championship, 225
World Championship, 129
Traung, Dorothy, 96, 99
Tull, Albert, 92
Turpie, Marion, **223**

U

United Golf Association. *See* U.G.A.
United States Golf Assoc. *See* U.S.G.A.
University of Minnesota Women's Intercollegiate Fund, 127
U.G.A., 215, 217
Underhill, Ruth, **35**
U.S.G.A., 31, 45-46, 62, 89, 168, 216-17, 266, 288
Upham, Henry, 30

V

Vagliano, Andre, 45
Vagliano Cup, 46
Valentine, Jessie, 115, **118,** 119

Vanderbeck, Mrs. C.H., 60
Vanderbilt, Cornelius, 30
Van Wie, Virginia, 46, 96-99, **97,** 227
Varangot, Brigitte, 177, 178, **181,** 184, 220, 229
Vardon, Harry, 201
Vare, Glenna Collett, xiv, 44, 46-49, **46,** 54, 58-60, **64, 68,** 69-73, **73, 74,** 74-82, **79,** 93, 96, 98-99, 109, 115, 126, 136, 225, 227-28, 241, 243, 303-04, **304**
Vare Trophy, 102
Vardon, Harry, 66
Veblen, Thorstein, 26
Victoria, 7
Volpe, Ray, 260, 280

W

Walker, Colleen, 299
Walker, Michelle, 300
Ward, Bud, 246
Ward-Thomas, Pat, 212
Watson, Mrs. J.B., 46, 79
Weil, Mrs. Burt, 128
Wellesley College, **37**
Western Women's Golf Association, 127
Wethered, H. Newton, 65-66
Wethered, Joyce, 15, 46, **46,** 57, 65-69, **67, 73,** 73-83, **80,** 88, 96, 98, 107, 152-53, 181, 202
Wethered, Roger, 65-66
Wheeler, Sherry, 204
White, Barbara Fay. *See* Boddie.
Whitney, Payne, 94
Whitworth, Dama, 255, 257-58, 260
Whitworth, Kathy, 123, 131, 180, 189, 194, 199-200, 211, 232, **248,** 249-66, **250, 251, 252, 253, 256, 261,** 275, 295, 300
Whitworth, Morris, 255, 258, 260-61
Wilkinson, Bud, 124-25
Williams, Ted, 141
Wilson, Enid, 46, **84,** 85-92, 109, 114, 160, 239
Wilson, Helen Sigel, 220, **221**
Wilson Sporting Goods Company, 120, 141, 152, 268
Wind, Herbert Warren, 30, 202
Winthrop, R.D., 32
Wirtz, Lennie, 188, 191, 193, 204

Woman Golfer magazine, 286
Women,
    American housewife, 26
    Emancipation of, 87
    In World War I, 41, 44, 60-61
    In World War II, 50, 111-14,
        128-30, 153-54
    Liberation, 222
    Minority rights, 214-222
    Political advances, 21
    Suffrage, 22, 24, 32
    Title IX, 276, 305
    Victorian, 5-7, 14-15, 21
Women's Air Force Service Pilots,
    154, 169
Women's Army Corps, 154
Women's Auxiliary Air Force, 113
Women's National Golf & Country
    Club, 92
Women's Professional Golf Assoc.,
    155, 160
Women's Royal Naval Service, 113
Women's Western Golf Assoc., 127

Woodward, Ruth, 160
Worsham, Lew, 171
Wragg, Mable, 78
Wright, Arthur, 209, 212
Wright, Kathryn, 209
Wright, Mickey, xi, 57, 123, 144, 146,
    160, **168,** 171, 173, 177, 177, 180,
    185, **187,** 188, 192, 194, **198,**
    199-212, **202, 203, 204, 205, 206,**
    211, 214, 220, 250-51, 258, 260,
    265-66, 271, 279, 291, 294

Z
Zaharias, Mildred "Babe"
    Didrickson, xii, xiv, 57-58, 102,
    123-24, **124,** 129, **132,** 133-47, **134,**
    135, 138, 139, 140, 142, 143, 145,
    149, 152-53, 159-62, **161, 164,**
    164-65, 169, 172, 200, 202, 207-08,
    243, 269, 279
Zaharias, George, 137-38, **138,** 140,
    140, 142, 143, 144, 156, 159
Ziske, Joyce, 260

Photography

All photographs are courtesy of Golf House/USGA with the exception of the following:

The Greenbrier—x; Bettman/UPI—2; Suffolk County Historical Society—4; Rhonda Glenn—13a, 13b, 37b, 154, 164, 228, 268, 269, 273b, 273c; Wide World—47, 49b, 89; Temple University—52b, 59; Tufts Archives—29, 90a, 221a, 223c, 224b; Polly Riley—90b; Wilson Sporting Goods—108b, 120, 125, 129b, 129c, 131; Bertha Bowen—132, 134, 138, 139, 142, 145; Helen Hicks—151; Ruth Gilman—189; Mickey Wright—202-205; Ann Gregory—213, 215, 216, 218; Tish Preuss—221b; Robie Ray/*Norfolk Virginian Pilot*—248; Kathy Whitworth—252, 253, 256, 261, 264; Lewis Portnoy—270, 271, 273a, 278; Dost & Evans/Focus on Golf—281; Judy Bell—287.